THE THINKING PERSON'S NEW BOOK OF QUOTES, APHORISMS, QUIPS, PHRASES, AND INFAMOUS ONE-LINERS FROM THE DISTANT PAST TO THE PRESENT AND INTO THE BEYOND

THE THINKING PERSON'S NEW BOOK OF QUOTES, APHORISMS, QUIPS, PHRASES, AND INFAMOUS ONE-LINERS FROM THE DISTANT PAST TO THE PRESENT AND INTO THE BEYOND

BY HAROLD M. ELLIOTT

SECOND EDITION

Midascat Press
Philadelphia, Pennsylvania, USA

Cover image:
Rodin's "The Thinker," Paris
https://commons.wikimedia.org/wiki/File:Jard%C3%ADn_Mus%C3%A9e_Rodi
n_Pensador_01.JPG
Image by Miguel Hermoso Cuesta
Attribution-ShareAlike 4.0 International (CC BY-SA 4.0)
Public Domain Image

First Printing: 2019

ISBN: 9781797435671

OTHER BOOKS BY HAROLD M. ELLIOTT

*The Thinking Person's Big Bathroom Book of Eternal
Quotes and Obscure One-Liners from the Beginning
to the Present to the End*

The Elliott and Marshall Family Tree

*The Structure and Evolution of the Geographic System:
A Study in Cultural Change*

*A Historical Atlas of the Domestic Trunk Airlines
of the United States*

A 001

BEFORE THE BEGINNING

Before the beginning, there was Nada .... *Dios*
Before the beginning, there was the Logos ....*Plato*
Before the beginning, there was the Dao............................*Laozi*
Before the beginning, there was Bupkis ....*Yhwh*
Before the beginning, there was Oy .... *Moses*
Before the beginning, all was null and void....................... *Jehova*
Before the beginning, there was Tian ....*Shangdi*

A 002

Before the beginning, was Yin, Yang, & Qi................... *Zhou Yan*
Before the beginning, there was Unity........................ *Baha'u'llah*
Before the beginning, there was Asha...................... *Zendavesta*
Before the beginning, there was Onkar ....*Guru Nanak*
Before the beginning, was darkness........................*Angra Mainu*
Before the beginning, there was Nichts .... *Gott in Himmel*
Before the beginning, there was Om (Aum)...... *Katha Upanishad*

A 003

Before the beginning, everything was calm, silent,
motionless, and in the sky, there was
nothing but darkness......................................*Mayan Popol Vuh*
Before the beginning, there was no sky
and no earth... *Mother Nature*
Before the beginning, all was black
and formlessness.. *The Wujing*
Before the beginning, there was nothing
except featureless chaos............................... *Xu Zheng*

A 004

Before the beginning, there was good and evil
and nothing in between .... *The Prophet Mani*
Before the beginning, there was
absolute darkness ....*The Magian scriptures*

1

A 005

Before the beginning was the ultimate reality that was Brahman,
with whom was the word Om, and
the word was Brahman.. *The Yajurveda*
Before the beginning, there was neither existence nor
non-existence. All was chaos, void and formless.................. *The*
Mahabharata

A 006

Before the dawn of time, there was darkness,
which predated all creations .... *The Book of Enuma Elish*
Before the beginning were the ways of
nature, existing before heaven and earth,
silent and void..*Laozi's Dao De Qing*
Before the beginning was the Word (aka the Logos) that lives on
in Christianity as the spiritus sancti.................*Philo of Alexandria*
But, neither the "Logos" nor the "Word" were in the
Hebrew, texts so neither of them were included
in my Vulgate... *Jerome of Illyria*

A 007

IN THE BEGINNING

In the beginning, God created heaven and earth, and
the earth was void and empty, and the dark was
upon the deep, and the spirit of God moved
upon the waters .... *The John Tyndale Bible*
In the beginning, Ahura Mazda made
light & brightness..................................... *The Avesta and Gathas*
In the beginning, Lord Brahma made the
earth out of nothing.. *Vedic scriptures*
In the beginning, there was chaos and many gods
El (Enlil), Enki (Ea), Marduk, Ba'al, Ishtar,
and more gods than can be
counted............................... *Mesopotamian & Canaanite priests*

A 008
And I created Babylon..*Marduk*
At the dawn of time was an epic battle among the gods, and
Marduk emerged victorious and became the highest god in the
Babylonian Pantheon...*The Enuma Elish*
Then, at the start of everything, Marduk made light. Then he
divided the waters, and created dry land with a barrier keeping
out the ocean waters............................*The Book of Enuma Elish*

A 009
When God began to create heaven and earth, the earth was
unformed and void, with darkness over
the surface of the deep...*The Tanach*
In the beginning, God created the heaven and the earth, and the
earth was without form and void, and darkness
was upon the face of the deep, and
God said "Let there be light"......................*The King James Bible*
In the beginning of creation, God made heaven and the earth,
and the earth was without form and void......................*The New
English Bible*

A 010
In the beginning, God seide maad of naught, heaven and Earth.
And in truth, the earth was idle and void, and darknesses were
on the faces of the depth. And the Spirit of the Lord
was bourne on the waters, and God said be maad light, and light
was maad...*The John Wycliffe Bible*

A 011
In the Beginning, God createth heaven and earth, and all things
therein, in six days, and God said be light made. And light was
made. And then God made a great firmament and divided the
waters .... *The Douay Bible*

A 012
AFTER THE BEGINNING
Afterwards, Chronos made Aether & Chaos...................*Hesiod's
Theogony*

Then was the Eridu Genesis......... *The Sumerian Adobe Cylinder*
Then was the creation .... *The Babylonian Seven Tablets*
Then we made the Black-headed
(Sumerian) people .... *The gods Enlil, An, & Enki*
We are also called the Black-headed
people .... *Ancient Chinese sages*
After the beginning were the teachings of the
Dao* de Jing (Daojiao)... *Lao-tse*

*Dao in pinyin, *Tao in Wade-Giles*

A 013
Then Yahveh created man and out of dust and clay in his own
image. And Yhwh then took a rib from Adam and made a woman
with it .... *The Torah*
Marduk then took lumps of earth and kneaded them with his
blood and created man and woman.................... *Clay tablets from
Ashurbanipal's Library*

A 014
After creating the world and the universe, Lord Brahma gave
form to man and woman, and named them Manu and Shatrupa,
from whom all people thereafter descend. Both Manu and
Shatrupa emerged by themselves out of Brahma's
own body, and Brahma then gave the two of them
dominion over the Earth.................................. *The Mahabharata*

A 015
After the beginning, Allah created man from out of a
clot of blood and gave the man a pen and taught him how to
read and write .... *The Koran, Surah 96*
And from man and woman there was made
nations and tribes .... *The Koran, Surah 49*

A 016
After the beginning, God said, "Let there be lite beer"............ *The
Burgermeister Bible*
And after the beginning, God made little
people .... *The Book of Gnomes*

After the beginning, there were the
words of Jehovih (sic)........................ *The New Bible of Oahspe*
Praise God and pass the ammunition....... *The John Wayne Bible*
Praise God and let there be animation ...... *The Walt Disney Bible*

A 017
THE BIG BANG
All are atoms that everything else is made from ....*Democritus*
Before the beginning, there was a primordial atom (or singularity)
of infinite density ....*Lemaitre*
Then there was the Big Bang .... *Double, Bubble,*
Hoyle, & Hubble
Speculation about what was there before the singularity or
what the elements of it may have travelled through after
the Big Bang remains undefined .... *Stephen Hawking*

A 018
After the Big Beginning and many eons and geologic time
periods, there were glaciers and drifting continents. Then there
was *Homo erectus*, Heidelbergensis, Neanderthalensis,
Denisovanensis, and finally Modern Humans, who spread
out of East Africa into the rest of the world .... *Svante Paabo*

A 019
After several thousands of years, the ancient Proto Indo-
European peoples began to spread westward into Europe ca.
5,000 BC. These westward migrants have been widely
associated with the Kurgan people living on the steppes north of
the Black Sea. They also spread southward into Iran and India,
and eastward into Central Asia sometime
after 4,000 BC........................*Gordon Childe & Marija Gimbutas*

A 020
IMPORTANT INDO-EUROPEAN FATHER GODS
After the beginning, there was the Proto Indo-European high
father god Dyeus Phter .... *Ancient Indo-Aryan shamans*
After the beginning, there was the high father god
Dis Pater (Father Dis)... *Irish druids*

After the start, there was the supreme god of the universe,
Deivos ....*Ancient Slavic shamans*
After the beginning was the early Avestan god of Persia,
Daeva.. *Ancient Iranian shamans*
After the beginning was the god Dyaus Pitr ....*Ancient Indic shamans*
After the big start up was the god Dievas or Deivs........... *Ancient Baltic shamans*
Dei Patrous...*Ancient Illyrian shamans*
After the beginning, there was the god Djous Pater .... *Proto-Italic shamans*
Ius Pater...*Ancient Italic shamans*
Jovis Pater.. *Early Roman sacerdos*
Jove, & Jupiter.. *Later Roman sacerdos*

A 021

OTHER INDO-EUROPEAN FATHER GODS

After the start of things
was the high god Tiwaz ....*Early Hittite sacerdotes*
After the beginning, there was the
high god Zeus... *Early Hellenic priests*
After the beginning was there was Ziu or Tiwaz................... *Early Germanic shamans*
After the beginning was Tiw............... *Old Anglo-Saxon shamans*

A 022

GREAT PREHISTORIC STRUCTURES IN EUROPE & ANATOLIA

We have forgotten why we built or why we buried these
wonderful stone monuments in
south-central Anatolia .... *Builders of the Gobekli Tepe temples*
This great Irish burial mound also marks
winter solstices .... *Officiants of Newgrange*
These giant stone circles can predict seasons
and eclipses .... *Officiants of Stonehenge*
We've forgotten the purpose of all these
stone alignments .... *Officials of Carnac*

These standing stone alignments
are still mysteries .... *Overseers of the Ring of Kerry*

A 023
GOBEKLI TEPE
Recently, near the town of Sanliurfa in modern day Turkey, I
discovered a complex of several circular complexes containing
five large T-shaped stone pillars and other smaller standing
stones surrounded by small uncarved stone walls located on Pot
Belly Hill in south central Anatolia. No one knows why or how
they were built..*Klaus Schmidt*

A 024
The Gobekli Tepe complexes were constructed between the
10th millennium BCE and were buried and abandoned by about
the 8th millennium BCE. They are among the oldest known
ancient structures in the prehistoric past, and so far, they are
mysteries......................................*Klaus Schmidt, J. Peters, et al.*

A 025
It is also thought that the Gobekli Tepe complexes were built at
or sometime before the agricultural revolution and located near
where wheat and barley were first domesticated ca. 10th
millennium BCE............. *Andrew Curry, A. Surry, & E.B. Banning*

A 026
DEISTS & DEISM
Deists before and after the Italian Renaissance and the French
and British Enlightenment believed there was Nature's God, who
made the universe and all life forms,
and then went away .... *Many Free Masons*
in Europe & America

Then the divine draftsman went
to work elsewhere .... *William Blake*
Many of the Founding Fathers of America shared this
belief, so here is a deistic version of the Bible..........*The Thomas*
Jefferson Bible

A 027

THE GARDEN OF EATING

During the creation, God made a vegetable garden in the
desert with four rivers running through it called the Tiger,
the Ganiff, the Pisha, and the Euthenasia...... *The Book of Hebes*
Then God created woman and man
in his own likeness.................................... *The Book of Genius*
Who are we? How did we get here?
And where are we going? .... *Book of Questions*
Nobody knows................................... *Says the great bell of Bow*
Would you like a turnip? .... *Eve, the 1st woman,*
    whose mitochondrial DNA is in all women and men today
No, go find me a zucchini .... *Adam, the 1st man,*
    whose Y chromosome DNA is in all men today
Gimme one too...................................... *The Montypython*
And then God said "Go, be friendly, and multiply"......... *The Book*
    of Adam & Eve

A 028

In ancient Iran, Ahura Mazda created the universe and the
primordial giant Gayomard, the first human being, from whom all
men and women descend..*Zoroaster*
Also in ancient Iran was another first man named Mashya, and
the first woman named Mashyana. Then the two became fruitful,
multiplied, and populated the earth................... *The Zend Avesta*

A 029

FECUNDITY

Then the high Norse, Greek, and Roman Gods said to us, "Go
and find mates and multiply" .... *Freyja, Demeter,*
    Aphrodite, and Venus
Then the high Hindu consort goddess Lakshmi came and said to
us, "Here is the *Kama Sutra* and you all may now go and be
fruitful" .... *Sarasvati & Cybele*
Too much of a good thing is too much.
We are now too many.. *Thomas Malthus*
There's no such thing as too much of this...................... *Dr. Ruth*

A 030

Y CHROMOSOME DNA & MITOCHONDRIAL DNA

Then Adam's Y chromosome DNA began to be passed down to
all men living today, starting about 125,000 to 156,000, or
200,000 years ago. At about the same time, Eve's
mitochondrial DNA began to be passed down
to all subsequent women on earth, starting about 99,000 to
148,000 years ago ....*Wilson Sayers & Carlos Bustamonte*
And the first man and woman
were Ash & Elm....................................*Early Germanic shamans*

A 031

THE GREAT ICE CAP MELTINGS

When Earth became warmer, the world's glaciers began to melt
(with no human input of any of the modern
satanic gasses) .... *Robert Balling*
Following the end of the Pleistocene, many large floods
inundated coastal areas all over the world and sea
levels rose by 200–300 feet...*USGS*

A 032

RISING ANCIENT SEA LEVELS

Several thousand years ago, as warming occurred, the Black
Sea rose as incoming salt water gushed in from the
Mediterranean and flowed north through the Bosporus and
mixed freely with all the fresh water until there was
no fresh water left..*Poseidon*
Then all the fresh water life forms died out and were replaced by
salt water plants and animals (i.e., fresh water snails
versus salt water snails) .... *Neptune*

A 033

GILGAMESH

I spent a lot of time searching for the secrets of eternal life.
Instead I came to the great sage Utanapishtim, who told me
about the great flood from long ago.............................*Gilgamesh*

A 034

ATRAHASIS

Before Gilgamesh and Utanapishtim, there was the great god Ea
of ancient Mesopotamia, who told Atrahasis, a good man of
Akkad (later called Ziusudra), that a huge universal flood was
coming and that Atrahasis must save himself and his family by
building a large ark and fill it up with animals and ride out the
deluge .... *The Akkadian & Babylonian Flood Epic*

A 035

UTANAPISHTIM

Before the great flood came, the god Enki said to get rid of
everything and build an ark. Enki then said to fill the ark with
family, friends, neighbors, animals, and lots of grain.
And then it rained .... *Shamash-Utanapishtim*
When the rain stopped and our ark went aground, and when the
birds I sent out didn't return, we all disembarked
and went swimming ....*Utanapishtim*
Row, row, row your boat. .... *Gilgamesh*

A 036

NOAH ZARK

Before the great flood came, God told me to build a zark and
stock it with food and condiments and all the animals I could
find (no dinosaurs). Then I and all my sons and their families
boarded the great ship. Then it rained .... *Noah of Sumer*
Those who had ridiculed me drowned in
the great deluge..*Noah*
When the rain stopped and our ark came to rest on Mt. Ararat,
and when the birds I sent out didn't come back,
we disembarked and went away...................... *The Book of Noah*

A 037

And it rained for 9 days and 9 nights.............................*Hellanicus*
And it rained for 12 days and 12 nights....................*Utanapishtim*
And it rained for 40 days and 40 nights................................*Noah*
And the water rose after many days .... *Atrahasis*

A 038

NOAH, SHEM, HAM, & JAPHETH

Shem and his family went south into Mesopotamia and Arabia, and in time became the Semites. Ham and his family went west into northern Africa and became the Hamites, and Japheth went with his family north into Anatolia and beyond and became the Ashkenazim, Medes, Russians, and everyone else in between.......................... *The Book of Noah*

A 039

OGYGES & DEUCALION

In Ancient Greece, there were the accounts of three great floods. The first was the flood of Ogyges, which is said to have covered the whole earth..*Ogyges of Thebes*
The second was the flood of Deucalion, who at the behest of Prometheus, made me a large wooden chest, which I filled up with food. When the rains came, my wife and I floated around on top of the food chest for 9 days and nights.................... *Deucalion in the Book of Hellanicus*

A 040

MANU & THE FISH

In India, one day after work, I was washing my hands and saw a small fish in the basin who told me a great flood was coming ....*Manu*
The fish (an incarnation of Vishnu), told me to build a boat and fill it with seeds and two each of all animals. I put the fish into a tank of water and it kept getting bigger and bigger. Instead of eating the fish I threw it into the ocean and let it go (free willy).......*Manu*

A 041

When the sea level rose, I pushed the boat into the water and attached a cord to the talking fish, who guided my boat through the currents and eddies of the storm ....*Manu*

A 042

The fish then dragged my boat to the northern mountains, and when the rain stopped, I let it go aground on the shore. Shortly

thereafter, the gods presented me with a young woman and we
lived happily thereafter, while we repopulated the earth...... *Manu*

A 043
DARDANUS & THE ANIMAL SKIN
The third was the flood of Dardanus. My family and I lived on a
mountain that after the flood became the island of Samothrace in
the northeast of the Aegean. From there, I paddled away on a
large inflated animal skin to find a place to live. I landed
on the eastern shores of the Aegean and
we settled there ....*Dardanus in the Theogony*

A 044
Fearing another deluge, I decided not to build a city there. The
land overlooking the Hellespont then came to be known
after me as the Dardanelles...*Dardanus*
All peoples throughout the entire earth who lived on or near the
coastal plains drowned. Those who lived in the mountains
survived until the rain stopped and the flood waters subsided.
Then they all walked away...*Dardanus*

A 045
ANCIENT EGYPT
In ancient Egypt, there was the all-powerful and self-created sun
god Amun-Ra. Also was the god Ptah, who created the world
and the material universe. Many other Egyptian deities brought
order out of chaos and kept chaos from overcoming order.
Deceased Egyptian notables had to be embalmed and laid down
in tombs before their spirits could enter the Field of Reeds
(Aratu) .... *The Egyptian Book of the Dead*
& The Pyramid Texts

A 046
PREDYNASTIC EGYPT
Before the Predynastic period in Egypt, the ancestors of the
ancient pharaohs lived and ruled over early settlements located

many miles to the west of the Nile, where the spring and summer
rains came every year and the waters filled up the lakes and the
desert turned green, from ca. 8000 BC to ca. 5,000 BC.
After this period, the earth's wobble changed slightly, the rains
ceased to come, and permanent dry desert conditions returned
Egypt to what it is today ....*R. Kuper, J. Kutzbach, &*
W. Ruddiman

A 047
After the summer rains stopped coming, the people of the
western desert departed and traveled to Egypt, settling first
around the Fayyum Oasis and then up
and down the Nile ....*Andrea Bekker-Collona*
Imhotep, the great Vizier of Egypt, built the
first pyramid .... *The Pharaoh Djoser*
Cheops built the Great Pyramid of Gizeh,
and then he felt better ....*Will Cuppy*
Many centuries later, I wrote the *Aegyptiaca*,
the great history of Egypt ....*Manetho*

A 048
ANCIENT EGYPTIANS
The priests of early Egypt taught everyone that the sun flew
through a hole in the sky on a great celestial boat, which was
being chased by a huge pig that stopped every month or so to
swallow up the moon. Centuries later, this was called the
"Wisdom of the Ancients" ....*Will Cuppy*

A 049
All Egyptians now must now worship my new god,
Aton ....*Ikhnaton*
That didn't work out very well .... *Nefertiti*
It didn't work out for me either ....*Tutankhamen*
Akhnaton is now dead, and
all his works will be expunged ....*Priests of Aman-Ra*

A 050

HOT CLIMATES AFFECT HUMAN CULTURES

Egyptians and the Libyans who live above (south of) the first cataract live in hot climates and thus lack manly courage and the ability to endure suffering and willingness to work, and live only for pleasure .... *Hippocrates*
But the art and technology of the
Egyptians are awesome ....*Herodotus*
Please note that since the 1940s, climatic and environmental determinism are regarded as horrible fallacies that
refuse to die.............................. *Modern Academic Geographers*

A 051

I visited Egypt, where the Nile surpasses all rivers upon the earth. The river water is sweet and lengthy. No rivers on earth can show such a continuous series of villages and towns along its banks .... *Ibn Battuta*
Egyptians are dominated by joyfulness, levity,
and no future .... *Ibn Khaldun*
I translated the Egyptian hieroglyphics..................... *Champollion*

A 052

Early Egyptians kept pigs on the temple grounds and ate them. Then, with the coming of the Hyksos Kings (aka, the desert or shepherd kings), pork became forbidden, and the keeping of pigs on temple grounds ceased. The Hyksos kings were migrant herders of sheep and goats. To them, pigs could not be herded from place to place and thus were seen as alien and unclean animals... *Frederick J. Simoons, et al.*

A 053

Most Egyptians are pale and ugly............................. *Jean Bodin*
Ancient Egyptians thought it is good luck to run into a swarm of bees while on a road. What they considered bad luck is not known.. *Wm. Cuppy*

A 054

NORTH AFRICAN TROGLODYTES

To the west of Egypt and north of the Sahara live the
Garamantes, who hunt Ethiopian Troglodytes (who live in
dugouts and holes in the ground) .... *Herodotus*
These Troglodyte people eat snakes and lizards, and speak a
language that includes many bat-like squeaks .... *Herodotus*
A click-language in ancient northern Africa?
Most interesting .... *Merritt Ruhlen*

A 055

THE PYGMAEA & LOTOPHAGI

The Pygmaea live upriver (south) from Egypt and south
of the city of Meroa .... *Homer*
The Lotophagi (lotus-eaters) live on an island to the west
of the Nile .... *Homer*
The Pelasgian Arimii live in northeastern Anatolia between
the Lacus Solis (Caspian Sea) and to the southeast
of the Black Sea .... *Homer*

A 056

NATIVE PEOPLES SOUTH OF THE SAHARA

People in the south of the Sahara are savages and barbarians.
They prefer glass trinkets over gold. It is impossible to believe
that they are men, and one can scarcely believe that God has
placed souls in such dark and ugly bodies .... *Jean Bodin*

A 057

Africans south of the Sahara are small, curly-haired, blubber-
lipped, ugly, and bald. Their self-control is so deficient that they
indulge in horrible excesses. The common trait of promiscuity of
men with animals explains why there are so many
monsters there. .... *Jean Bodin*
On my island, I've created many of these so-called monsters (my
children). Their first rule is not to walk on all fours. They all ask
me, "What are we Father?" .... *Dr.*
Moreau

A 058

NILOTIC PEOPLES OF KUSH

Long ago, in northeastern Africa, the ancient Nilotic kingdom of
Kush was located in the modern state of Sudan at the
confluence of the Blue Nile, the White Nile, and the
Atbara. This ancient Kushitic state lasted from
785 BC to 350 CE..*John N. Wilford*

A 059

NILOTIC PEOPLES OF NUBIA

During ancient times, there were other Nilotic peoples who lived
in the African kingdom of Nubia, located along the upper Nile.
They later built a new capital to the north at Meroe in ca. 300 CE
and built many pyramids in the vicinity. They fought with the
Romans, the Egyptians, and sometimes actually ruled
Egypt as pharaohs during several
Nubian Dynasties ....*Stuart Tyson Smith*

B 001

LIBYANS & OTHER ANCIENT PEOPLES

Ancient North Africa (aka, Ancient Libya), through which comes
water (from the upper Nile flowing northward down to the Nile
delta) is nothing but sand, and is full of wild beasts, weeds, and
very few people ....*Herodotus*
West of the Pillars of Hercules live the Celts and
Gades (Cadiz) ....*Herodotus*
Ancient Minoans lived on the island of Crete, south of the
Aegean Sea..*King Mynos*
To the north of Greece are the Thracians, who are among the
strongest men in the world...*Antonitus*

B 002

ANCIENT HEBREWS

Let my people go ....*Moses*
Let those people go ....*Ramses*
Watch my people go..*Moses*

B 003
Watch me part the Red Sea .... *Heston*
Forty years wandering in the wilderness, Oy .... *Moishe*
Watch the walls of Jericho come tumbling down .... *Joshua*

B 004
After the beginning, God made a Golem (a giant being) out of
clay and mud, which protected Israelites and Jews
for many centuries..*Book of Palms*
We've only been here in Israel for at least
4,000 years ....*Benjamin Netanyahu*
The real protection of modern Israel is our
Israel Defense Force (IDF).. *Golda Meir*

B 005
Delilah cut my hair off, and I can't even stand up. When I get my
strength back, just watch me pull down the pillars of this
goyish temple..*Samson*
Later, at the battle with the Philistines (one of the Great Sea
People migrants), I struck Goliath with a rock from my sling-shot
and knocked him unconscious. Before he woke up, I cut off his
head, and all the Philistines ran away ... *David the Shepherd Boy*
Nobody ever cheers for Goliath.........................*Wilt Chamberlain*

B 006
We must now leave the wicked cities of
Sodomy and Gonorrhea .... *Abraham*
Keep moving, woman, and don't look back ....*Lot*
Now, let there be airstrikes...*God*

B 007
ANCIENT PHOENECIANS, AKA THE KANAANI
The life's work of the great Phoenician historian Sanchuniathon
recorded the histories of Phoenicia, Byblos, Uruk, Sidon, and
Tyre (some of the world's oldest cities at the time)...........*Philo of
Byblos*

A long time ago, a Phoenician, or Carthaginian, ocean fleet
circumnavigated all of Africa in just three years ....*Herodotus*
And the western seas are ours ....*Carthaginian navigators*

B 008
THE PELASGIANS
The Pelasgians (original non-Greek inhabitants of ancient
Greece and other nearby lands) speak
barbarous languages...*Herodotus*
The Lacedaemonians (Spartans) are a
well-governed people..*Herodotus*
But they don't have any fun .... *Will Cuppy*
The Aegean isles of Lemnos and Imbrus are still
inhabited by Pelasgians...*Herodotus*
All men in Laconia (Sparta) inherit the occupations
of their fathers..*Herodotus*
This custom is the same as in India, except we
call it caste..*Arjuna*

B 009
ANCIENT GIANTS
And there were giants in those days..............*Book of Genetics &*
Numerals
These giants, called Nephrolites, were the children of the
Abanakis, who were believed by some to be
messengers from God .... *The Book of Eunuch*
When they grew old, they left their home in the East
and removed to the western land of the seals...............*The Book*
of Giants
B 010
THE OLDEST ALPHABETS
The 1st alphabet was created long ago by the Phoenicians and is
the one that most other scripts throughout the world come from.
Earlier scripts include Cuneiform, Harappan, Egyptian Hieratic,
and/or earlier scripts from the old city of Ebla in Syria.........*Paolo*
Matthiae

B 011
DOING & EXISTING
First, do no harm ....*Hippocrates*
To be is to do .... *Kant*
To do is to be .... *Sartre*
To do or not to do? .... *Omelet*
Skoobie doobie do .... *Sinatra*
I am what I am ....*Burning bush*
I am the great I am .... *Prince Charles*
I do not like this spam.. *Steve Jobs*
I yam what I yam...*Popeye*
I do not like green eggs & ham................................... *Dr. Seuss*

B 012
SEEKERS
Are there any honest men? ....*Diogenes*
Are there any righteous men? .... *Abraham*
Are there any straight men? ....*Lot*
Are there a few good men? .... *Tom Cruise*
Are there any sober men?...*Alanon*
Are there any learned men?..*Socrates*
Are there any men who can play this game?......................*Casey*
of the Mets

B 013
BRAHMA, VARNA, & CASTE IN ANCIENT INDIA
After the beginning, in ancient India, the god Brahma created the
earth and the heavens. Then Vishnu created Manu (the first man
on earth) and the god Parusa. From out of the god Parusa came
the first peoples (the higher and lower varnas
and castes) ....*The Vedas and Puranas*

B 014
Brahmins (the highest caste group, or varna, are priests,
teachers, and white people) came out of Parusa's head, eyes,
mouths, and ears ....*The Vedas and Puranas*

The next highest varna (major caste group, whose color is blood red) are the Kashatriyas (warriors, administrators, and royalty), who came out of Parusa's torso and arms .... *The Puranas and Vedas*

B 015

The third highest varna, the Vaisyas, came from out of the legs and lower body of Parusa. They are yellowish or saffron, and their occupations include craftsmen, land owners, merchants, bankers, money lenders, and followers of other highly skilled occupations, such as corporate administrators and lawyers) .... *Vedas and Puranas*

B 016

These three higher varnas are today called forward castes. The fourth, or lower varna, includes what generally are called the lowest castes; specifically, Shudras, many of whom are black people who came out of Parusa's feet. Shudras are laborers, farm workers, menials, and unskilled workers..........*The Vedas & Puranas*

About half of all the people of India are Shudras (however defined) .... *Time & Newsweek*

B 017

Approximately one-quarter of the people in India are of forward castes ....*Census of India*

160 million people in India are Untouchables (Dalits) and scheduled (lower status) tribals. Some 4.5 million Indians are Jains, ca. 8.5 million are Buddhists. Some 70 million are Muslims, and 28 million are Christians.................*Census of India*

B 018

Some authorities claim that the colors don't describe physical appearances, but are simply memberships in particular social groups (much like athletic teams, schools, and school colors). Yet the term varna in Hindi and ancient Sanskrit still means skin color, and black people in India are still looked down upon, whether they're black or not....................................*Jagjivan Ram*

B 019

ANCIENT IRANIANS (ARYANS), PERSIANS, & ZARDUSHTS

Our most important sacraments are our Fire Temples, where the
sacred fires are never extinguished, and our Towers of Silence,
where the bodies of our deceased are laid out on top of the
Towers of Silence and consumed by birds .... *Zoroastrian &*
Mazdaist priests

The practice of sky burial is also practiced in Tibet, ancient North
America, Bhutan, Nepal, Inner Mongolia, Qinghai,
and Sichuan .... *Buddhist Lamas*

B 020

ANCIENT ZOROASTRIANS

I am the keeper of the Zoroastrian Chinvat Bridge.
All must pass by me ....*Mithras*
Zardushts and Parsis who have had good thoughts and good
deeds can cross over this celestial bridge into paradise. All
evil-doers will fall off into the fiery abyss below.................*Mithras*
Persians are admirable because of the
teachings of Zoroaster.. *G.W.F. Hegel*

B 021

SCYTHIANS & PERSIANS

The Scythian nomads in the north of Central Asia (who are
related to and ancestors of Persians, Afghans, Tajiks, and
others) drink too much fermented mare's milk................... *Strabo*
The Scythians drink wine unmixed with water,
which is not very good.. *Herodotus*
Persian nobles prefer to discuss important matters when they
are drunk. Then they come back later to finish the various
deliberations when sober .... *Herodotus*

B 022

Persia is a scene of despotism and tyranny .... *Georg F.W. Hegel*
I hosted the mother of all garden
parties at Persepolis... *The Shah of Iran*
All are in the Satanic Verses ....*Salman Rushdie*

All are fatwas, assassins, and murderers.
(We are so corrupt)....................................*Ayatollah Khomeini*

B 023
ANCIENT & MODERN GNOSTICS
From out of ancient Zoroastrianism and Manichaeism came a
family of religions called Gnosticism (from gnosis, meaning
knowledge). These beliefs are held by divergent groups of
Christians and many others who believe that in the beginning,
there was a pure and perfect god (who made the intelligent
and spiritual world), along with an imperfect Demiurge, who
created the impure, hateful, and flawed material
world..............................*Ancient Mystery teachings and practices*

B 024
Ancient Gnostics who master hidden, mystical, esoteric, and
secret knowledge could achieve enlightenment, salvation, and/or
mental contentment .... *Al-Hakim bi-Amr*

B 025
A different path to achieve gnosis and/or salvation was
participation in mystery rites, as with the sacrificial Mithraic
Tauroctony (bull sacrifice), followed by periodic communal ritual
feasts and heavy drinking ....*Priests of Mithras*
Today, there are many small populations of Arabs, Greeks,
Turks, Iranians, Israelis, Kurds, and many other little-known
religious groups whose beliefs can be traced back to ancient
Gnosticism...*John B. Noss*

B 026
Today, modern Gnosticism can be found among the Mandaean
Marsh Arabs in southern Iraq, Sabaeans in Yemen, Dervishes in
Turkey, Yazidis in northern Iraq, and Druzes in southwestern
Lebanon, southern Syria, and in northern Israel ..... *Sultan Pasha*

B 027

OF WATER

All is water and change .... *Thales*
Oh, the water goes down and around and around
and it comes out here ....*Archimedes*
Water, water, everywhere, and not a drop to drink .... *Coleridge*
We do not live in water ....*Arachnids*
He who is now dead was found drinking from our well ....*Omar Sherif*
I have drunk from your well .....................................*T.E. Lawrence*
You are welcome ....*Ali of the Ruala*
Here, can you carry my water bag? .... *Lawrence*
The Ruala do not carry water .... *Sherif Ali*

B 028

EARLY ARCHAEOLOGICAL DISCOVERIES

I discovered Knossos on the island of Crete .... *Minos Kalokairinos*
I led the excavations of Knossos .... *Sir Arthur Evans*
I was the first to recognize how old the
Harappan ruins were ....*John Marshall of the Raj*
I discovered Gobekli Tepe, the oldest
stone temple on earth .... *Klaus Schmidt*

B 029

ANCIENT GREEK EXPLORERS

Long ago, we explored the Black Sea and never found any
golden sheepskins. But we did explore all around the Pontus
Axinus (Black Sea) .... *Jason and the Arguments*
The Odyssey is a compilation of stories about Greek exploration
of the western Mediterranean .... *Homer*
Many of these stories are included in my Aeneid .... *Virgil*

B 030

GREEK LAWGIVERS

After the time of Jason, there were many things in Athens, and
some of them were written down. Yet, there was no written
comprehensive legal code, and I was commissioned to write

one. I codified old laws and invented new ones. Some were
regarded as too severe and came to be called "draconian." I told
everyone that such laws were frequently draconian ....*Draco,
the 1st Lawgiver of Athens*
Years later, I modified Draco's harsh Athenian law code and
eliminated those laws deemed too severe and unfair......... *Solon,
the 2nd Lawgiver of Athens*

B 031
HELEN of MYCENAE
They say I had the face that launched a
thousand ships ....*Helen of Mycenae*
And that I was the wife of King Menelaus of Achaea, Sparta, or
Laconia. Some say I was the wife of King Agamemnon, the King
of Mycenae. One day, I was abducted by Paris, Prince of Troy
(in western Anatolia overlooking the Dardanelles) and was kept
hostage behind the massive walls of his city......*Helen of Laconia*

B 032
HELEN OF TROY
And for whatever it's worth, Paris really wasn't very
good in bed..*Helen of Troy*
Yeah! Whadidya expect? All those Greeks & Trojans
were just !*#+!^#*%*! faggots who only stuped
each other ....*Iliza Vie Shlesinger (The Elder Millennial)*
Imitation is the greatest form of flattery .... *George Carlin*

B 033
THE TROJAN WAR
A war ensued where the Trojans were defeated after the
Mycenaean Greeks gave them a bogus wooden horse, which the
Trojans hauled in through the great walls into their city.
(God, were they dumb) .... *Homer*
I discovered the modern ruins
of the ancient city of Troy..............................*Heinrich Shliemann*
I don't believe that any of the Achaean Greeks would send an
army just to free one small woman from far away.
This does not compute ....*Herodotus*

B 034

SALAMIS & MARATHON

The Persians are invading Greece again............... *King Leonidas*

Wooden walls will not fail .... *Delphic Oracle*

We won a great naval battle at Salamis .... *Themistocles*

We've won at Marathon. *pant, pant, pant, thud*..... *Pheidippides*

B 035

ICARUS & DAEDALUS

Now where did those two go? .... *King Minos*

Watch me fly really high .... *Icarus*

Don't fly too high, the sun will melt your wax wings ....*Daedalus*

Don't listen to him, fly as high as you want................... *Jonathon*
Livingston Seagull

A man can't soar too high, when
he flies with just his own wings............................. *William Blake*

I flew too far on borrowed wings.....................*Charles Van Doren*

I believe I can fly .... *R. Kelly*

Let's fly away .... *Frank Sinatra*

B 036

ALEXANDER THE GREAT

I conquered Greece, Anatolia, Mesopotamia, Persia, NW India,
and Egypt. Before I died, I founded the Egyptian city of
Alexandria in the northwestern part of the Nile Delta. I also
founded the great library there, which was built shortly thereafter
by Ptolemy I Soter, one of my generals.......................*Alexander*

B 037

Many years later, the library was accidentally burned by troops of
Julius Caesar and later by Aurelian. This and later fires
destroyed much of it..*Eratosthenes*

I ordered the final blow that destroyed all
its pagan writings .... *Coptic Pope Theophilus*

B 038
ANCIENT FOOD AVOIDANCES
Ancient Gauls avoid eating rabbits and hares..................*Caesar*
Pythagoreans must not eat beans; particularly,
castor and fava beans .... *Pythagoras*
Jews must not eat pork, oysters, clams, shrimp, lobsters, and
any other bottom-feeding aquatic animals, the rear half of cows,
or anything else that's treif and unclean........... *Book of Levitation*

B 039
Ancient Mongols and Turks, before Islam,
did not eat pork ....*Book of No Eats*
Chinese do not drink milk and also avoid
cheese and butter.. *Chinese menu*
Jurched Manchus do not eat dogs and are angry
that Koreans do .... *Korean menu*
Armenians and Greeks seldom ate pork, but there were no bans
against it... *F. Simoons*

B 040
JAIN & BUDDHIST FOOD AVOIDANCES
Jains avoid eating meat and don't grow crops where
ploughing kills innocent insects and other
small creatures .... *The Jain Agamas and Jaina Sutras*
Buddhists avoid eating meat..... *The Tripitaka and the Pali Sutras*
Modern Vegans don't eat meat.............. *The Annals of No Meats*
At all our beef delis, we have the meats............... *Ving Rhames &*
James Earl Jones
Early Muslims did not eat pigs, dogs, carrion, donkeys, snakes,
hyenas, insects, or anything else that wasn't Halal................ *The*
Hadiths

C 001

IBN BATTUTA & HIS EARLY JOURNEYS

I was born in Tangier, Morocco into a Berber family. I was a scholar and explorer. For thirty years, I travelled widely throughout most of the Islamic world and visited many non-Moslem places as well ....*Mohammed Abdul Ibn Battuta*

C 002

In 1325, from Gaza, I travelled to Hebron. I saw there a mosque that housed a tomb, within which were the graves of Abraham, Isaac, and Jacob, along with another three graves containing the remains of their wives. It is said that the mosque was built by Solomon, who commanded a jinn to build it .... *Ibn Battuta*
I also saw the tomb housing Adam and Eve's earthly remains in Jeddah... *Ibn Battuta*

C 003

Soloman's mosque also contained the grave of Joseph, and nearby was the tomb of the ancient prophet, Lot. A short distance away was Lot's Lake (the Dead Sea), which is highly brackish. Below the current surface of the sea lies the drowned settlement of Lot's people .... *Ibn Battuta*

C 004

I then travelled to Jerusalem and entered the al-Aksa Mosque, near where the site of the Dome of the Rock exists, which houses the place where Mohammed ascended into heaven on his mystical nocturnal journey .... *Ibn Battuta*

C 005

LATER MANICHAEANS

Long ago, there were the Gnostic Manichaeans in ancient Rome and the Middle East, who sought to master hidden, mystical, and secret knowledge simply by passing through an esoteric ritual that could by itself help them to achieve fulfillment and/or a higher status in society.............................*Al-Hakim bi-Amr Allah*

C 006

From Manichaeism came many Gnostic beliefs. In ancient Rome
and the Middle East, many esoteric Gnostic groups slowly
became sparse and many left and died out. And I was one of
them for years.. *Saint Augustine*

C 007

ANCIENT & MODERN GNOSTIC BELIEVERS

Today, there are many small Arab, Greek, Turkish, Iranian,
Israeli, Kurdish, and many other little-known religious groups
whose beliefs can be traced back to ancient Gnosticism (that the
material and carnal world is evil and was created by an evil and
defective god). On the other hand, the spiritual world is good and
beautiful, and was created by a good and perfect god who is still
worshiped today by some believers .... *Modern Gnostic sects*

C 008

MODERN MANDAEANS

One of these Gnostic groups is the Mandaean Marsh Arabs in
southern Iraq (who lived in the marshes of the deltas of the Tigris
and Euphrates rivers). Notably, they especially revere John the
Baptist. In the 1990s, Saddam Hussein dried up the marshes by
diverting both of the two rivers .... *BBC, NY Times*

C 009

MODERN YAZIDIS, DRUZES, ALEVIS, & PARSIS

The secretive Gnostic Yazidis live in northern Iraq, while Gnostic
Druzes live in northeastern Lebanon, southern Syria, and
northern Israel .... *Suliman Bashear*
I was the spiritual leader of the modern Druzes in Israel
until 1993...*Amin Tarif*
Other Gnostic-like communities today include Muslim Dervishes,
Alevis, and Alowites in modern Turkey and Iran. Other such
groups include the modern day Parsis in Bombay and elsewhere

in India. Many Jains have emigrated to the United States and the
European Union .... *AP, UPI, BBC, NYT, AL-JAZEERA*

C 010
MESOPOTAMIA & HINDUSTANI BEGINNINGS
In early Mesopotamia, after the floods, there was extensive trade
between the Phoenicians, Egyptians, the ancient Indian cities of
Dholavira, Harappa, Mohenjo-daro, and the Elamites in the
Zagros Mts. .... *Sumerian clay ledgers & edicts*
I was the last Sumerian king before
the Akkadians came ....*Lugalzagesi*
All laws are now written in stone ....*Sargon I of Akkad*
Later, Amorite herders came into Mesopotamia from
farther west .... *Lugalbanda Text*

C 011
THE GREAT TOWER OF BABYLON
We built the Great Neo-Sumerian Ziggurat of Ur ....*King Shulgi*
I am bored. Let's build another tower that will reach up
into the sky .... *Nimrod*
OK, and we will call it the Great Erection of Babylon ....*King Ur-
Nammu*
Whom the gods would destroy, they first scramble
their brains ....*Sopheranidas*
I can't understand anything you
Babyloniacs are saying ....*Cyrus the Great*

C 012
AFTER THE GREAT CONFUSION OF TONGUES
Most languages on Earth are related in some way to many other
languages and dialects, either by borrowing or by conquest and
absorption. Other tongues originate from splitting into several
offspring languages, which evolve into different forms as a result
of isolation from others, such as Latin (splitting into Italian,
French, Spanish), and isolation of Romanians, from Portuguese
& Gallegos. Also is early Germanic (evolving into Dutch, Yiddish,
Danish, Friesian, and Cockney). Also are "language isolates"
(living or dead) that are remote from and not related to any other

lingo on earth (Basque, Ainu, Etruscan, Sumerian, Haida, Andaman, Elamite, and Gilyak) .... *Merrett Rhulen, et al.*

C 013

FOUNDERS, TRADERS, & CONQUERORS OF ANCIENT MESOPOTAMIA
In the beginning were the ancient Sumerians (original peoples)
Then came Phoenician traders (Semitic)
Then came Egyptian traders (Coptic)
Then were the Assyrians (Semites)
Then were the Babylonians (Semites)
Then were the Akkadians (Semites)
And then came the Amorites (Semites)
Then were the Hittites (Indo-Anatolians)
Then came the Kassites (Indo-Aryans)

C 014

Then were the Chaldeans (Semites)
Then came the Mitanni (Indo-Aryans)
Then the Medes arrived (Indo-Iranians)
Then the Persians came (Indo-Iranians)
Then the Greeks (Indo-Europeans) came
Then came the Romans (Indo-Europeans)
Then came the Parthians (Indo-Iranians)
And then came the Arabs (Semites)
Then came the Mongols (Altaics)
Then came the Turks (Altaics)
Then came the British (Indo-Europeans)
Then came the Americans (Indo-Europeans)
Then came the ISIS Caliphate (Arabs and others)
And then the Americans came (again)

C 015

THE TUNGUS OF SIBERIA
After the beginning was the god Buga
and the primordial sea .... *Tungusic shamans*
Ancient Proto-Russian Slavs worshipped
their uber god, Buhkh ....*St. Methodius*

C 016

JAPAN'S MYTHICAL BEGINNINGS

Long ago, all was mixed up together in darkness .... *The Kojiki*
After the beginning, there were gods and demons who churned
up the Sea of Japan and made the elixir of life .... *Watatsumi*
the sea god

C 017

After the beginning, Izanagi and Izanami stirred up the primeval
sea with their wands and created the Islands of Nippon. Then
they begat the Sun Goddess Amaterasu in 680 BC, from whom
all Japanese emperors are descended .... *The Nihon Shoke*
Also is Ryujin, the dragon god, who rules all the seas and
oceans .... *The Nihongj*

C 018

THE AINUS & ANCIENT JAPAN

Bears and Mt. Fuji have always been sacred
to the Ainu people .... *Ainu shamans*
Old Japan is generally known by the Chinese as the
land of hairy dwarfs .... *Han Scripts*
We Ainus (aka Ezo) used to live all over Japan, but now only a
few of us remain, and we now live only in Hokkaido
and northern Honshu .... *Shigeru Kayano*
We all originated in ancient Siberia and came from what is now
the Maritime Kray in Russia about 20,000 years ago via a land
bridge to the island of Sakhalin. Many ancient Ainu also came to
Hokkaido, directly from the EastAsian Mainland ..... *Hirofumi Kato*

C 019

JOMON & SATSUMA PEOPLE

Recent research places the origin of the ancient Ainu people
from the ancient Jomon, Satsuma, and the northern Okhotsk
archaeological cultures of Sakhalin, Kamchatka, and the Kurile
Islands. The Ainu language is unrelated to any other languages
on Earth, for a long time, which indicates that the early Ainu lived
away from other human groups and had
few contacts .... *L.L. Cavali-Sforza & Mark J. Hudson*

C 020

For a long time, Ainus were thought to have been the original inhabitants of Japan, who are usually associated with the ancient Jomon culture several thousand years ago............*Ainu shamans*

The Ainu people, who came largely from the Jomon culture, are also believed to have migrated to Japan from
Southeast Asia .... *Alex Iwasaki*

Early Jomon cultural artifacts have been
found in Chile.. *Betty Meggars*

C 021

ANCIENT ORIGINS & SPREAD OF THE JAPANESE

Early explanations of who and where the Japanese people came from follows accounts of the Yayoi culture, which spread southward from Siberia and spread through Korea and across the Tsushima strait into the western part of the Inland Sea, and then spread eastward to Kansai (Osaka-Kobe) and became the Yamato Japanese......................................*Reichauer & Fairbank*

C 022

At the same time (possibly earlier) the Jomon people spread northward through the Ryuku Islands into the southern part of Kyushu and became the Satsuma people, who then spread into and around the Inland sea ....*Fairbank & Reichauer*

C 023

TUNGUSIC & YAYOI PEOPLE

Many years ago, it was thought that the Japanese and Korean Yayoi culture arose among the Tungusic people of eastern Siberia. Now, the Yayoi culture is thought to have arisen along the lower Yangzi in eastern coastal China. From there, the Yayoi people diffused eastward into the Ryukyu Islands, and later became the people of the ancient Okinawans, south Koreans, and the people of southern Kyushu .... *Alex Iwasaki*

C 024
The modern Japanese are now thought to have descended
from both the ancient Jomon and the
ancient Yayoi cultures .... *Alex Iwasaki*

C 025
The Ainu people are thought by some to have arisen in
Sundaland where most of today's Indonesian islands were above
sea level during the last ice age. Much of the Southeast
mainland was above sea level. There, they mixed with the
nearby Austronesian peoples and the hairy Australoid peoples
(maybe farther south). As this was taking place, they travelled
northward to southern Kyushu and brought the Satsuma
Austronesian people with them .... *Iwasaki*

C 026
Then the Jomon people, along with the similar Ebisu and Emishi
people, spread around most of the Setto
Naikai (Inland Sea).. *Iwasaki*

C 027
THE YAYOI & YAMATO PEOPLE
And later came the Yayoi people from out of southern Korea,
and then from the western part of the Setto Naikai (Inland Sea).
The later-arriving Yayoi people had a metallurgical advantage
that they brought with them that enabled them to make hotter
fires in their metal smelting technology. This enabled them to
make stronger metal weapons than the
Jomon Ainu .... *Edwin O. Reichauer &*
John K. Fairbank

C 028
Years later, the Yamato Japanese people extended eastward
into the farthest edge of the Setto Naiki (Inland Sea), called
Kansai (the western gateway, which became the area around
Osaka). There they founded a state called Yamatai, which was
noticed briefly by the Chinese .... *Spring & Autumn Annals*

C 029

Eventually, the Yamato Japanese pushed north and eastward and settled in the region they called Kanto (eastern gateway and Tokyo), and then farther north into Tohoku (east-north) in northern Japan ....*Reichauer & Fairbank*

C 030

As they spread to the east and then into the north, the primal Yamato Japanese pushed the Ainu northward into Tohoku, northern Honshu, and then finally into the northern island of Hokkaido ....*Louis F. Nussbaum, Delmer M. Brown*

C 031

THE ETAS OF OLD JAPAN

There are separate ethnic groups in Japan that include the Etas (aka, Burakumin) and other out-castes, who live in Japan's larger cities, where many are associated with the Yakusas (underworld Japanese crime syndicates) ....*Tokyo Police*

C 032

MODERN NIPPON & THE JAPANESE

After many centuries, the Islands of Japan came to be called Nippon and Nihon by the court of the Emperor, Daimyos, and the Shogun. Many years ago, a Mongol/Chinese naval attack on our homeland was blown away by a great typhoon, which will always be known in Japan as the divine wind (Kamikaze)....*The Go-Uda Emperor*

C 033

About the same year, during the reign of The Great Khan in China, some Italian tourists, named Polo, learned of us and referred to our island nation as Cipango or Zipango and the land of the hairy dwarfs ....*The Kameyama Emperor*

C 034

THE JAPANESE MEIJI RESTORATION & MODERNIZATION

First was the Bokafu, then the Meiji period .... *Sydney Brown*

We restored the Emperor in the Meiji Reformation and tossed
out the Shogun. We also tried modernizing Japan into a modern
industrial superpower and building a modern
navy and military .... *Okubo, Okama, Ito Hirobumi, & Mitsubishi*
We sent observers and emissaries to America and Europe to
learn how to industrialize and modernize Japan .... *The Iwakura*
Mission

C 035

THE JAPANESE SHOWA RESTORATION

We must continue to modernize and industrialize the Japanese
people under a militarized emperor. At the same time, we must
also keep our sacred doctrines of Kokutai (national ethos) and
Bushido (the ethos of the ancient samurai and the Japanese
military). These were the guiding lights of the Cherry Blossom
Society, who envisioned a modern military state and a military
ideology for all the Japanese people .... *Kita Ikki*

C 036

Japan is now called the England of the East for bringing
advanced civilization to the whole
of eastern Asia .... *Ellen Churchill Semple*
The Japanese have perfected good manners that have made
them indistinguishable from rudeness .... *Paul Thereaux*

C 037

How curious is the Japanese, he always says, "Excuse it,
please." He climbs into his neighbor's garden, then smiles and
says, "I beg your pardon." He bows and grins a friendly grin, and
calls his hungry family in. He grins and bows a friendly bow; "So
solly, this my garden now" .... *Ogden Nash*

C 038

JAPAN & THE GREAT PACIFIC WAR

We needed all that scrap iron and oil that was cut off... *Japanese*
General Staff
Banzai, banzai, banzai .... *Yamashita*
All Americans are soft and lazy .... *Tojo*
Why are the waves so restless? .... *Hirohito*

Tora, tora, tora..*Fushida & Genda*

C 039
All we've done is to awaken a sleeping giant...................*Admiral Yamamoto*
The Pacific War has turned out not necessarily to our advantage, and we must now endure the unendurable ....*The Emperor*
The Americans occupied our country for several decades ....*Japan's new government*
And we have once more become an industrial giant.....*Japanese Salarymen*

C 040
Many customs were changed. One innovation was the changing of roles of women and their entrance into the workforce. This has resulted in a falling birth rate. Many women have postponed marriage and some Japanese men must find wives from overseas; more specifically, from Thailand and Vietnam .... *National Census returns*
Japan's best university is still the University of Tokyo (aka "To-dai")...*Shinzo Abe*

C 041
ZAIBATSUS & GAIJIN OF MODERN JAPAN
Another category of people in Japan are the Gaijin (aka, Kikoushijo or Beikokujin). They are people from Japanese families, who were born and/or grew up in other countries. Most of these have come came back to Japan with their parents, who've lived abroad for many years as diplomats or representatives of Japan's Zaibatsus (industrial and business cartels). Many Gaijin (adults and children) must study how to speak modern Japanese, and take lessons on how to behave in modern-day Japan.. *Asahi Shimbun*

D 001

CHINA'S ANCIENT CREATION STORY

In the chaos of the primordial universe, things coalesced into a cosmic egg, where the forces of yin and yang existed in perfect harmony. Then Pan-gu emerged from the egg and commenced to create the earth and the sky .... *Xu Zheng*
After many eons of creating everything, Pan-gu became bored, faded away, and expired, leaving the world intact and in proper balance ....*Xu Zheng (Shoo-Jung)*
OK, people, it's halftime at Super Bowl 51, so let's hatch this giant egg .... *Lady Gaga*

D 002

NORTHERN CHINA'S GREAT HUA BEI PLAIN

In the beginning, I created the great Yellow-colored Loess Plateau in northern China. Then I created a mighty river that crossed the plateau and eroded down through it and took on the yellow color of its soft earthen plateau. Then the river, which the Chinese named the Huang He (Yellow River), periodically floods every few years or decades all over the flat North China Plain. At the same time, the sluggish river drops all its load of yellow silt and sediment as it flows all over the great northern plain, and thousands die; hence the name it's often called is "China's Sorrow" .... *Pan-gu*

D 003

CHINA'S EARLIEST MYTHICAL EMPERORS & KINGS

Before the Eight Kings (number three plus number five) period was the Chinese Neolithic, lasting from ca. 8500 to 2070 BC. The reigns of the Three Sovereigns and the Five Emperors (a total of eight kings) make up the earliest quasi historical periods in ancient China. The eight kings had magical powers and created the Chinese landscape and created
the Chinese people .... *Xu Zheng*
(a historian and court official living in the 3rd century BC, who wrote and codified the "Three-Five" Histories)

D 004
These two ancient time periods of the eight supernatural or human kings (aka, august ones) have been assigned modern dates by historians from ca. 2852 BC to 2070 BC, when the (earliest) Xia Dynasty began (from 2070 to 1600 BC). The earlier periods (3 kings or sovereigns) (ca. 2852–2205 BC) were named Fuxi, Nuwa, and Shen-nong ....*Xu Zheng*

D 005
The later period (5 emperors) started with Huang di (the Yellow Emperor, the earliest of several rulers with that reign name). The next four emperors were Zhuanxu, Ku, Yao, and Shun (ca. 2205–2070 BC). Each of these prehistoric figures performed and created important environmental and social elements of Chinese history, geography, culture, and identity.......................*Xu Zheng*

D 006
ANCIENT CHINA'S GREAT FLOOD
In ancient China, there was a great deluge, which was called the Great Flood of Gun-Yu, who was a prince ordered by the Emperor Yao (one of the eight august kings) to tame the flooding of the great Huang He (Yellow River) in northern China so the people could come back home .... *The Bamboo Annals*

D 007
Since the elevation of the entire eastern part of the Huabei Plain is close to sea level, the Great Chinese Flood (and perhaps many earlier floods) also should have been caused, in part, by rising sea levels, just as was the case of the great floods along the coasts of lower Mesopotamia, the eastern Mediterranean, the Black Sea coast, India, and the low-lying coasts along the North Sea and the Baltic, (around the same general time period) .... *Chinese hydrologists & Feng Shui masters*

D 008
Some sources have written that the flood (caused by a large
landslide) lasted for 30 or 40 years and drove away most of the
people living on the flat Huabei Plain. Some estimates place this
flood on the Huang He to the third millennium (3000–2000 BC).
The earliest documentation of the Gun-Yu Flood include the *Shiji*
and the *Shujing* (Book of Documents) from the mid first
millennium (1000–2000 BC), which do not record any
catastrophic rainfall events........................ *Wu, et al. (see below)*

D 009
Emperor Yao's court scribes recorded that the water of the Great
Flood reached as far south as the Chang Jiang (Yangzi,
Yangtze). Around 1920 BC, there was a flood on the Huang He
caused by a great landslide that created a large dam on the
river. After several months, the dam broke and a large flood
resulted that may have played a role in the rise of the Xia
dynasty .... *Michael Greshko & David Cohen (2016)*

D 010
The dynasties of this time that would have been affected by the
flood were in the earliest stone age and Neolithic Xia Dynasty,
lasting from 2070 to 1600 BCE (if it really existed), and the
Bronze Age Shang Dynasty from 1600–1046 BC............*Chinese*
Bamboo Annals

D 011
This flood and its connection to the Great Flood of Gun-Yu and
the origins of the early and mythical Xia Dynasty has provoked
comments of contemporary scholars.......*Wu, Zhou Liu, Granger,*
Wang, Cohen, Wu, Ye, Bar-Yosef, Lu, Zhang, Yuan, Qi, Cai, &
Bai, in the journal Science, Vol. 355, (Mar. 2017)

D 012

CHINA'S FORTUNE TELLERS & THE I-JING
Long ago, there were many ways of divining the future, and there
were many Chinese fortune-tellers and charlatans who recorded
them in a book that came to be called the *Book of Changes*, also
known as the *I-jing*............................. *Fuxi & Ancient Folk Beliefs*
The *I-Jing* is hen bu hao,
la shi, silly, and worthless .... *Confucius & Confucians*

D 013

After the beginning were the teachings of the Dao* de Jing (also
Daojiao), which were written down ca. 500 BC by the sage Lao-
tse (Laozi) as he waited to cross the Chinese border into Tibet
(most likely). He was then ordered by a border guard to leave
behind in China all his possessions. He said all he had was in his
head. The guard then ordered him to write everything down
before he could leave .... *Daoist* traditions*
Dao written in pinyin,
Tao in Wade-Giles (both pronounced Dao)

D 014

THE FIRST EMPEROR & THE GREAT WALL OF CHINA
I'm the first historical emperor, and all imperial history begins
with me ....*Qin Shi Huang Di*
Seek virtue and proper behavior in society .... *Master Kung*
I completed much of what became the Great Wall, which was
designed to keep the northern degenerate Xunu barbarians out
of China...*Ch'in Shih Huang Ti*

D 015

The Hsiung-nu (Xunu) barbarians, pronounced in both writing
forms "Shoo-noo," have always ravaged north China ......*Ssu-ma*
Ch'ien
Throughout history, China also has had many communist
regimes (including mine) with many land
reform edicts.. *Wang Mang*

D 016

THE GRAND CANAL OF CHINA

I started and completed much of the Grand Canal, which made travel from the mighty Yangzi in the south to the Huang He (Yellow River, aka, China's Sorrow) much easier......*Sui Yang Di*

D 017

THE CHINESE & FENG SHUI

A long time ago, Chinese naturalists seeking harmony with nature found ways of reading landscapes, wind, and water, so as to correctly orient homes, bedrooms, graves, roads, buildings, offices, outhouses, and tombs...........*Ancient feng shui* masters,*
**pronounced "fung shway"*

D 018

INDO IRANIANS (ARYANS) IN NORTHWESTERN CHINA

Long ago, there were Ancient Indo-European Tocharians living in the northern part of the Tarim Basin in XinJiang province, along the ancient Silk Road from about 4000 BC to about 1800 BC. Some of them had "red hair" and spoke a Centum (western) Indo European language. Their burial sites in western China are called the Xiaohe tomb complex in Xinjiang province along and near the ancient Silk Route ...... *Li Chunxiang & Kristina Killgrove*

D 019

TOCHARIANS, KUSHANS, & SAKAS IN NORTHWEST CHINA

Some scholars believe the Tocharians originated from ancient Bactria .... *J.P. Mallory*
At an early date, there were also two other Indo-European "red-haired" barbarian tribes living along China's Hexi Corridor in Gansu province. The Chinese called them the Yueh-Chih and Wu-sun .... *Mallory*

D 020

THE ANCIENT YUEH-CHIH & THE WU-SUN

Eventually, both of these cultures were escorted out of China and later entered the Indus Valley, where they became known as the Kushans (first) and the Sakas (second). They both invaded northwest India and established two successor kingdoms there..*Mallory & Pulleybank*
Both the Kushan and Saka kingdoms declined, and were later taken over by the great Gupta Empire ......*Moreland & Chatterjee*

D 021

THE ANCIENT CHINESE

The Chinese are weak, misshapen, harmless, and vain... *Johann G. von Herder*
The Chinese are clever, but their artwork lacks beauty .... *George Frederich Hegel*
The Chinese are half-civilized, mild, intelligent, courteous and highly industrious, but also vain, timid, and jealous.............*Jesse Olney*

Chinese are skillful and clever, and are distinguished for their mental and physical abilities, but they have little respect for themselves or for humanity in general ....................*G.W.F. Hegel*

D 022

HUI SHEN'S JOURNEY ACROSS THE PACIFIC OCEAN

A thousand years ago, or during the 7th or 5th century CE, a Buddhist monk named Hui Shen claimed to have sailed a sea-going junk across the Pacific Ocean and had seen a land he called Fusang after a fabulous tree growing there, which was most likely southern Mexico judging by descriptions of the vegetation there...*George Carter*

D 023

HUI SHEN'S MYTHICAL ADVENTURE IN THE LAND OF FUSANG

Hui Shen claims to have sailed his ship across the Pacific some 3,000 or 20,000 Li from China to the west coast of America..*George Carter*

Nobody knows how long the ancient Chinese Li was and Carter
doesn't know what he's talking about ....*Joseph Needham*
& John Fairbank
I never sailed a ship from China to "Fusang,"
or anywhere else... *Hui Shen*

D 024
Some say the Chinese will eat anything with four legs, except
tables, but this is really not true .... *Wing Ding*
Everyone should have deep fried chicken
parts in every wok .... *General Tso*

D 025
ZHENG HE'S GREAT OCEANIC FLEET
During the Ming dynasty, I sailed out into the ocean with my fleet
of many huge sea-going junks. We sailed from China to the
South Seas, India, Arabia, Africa, and then returned with a
giraffe and many other gifts for the Emperor. But the emperor
was not impressed, and the Ming court destroyed all my ships
and sailing charts, and that was the end of Chinese exploration
into the outside world .... *Admiral Zheng He*

D 026
The ancient Chinese rulers were enlightened, but their views
were worldly and materialistic. Chinese philosophy says nothing
about humility, meekness, or returning good for evil. Otherwise,
China is a country of long-suffering coolies and crocodile-
gnawed sampans.................................*Hendrick Willem van Loon*

D 027
MOSLEM PARADISE & THE GREAT DOWN-BELOW
We are angels and recorders of deeds of those righteous
Muslims who wish to cross over the Bridge of Sarrat into
paradise (Jannah). The unrighteous will fall off into the burning
pits below (Jahannam) .... *Munkar & Nakir*
All Jihadistas will go directly to paradise
without passing Go.. *Mohamet al Sod*

D 028
ARABS & BEDOUINS
Arabs in the Maghreb are growing harder to distinguish from
Berbers..*Ibn Battuta*
Arabs who have left Arabia have not kept up the purity of their
ancestral lineages. True Bedouins are admirable, but other
Arabian camel nomads are the world's most savage people and
they all live like wild animals .... *Ibn Khaldun*
After ingesting much hashish, my fanatical Assassins will murder
Crusaders in their beds..*Hassan Sabbah*
(aka, The Old Man of the Mountain)

D 029
Just me and my camel..*Ahab the Arab,*
Sheik of the burning sand
I found a girl with a seven-year itch, and she came
with me to the casbah..*Ahab*
Get rid of Ahab, I said, and Fatima came with me
to the casbah...................................... *Rudolph Valentino*
Rock the casbah and do the Mestapha Dance.......*Joe Strummer*
of the Clash
Then walk like an Egyptian .... *The Bangles*

D 030
Arabs and Bedouins are ignorant, savage, illiterate, and
barbarous. Those living along the Barbary Coast are pirates.
Those in the interior are robbers. The Arabs of the shores of
Tripoli are also ignorant, rapacious, and cruel...........*Jesse Olney*

D 031
Arabs are a careless people and provide nothing
for the winter...*George W.F. Hegel*
Arabs are a race of robbers equally addicted to theft
and trade ....*Ellen C. Semple*

D 032
Arabians are a hard people who rarely smile or play. They can't
be corrupted by material wealth because their needs are so
simple ....*Hendrick Willem van Loon*
Keep smiling and sailing the seven seas...........................*Sinbad*
Keep the genie in the #~x*^!v+; bottle ....*Aladdin*
Open the gates for me and my 40 thieves...................... *Ali Baba*
Open the gates for me and my 40 wives .... *Joseph Smith*

D 033
CHINA & KUBLAI KHAN
While ruling China, I sent a large invasion force against the
eastern sunrise Islands of Jih-pen-guo (aka, Zipango or
Cipango), also known as the land of the rising sun and the hairy
dwarfs. But my Chinese river junks were poorly made, a huge
typhoon sank them all, and our great
attack failed.. *The Great Khan*

D 034
IBN BATTUTA & MARCO POLO IN CHINA
While at the court of the Great Khan, I witnessed a rope trick
exhibition where a boy "levitated" up a rope and then slithered
down it. When he came down, his master became angry and
killed him with a sword .... *Ibn Battuta*
We visited the court of the Great Khan while travelling through
from western China in the year 1266. And the Chinese eat
spaghetti just like us...*Marco Polo*

D 035
China was beautiful, but it didn't please me. Pagans and Infidels
ruled in all the land. Whenever I went outside my residence, I
saw many disturbing sights, so I tried to stay inside as much as I
could. Sometimes, when I was outside, I would see some
Chinese Muslims, who seemed to me to be members of
my own family .... *Ibn Battuta*
I then filled up my ships with trade goods acquired in
China and sailed home... *Ibn Battuta*

D 036

END OF IBN BATTUTA'S JOURNEY

On the way back to the Mediterranean from China and India, we
stopped off at the Maldive Islands south of India, and partook of
the local custom of providing "temporary wives" for the pleasure
of travelers. Their dowries were very low and I "married" four of
them. And then we left..*Ibn Battuta*

D 037

My journey from Morocco to China and back lasted from 1325 to
1354 CE. From there, I travelled back home to Tangier.
Extensive travel leaves a person speechless and turns one
into a storyteller. It also makes one a stranger in
one's own land...*Ibn Battuta*

D 038

Toward the end of my life, the Sultan of Morocco insisted that I
dictate to one of his court scholars an account of all my travels
so that my experiences would live on forever. It came to be
called the Rihla, or "My Journey" ....*Ibn Battuta*

D 039

CHINA'S GREATEST TEACHERS

Seek harmony in nature and practice simplicity, patience, and
compassion ....*Laozi*
(aka, Lao-tse)
First know your place in society .... *Kungfuzi*
Then seek harmony in society .... *Confucius*
Practice ethical behavior in society................................*Mencius*
Seek and practice universal love ....*Mo Di*
Bend with the wind like the wise bamboo........................*Lao-tse*
(aka, Lao-tzu)

D 040

MONGOLIANS

I have fathered hundreds of children living in Mongol lands from
the Altai Mountains to the Black Sea and throughout all of central
Asia ....*Genghis Khan*

Years ago in Xanadu, a stately pleasure palace
I did decree ....*Kublai Khan*
How many Mongols does it take to make a horde? .... *Genghis*
Wong
I'm just a nice clean-cut Mongolian boy...................... *Yul Brynner*
We're all born bald ....*Telly Savalas*

D 041
THE GOLDEN HORDE
Is the Golden Horde really composed of yellow-skinned
Mongols? .... *Prince Rurik of the Varangian Rus*
No. It comes from our yellowish felt yurts (tents) .... *Jaghatai*
Khan

Ah, yes. Now please try my
kosher Mongolian BBQ .... *Genghis Cohen*

D 042
Mongols resemble beasts of prey. They have prominent, brutal
ears and projecting, bone-gnawing teeth. They are addicted to
gulping large quantities of warm liquors (fermented mare's milk)
that enfeeble their entire digestive tracks daily. The Kalmucks
and the Kipchak Mongols are the most wicked of all. They are all
lazy and live by thievery and banditry.................... *Hadud al-Alam*

E 001
HINDUS & EARLY INDIA
India today is divided into two great language families: Indo-
Aryans in the North and Dravidians in the South (along with
many small pockets of unrelated tongues in between). For many
years, it was assumed that the Indo-Aryans came from the
northwest into India through the
Khyber Pass ca. 1500 BC .... *Max Muller*

E 002
That version of pre-history has changed, and many alternatives
are putting the arrival at about 1800 BC. Others put the arrival as
far back as 3000 BC, or more. Some "Saffron Hindu Nationalists"

even argue that the Indo Aryans are the original natives of India and didn't come from anywhere.........................*Hindustan Times*

E 003

"Saffron Hindu nationalism" refers to the color of the yellow-orange flames of crematory bonfires of dead Hindus. It is also the orange/yellowish color on the Indian flag that symbolizes Hindus in India. The other color on the flag is green, which symbolizes Islam in India....................................*Brahman Priests*

E 004

In ancient times, the Aryan ancestors of modern-day northern Hindustanis worshipped many different gods. Many of these were their own Aryan gods from whence they all came, and some were borrowed from the people they encountered as they migrated into India from the north
and west of the mountains................................. *The Early Vedas*

E 005

HINDU GODS

There are thousands of gods in India. Many of them are equal, but some are more equal than others. There are, however, three of most powerful and favorite uber gods that most Hindus worship. These three, called the Hindu Triumvirate, are Brahma (the creator), Vishnu (the sustainer, observer, and helper), and Shiva (the terrible destroyer of everything
at the end of time)... *The Puranas*

E 006

These three uber gods are, in turn, manifestations of the divine presence and ultimate reality of nature, Brahman, the one superior over-arching mystical "ultimate reality" that is the source of all of the gods, spirits, and everything else, forever. All gods and spirits in India are derivatives of Brahman.............. *The Upanishads*

E 007
ANCIENT INDUS VALLEY CIVILIZATION
The earliest accounts of the Indo-Aryans coming into the Indus
Valley and their encounters with the already existant inhabitants
living there are recorded in some of the oldest books of
Hinduism. Some of these natives were described as living on
cultivated lands. They lived in villages and towns, while others
lived in the woods and forests. Some were called devils, while
others were called monkeys, and both were described as being
black .... *The Rig Veda, Max Mueller*

E 008
Some Indian scholars dispute the notion that the Rig Veda
described these people (Dasas and Dasyus) as
being black.. *Berghe,*
Clementin-Ojha, Deshpande, et al.

E 009
I am the seventh avatar of the god Vishnu .... *Rama*
I am the eighth avatar of the god Vishnu .... *Krishna*
I am the twelfth incarnation of Dr. Who................................ *BBC*

E 010
EARLY HINDU CLASSICS
In ancient Indian literature, there are many descriptions of
cultural and religious influences spreading from the north of India
into the Deccan, which is everything south of the Narbada River.
The *Book of Rama*, for example, is the story of the diffusion of
influence from the northern lands of the Indus and Ganges River
Basins into the southern realms where Rama's wife Sita (like
Helen of Troy) was abducted by the evil Demon King Ravana,
whose kingdom was in Ceylon in the extreme southeast of the
Deccan Peninsula .... *The Ramayana*

E 011

RAMA & SITA

In this classic, King Rama took his army to the Demon King Ravana's kingdom in modern day Sri Lanka (Ceylon), which lies across the Palk Strait. On this journey, King Rama called upon Hanuman, the king of the monkeys, to help him get across the strait to rescue his wife Sita .... *The Earlier Ramayana*

E 012

HANUMAN

In this story, King Hanuman created a long hanging bridge of monkeys holding hands across the water, which enabled Rama to take his army across the water and rescue Sita. This bridge still exists as a line of dots on contemporary maps and is called Rama's (or Adam's) Bridge, where Rama rescued Sita and carried her back home to northern India, where Sita was reunited with Rama's court .... *The Later Ramayana*

E 013

HARAPPAN RUINS & ANCIENT INDIA

I first saw the ancient ruins of Harappa during a trip across the Punjab. It occurred to me that they were exceptionally ancient structures. The locals didn't seem to know or care that the ruins were all that old. The city, like other ancient city ruins in the far western part of ancient India, was laid out with a grid pattern of streets surrounded by a large brick and stone wall for protection or to keep flood waters out.................................... *John Marshall*
of the British Raj

E 014

ANCIENT RUINS OF MOHENJODARO

More recently, the age of the ruins of Mohenjodaro (on the middle course of the Indus) is considered by some to be much earlier, perhaps as much as 4,000 or 5,500 years ago, or as some say, 8,000 years ago. It was originally laid out with a grid pattern of city streets and a large wall surrounding the whole city..*Rajesh & Nalini Rao*

E 015

THE ANCIENT RUINS OF MEHRGARTH

Another ancient city, called Mehrgarth, situated near the Bolan Pass in Pakistan was discovered in 1974 and excavated until 1986. The city was dated between 7000 BC and 5500 BC. A later period of the city has been dated from 5500 to 2600 BC (or 500 BC).............................*Ahmad Hasan Dani, Hussein Sharar, Cat. Jarrige, Hasan Usman*

E 016

Modern Hindu "Saffron Nationalists" (wearing orange or yellowish robes) argue that the Indo-Aryans originated in India and were the builders of the ancient cities of Harappa (in the upper Punjab), Mohenjodaro (on the middle course of the Indus), and the ruins of Dholavira (in Gujarat) near the ancient, now dried up, Sarasvati River...................................*The Mahabharata*

E 017

Both Harappa and Mohenjodaro were constructed with a grid pattern of streets, and both were surrounded by massive stone or brick walls for defense against enemy invaders and/or to keep water out .... *S.R. Rao*

E 018

THE ANCIENT SUNKEN CITIES OF DHOLAVIRA & DWARKA

Near the ancient sunken city of Dholavira, there is another sunken city called Dwarka, located on the northwestern coast of Gujarat just south of the Rann of Kutch. It is under 70 feet of water and was an important ancient Indian seaport. It also is the site of a two-thousand-year-old temple dedicated to the god Krishna, who founded the city ....*Krishna worshippers*

E 019

Some believe the Dwarka is nine thousand or twelve thousand years old. It was laid out with a grid pattern of city streets and was surrounded by massive protective brick and stone walls. Based on underwater archaeology studies, it is estimated that Dwarka sank about 150 feet into the Indian Ocean during the

Second Millennium BC, as is described in the ancient Hindu
historical and religious classic, Mahabharata................*S.R. Rao,
A.S. Gaur, & H.K. Vora*

E 020

CASTE & COLOR IN INDIA

Many or most historical sources postulate that light-skinned Indo-
Aryan interlopers met indigenous dark-skinned Indians and that
these groups became the two extremes of the Hindu caste
system. Ancient sources refer to high caste Brahmins (priests
and teachers) as white; Kshatriyas (warriors) as red, Vaishyas
(merchants, artisans, and bankers) and Shudras (menials, serfs,
and migrant farm workers) as black people ....*Laws of Manu*

E 021

Untouchables in India are outcastes who are not born into any
caste/varna, and/or have been expelled from their castes by their
caste councils. All foreigners and non-Hindus are technically
outcastes who pollute high caste Hindus
by touching them .... *The Mahabharata*

E 022

EARLY INDIAN RULERS & TEACHERS

I was born the crown prince of the Kingdom of Maghada (modern
Bihar). When I became an adult, I withdrew from royal duties
and spent time meditating under a banyan tree at
Bodh Gaya in Maghada ....*Siddhartha Gautama*

E 023

THE BUDDHA

I then spread my teachings throughout India, and my disciples
later spread my thoughts and teachings throughout northern and
southern India, and to the many lands into the east and into
southeast Asia, where Hinduism already had an important
presence and influence.......................... *The Buddha (Siddharta)*

E 024

The foremost among my teachings is the doctrine of ahimsa (nonviolence toward all living beings), and following my eightfold path, which leads to Nirvana (release from pain and misery and away from the unending cycle of re-birth). And I also strongly reject the legitimacy of caste .... *Siddharta Gautama*
(The Buddha)

E 025

BODH GAYA

Bodh Gaya today is a place of constant celebration and immersing of oneself in the ancient reenactment of the drama of the life of Siddartha (the Buddha himself). There are today many Buddhist pilgrims who come to Gaya (in Bihar) from everywhere on Earth (many Chinese). There is a modern freeway that surrounds Gaya, which brings in Pilgrims.... *Bihar Highway Dept. & Buddhist Festival Committee*

E 026

JAINISM & MAHAVIRA

I envisioned and taught a more strict version of non-violence and a more strict vegetarianism than the Buddha. Specifically, eat no meat, grow no crops, and sweep the streets before walking (so as not to step on insects and other small creatures...*Mahavira the Jain*
Do not injure, oppress, enslave, torture, kill, or harm, or insult any living being or creature ....*Mahavira in the Jaina Sutra, the Kalpa Sutra, & the Acharanga Sutra*
Both Jains and Sikhs believe in karma and rebirth .... *Yadev Vidawat*

E 027

Today, Jains have a procedure whereby they can buy and eat vegetables, fruit, and grain from special stores that declare the foods they sell are "leftovers," which have been "rejected" by others, so Jains may eat the "garbage" without sin .... *Indian Grocers*

One might suspect that in any place outside India, might this
practice at some time involve widespread dumpster-diving
instead? Not really...*Padmanabh Jaini*
There are between 100 and 150 thousand Jains in the
United States (the largest community
outside of India)............................. *Rakesh Jain, Jagdish Sheth,*
Chitrabhanu Jaina

E 028
INDIA'S MAURYAN DYNASTY, BUDDHISM, & ASHOKA
When I became king of Maghada (modern Bihar state) in the
land of the eastern Ganges, I expanded the kingdom that later
became the Gupta dynasty and then the Mauryan Empire ruling
all India north of the Narbada River .... *Chandragupta Maurya*

E 029
Then, when I became emperor of the Mauryan Dynasty, I
expanded the realm from the north into almost all the southern
parts of the Indian landmass, except the small kingdom of
Kalinga, located just to the south of my old
territory of Maghada.. *Ashoka*

E 030
One day, several Buddhist monks came into my presence
preaching nonviolence and reverence for all life forms. I
responded by throwing them all into my dungeon down below
(aka, Ashoka's Hell) and later sent them away .... *The Emperor*
Ashoka

E 031
ASHOKA'S CONQUEST OF KALINGA
Later, after leading an invasion against the hostile kingdom of
Kalinga just south of my realm, I grew uneasy with the terrible
loss of life in that campaign. I then remembered what the monks
had said about killing and nonviolence, and then I accepted
Buddhism and its doctrine of Ahimsa............*Ashoka (aka Asoka)*

On all of these tall pillars are carved the symbol of my kingdom:
the wagon wheel of time, rebirth, and reincarnation.
Many centuries later, it also will adorn the flag of
modern India .... *Emperor Asoka*

E 032
PILLAR EDICTS OF ASHOKA

I issued many proclamations and had them inscribed on large
stone pillars throughout my empire promoting Ahimsa (non-
violence to all living beings) and adherence to vegetarian dietary
practices. On some of my pillar edicts, I ordered my subjects to
build retirement pastures for aged and sickly
farm animals ....*Ashoka's Pillar Edicts*

E 033
AHIMSA, KANISHKA, & MAHAYANA

In time, Ahimsa and non-violence came to be adopted by Hindu
Brahmins, and the original monastic form of Buddhism
(Hinayana) gradually disappeared from India. But the doctrine of
Ahimsa continued in Jainism, with a much more rigorous form of
Ahimsa.. *Brahman Priests*

E 034
THE KUSHAN DYNASTY IN WESTERN INDIA

From out of the Hexi corridor in Gansu province in north-western
China, we came down into India with my horsemen and
conquered much of the north and western part of the Indian sub-
continent. Later, in my court, many intellectuals debated
extensively with each other ....*Emperor Kanishka*
In Kanishka's court I proved a great number of mathematical
theorems.. *Aryabhata*
Under Kanishka, I wrote about stars and other astronomical
phenomena .... *Brahmagupta*

E 035
BODHIDHARMA & GUANYIN

During the second century CE, new interpretations of Buddhism
under the new school of Mahayana flourished in my court and

were written down as the Diamond Sutra. Also, our Indian
numerals diffused westward to the Arabs and then to the
Europeans......................... *King Kanishka of the Kushan Dynasty*
I took Mahayana Buddhism into Tibet and China.... *Bodhidharma*
I came later as the Bodhisattva of Mercy .... *Guanyin*

(aka Avlokishavara)

E 036
THE COMING OF ISLAM INTO INDIA
I was India's last Hindu king.................*Harsha of the White Huns*
I was the first to bring Islam into northwestern
India .... *Mahmud of Ghazni*
Later, after much bloodshed, I founded the
Sultanate of Delhi ....*Kutbu-d Din Aibek*

E 037
Upon becoming ruler, I decreed the evacuation of all the native
people in Delhi. Sick or lame people who refused to go were
dragged out by horses or shot over the city walls with
catapults.................*Muhammad bin Tughlaq ("The Mad Sultan")*

E 038
IBN BATTUTA IN INDIA
I came into India and saw the great Indus River. It resembled the
Nile in that it rises and falls according to the seasons. The lands
of the river's five northern tributaries are called
the Panj-ab (five rivers)... *Ibn Battuta*
The other major river is called the Ganga. Along its banks are
gathered Hindus on pilgrimages. And when they die, they burn
their dead and scatter the ashes into the river and believe the
ashes come from paradise....................................... *Ibn Battuta*

E 039
I also visited Sultan Muhammad Tughlaq's court, and he made
me a law judge of the city of Delhi. The sultan had a policy to
appoint foreigners to his professional offices. As such, I
remained there in that capacity for several years........ *Ibn Battuta*

E 040

TAMERLANE & THE MOGUL DYNASTY

From Samarkand in Central Asia, I invaded northern India and forged my vast Timurid Empire of Persia, Bactria, and Northwestern India .... *Tamerlane (Timur)*
Years later, I led my horsemen out of Central Asia and through the Khyber Pass into northern India and founded the magnificent Mogul Dynasty .... *Babur the Tiger*

E 041

BABA NANAK, SIKHS, & THE SIKH RELIGION

After Tamerlane died, I created Sikhism out of the best of Hindusm, Islam, Christianity, and other admirable religious traditions. In my new religion, there were no castes. All Sikhs are equal, and there is only one god (whose holy name must never to be uttered)................... *Baba Nanak, the 1st Sikh guru of India*

E 042

All male Sikhs must wear holy undergarments and clean turbans at all times. Sikh men must not cut their hair or trim their beards and must always carry a dagger for protection from attacks by Hindu and Moslem assassins................................. *Govind Singh*
There are no particular dietary prohibitions in Sikhism except for beef (while in India).. *Later Sikh Gurus*

E 043

Sikhs must not consume alcohol or opium. Police and military careers are popular among Sikhs, who are also encouraged to take the surname Singh. But not all Singhs in India are Sikhs. Some with that surname are Hindus........................... *Sikh Gurus*

E 044

Modern Sikh women have no dress codes and no particular dietary restrictions. We can attend universities and become British and/or United States citizens, members of parliament, governors of states, and for some, even become ambassadors to the United Nations... *Nikki Haley*

E 045

AKBAR THE GREAT

Years later, in my court, I brought together poets, teachers, philosophers, and gurus, and forged a new religion called Din-Ilahi, which blended together beliefs from Hindus, Muslims, Zoroastrians, Jains, Sikhs, and Christians. I also built a city near Delhi and called it Fatehpur Sikri, where my new religion could thrive .... *Akbar the Great*

E 046

SHAH JAHAN & THE TAJ MAHAL

I was the 5th Mogul Emperor of India and I built the Taj Mahal to house the crypt of my favorite wife, Mumtaz Mahal, who died after bearing my 14th child... *Shah Jahan*

E 047

Hindus invented forks long ago,
yet we still eat with our fingers ....*Mahatma Gumbah*
What's a fork?.. *Gunga Din*
Just don't eat or point with your left hand...............*Madhu Raghu*

E 048

THE BRITISH RAJ IN INDIA

We came to India to trade and get rich. At various times, we founded small trading missions, and then larger trading posts, which evolved into big cities, such as Calcutta, Madras, and Bombay. Before long, we began to govern the entire state of Bengal and many of us became rich...........*The British East India Company Chronicles*

Tyger Tyger! burning bright
In the forests of the Night...................................... *William Blake*

F 001

INDIAN EMPIRES RULING MOST OF THE INDIAN SUBCONTINENT

Eventually, we came and took over most of India, which then became one of only five realms controlled by us on all or most of the Indian sub-continent (i.e., Ashoka's Empire, the Sultanate of

Delhi, the Mogul Empire, the British Raj, and the soon-to-be
independent and modern state of India) .... *Lord Cornwallis*

F 002
RABINDRANATH TAGORE
During the British Raj, I founded a new religion in India and
called it Brahmo Samaj, which sought to revive some of ancient
Hindu monistic traditions (only one god). I also supported the
divine position of high caste Hindus in Indian society (caste
matters), as Krishna taught Arjuna in
the Bhagavad Gita .... *Rabindranath Tagore*

F 003
SUTTEE IN INDIA
Following the efforts of Raja Ram Mohan Roy, and the British
Raj in Bengal, we were able to abolish the ancient practice of
Suttee (aka, Sati) whereby widows throw themselves (or are
physically thrown) onto the funeral pyre of their dead husbands.
We expunged this barbarous practice .... *Governor-General
Lord William Bentick*

F 004
The Hindus are the gentlest people on earth. The Brahmins have
brought their people to a high degree of courtesy, temperance,
and chastity. Hindus are friendly, clean, simple, and harmless.
Hinduism is the most learned, humane, and most noble of all the
sects of Asia. And they have no vices ....*Johann G. von Herder*

F 005
I won the Nobel Prize for literature in 1913 for a blending of
Hindu and Western learning traditions and I came to be called
the Bard of Bengal. I was also awarded a knighthood from King
George V, but I turned it down................... *Rabindranath Tagore*

F 006
In 1947, India was partitioned into Moslems in West Pakistan
and East Bengal (which later became Bangladesh). Everywhere

else in India remained Hindu. Most, but not all, Sikhs chose to be part of Hindu India .... *Jarwaharlal Nehru*

F 007
It doesn't matter whether you are Christians, Sikhs, Muslims, Jains, Jews, British, or Communists. To us, you are all just simple untouchables..*Brahmin priests*
The same is true about foreigners. You may be powerful, but you are also untouchables, as you, sir, always will be ....*Brahmin authorities*
And you, sir, are a swarthy, sniffling, slithering, stunted little monkey, and you will always be one...........................*Edward VII*

F 008
SRI AURABINDO & THE GREAT PARTITION
In 1947, the Indian subcontinent was divided into Muslim India and Hindu India. The province of Bengal was split into West Bengal (Hindu) and East Bengal (Islam). East Bengal was later renamed Bangladesh. I went to Calcutta and joined a Hindu revolutionary organization that advocated uprisings against the British Raj. I was arrested twice and convicted for sedition and conspiracy ....*Sri Aurabindo*

F 009
Later, I became occupied with self-introspection, religion, poetry, and the arts, and wrote a number of books that led to a nomination for the Nobel Prize in 1943 and the Nobel Peace Prize in 1950...*Aurobindo*

F 010
THE HOLY GANGES & BATHING GHATS AT BENARES (AKA, VARANASI)
Along the Ganges River (aka, Ganga Mata or mother Ganges) are some of the most revered pilgrimage sites in India. The first

one is at the river's source, high up in the Himalayas. The river Ganga flows out of a large ice pillar (lingham, or phallus and/or wanker) inside a cave. In the summer, the site draws thousands of Hindu pilgrims from all over India .... *Attendant Brahmin Priests of Shiva*

F 011
THE KUMB MELA
Another important pilgrimage spot is where the Jumna River flows into the Ganges. Every few years, at this sacred spot, the Kumbh Mela celebration attracts more pilgrims than any other on earth................................*Attendant Brahmin Priests at Allahabad*

F 012
Further down the river to the sacred city of Benares (modern day Varanasi) is where the bathing ghats (stairways) are. Every day, thousands of pilgrims step down into the river and perform simple ablutions that wash away ritual pollution (i.e., contact with untouchables, dead animals, foreigners, forbidden foods, and excrement)...*Indian health tracts*

F 013
FUNERAL PYRES ALONG THE GANGES
Downriver, below the bathing ghats (staircases), are the burning ghats at Varanasi (formerly Benares) where the cremated dead are shoveled off into the Ganges. Where wood is scarce, many corpses are sprinkled with gasoline, lighter fluid, or gin, and set on fire before sending them down the river and hopefully on into East Bengal (Bangladesh) and then into the Indian Ocean.....................................*BBC, al Jazeera, NY Times*

F 014
NUMEROUS CREMATION SITES
In recent years, many Indian corpses are not fully consumed by funeral fires on the Ganges. The main reason is that wood is scarce and gasoline is dear. Their partially burned corpses eventually float out into the Bay of Bengal, where whatever

remains are eaten by fish, birds, sea worms, and crabs.
Occasionally, Indian fishermen and their customers wonder if
the fish they are catching in the ocean and selling at Indian
bazaars have eaten human flesh..................... *BBC & al Jazeera*

F 015

This also was the case recently when many islanders from the
eastern coasts of the Bay of Bengal were hit with a huge
earthquake and tsunami that carried many bodies to India's
Coromandel Coast. There was concern among villagers that the
fish they were buying from the fishmongers had earlier eaten
these corpses ....*Reuters, UPI, BBC*

F 016

PARTLY BURNED CORPSES

Upriver, along the Ganges, there are many other cremation sites
from which many half-burned corpses are consigned to floating
down the river into the bathing ghats at Benares. Floating
corpses from upriver often bump into pilgrims performing ritual
ablutions on the stair steps (ghats). Many floating corpses are
eaten by vultures, and some of them sink to the bottom of the
river ....*UPI, AP descriptions*

F 017

THE TOXIC GANGES

Water from the Ganges (aka, Ganga Mata or Mother Ganges) is
more toxic than that of any other river on earth, except perhaps,
for the burning Cuyahoga, the Chang Jiang (Yangzi), and/or the
Houston Ship Channel...................*al Jazeera, AP, Reuters, BBC*

F 018

Every year, many Hindus get sick and/or die from splashing
themselves in Ganges river water and drinking some of it.
Ganges holy water in small amounts are also available
throughout India for ritual ablutions. It is not known how many
people taste or drink some of this water. There is a widespread
market all over India for small vials of Ganges river holy water for
rituals...*U.N. World Health Organization*

F 019

NOTHING CAN KILL YOU BUT A BULLET

It used to be an urban legend along the Ganges that if one
survives drinking Ganges river water, then for the rest of one's
life, nothing will kill you but a bullet
(possibly true) .... *World Health Organization*
Diet and River Sanitation Inspectors

F 020

FLOATING CORPSES & TURTLES

Many decades ago, Indian governments tried to clean up the
floating corpse problem by introducing snapping turtles that
would chew up most or part of the floating corpses on their way
down the river, letting their remaining parts sink to the bottom to
be consumed by bottom-feeding crustaceans and river fish. But
starving villagers living upstream and downstream caught the
tasty turtles, cooked them, and ate them all up
themselves...................*Hindustan Reporter, UN Food Observers*

F 021

INDIAN TEMPLES & HOVALS

For poor Hindus, the preferred substance for covering floors in
their dwellings is cow dung. It is smooth, and when it dries, it
doesn't smell .... *National Geographic*
In India, putting cobras into one's dwelling will quickly rid it of
mice, rats, roaches, and unwanted guests. But then you would
still have those cobras.. *Will Cuppyjee*
Welcome to my new Garden of Krishna restaurant. Would you
like a nice drink of Bombay Gin and tonic with your yoghurt and
vegetables?... *Chandra Panditji*

F 022

How many damned temples and places of historic interest can
anyone see, enjoy, and understand in India? ....*Bala Senthil*
Kumar

In 1945, I walked through some Hindu temples in Calcutta. The walls of some were festooned with the bottoms of Coke Bottles plastered into the concrete. Also, the entire city of Calcutta stunk from who knows what .... *Vernon G. Elliott*

F 023
TIBET & LAMAS
On the road to Shangri-la .... *Hope & Crosby*
Along the way, we were greeted by "The Ever-Ever Man"
in "Never-Never Land" who sent his
greetings from Shangri-la .... *The High Lama*

F 024
PRAYER WHEELS
We keep the prayer wheels spinning. And the prayer flags flying
where the dead are exposed and consumed by birds from
out of the sky .... *Tibetan Monks*
The religion of Tibet is monstrous and inconsistent......... *Hegel &*
Herder

F 025
I never quite reached the top of Mt. Everest .... *George Mallory*
I was one of the first to climb Mount Everest....... *Tenzing Norgay*
Sherpa
I've climbed Mount Everest 22 times .... *Kami Reta Sherpa*

F 026
Tibet isn't really part of China .... *The Dalai Lama*
And I am not a fake lama............................... *The Panchen Lama*
Krishna worshiping lamas are everywhere......................... *Swami*
Bhaktivetivedanta
Rama lama .... *Hairy Krishnas*
Just me and my llama............................. *The Sesame Street Girl*
This llama is my llama .... *Bruno of the Altiplano*

F 027
PRE-MODERN CHINA
China is an admirable country with running water. Its people are
good craftsmen who make wonderful products..... *Hadad al-Aram*
Northern Chinese are comparable to Europeans, but the
Cantonese are more irresponsible and hot-blooded than their
northern neighbors .... *Ellen C. Semple*

F 028
China is an embalmed mummy, wrapped in silk, and painted with
hieroglyphics. The Chinese are a vain, misshapen people who
are ashamed of their bodies and distort their ears and force
women to bind their feet. They do this because Chinese men find
"Lilly feet" to be sexually attractive...................... *J.G. von Herder*
A major result of foot binding is that Chinese women whose
parents acquiesce to this barbaric practice cannot walk.
So they scoot around on the ground on their hands
and knees instead of walking. I saw this in Xi'an
and Huxien in 1945 .... *Vernon G. Elliott*

F 029
Swelling with Tartarian pride, the Chinese despise the merchant,
and yet they sell millions of pounds of enervating tea for the
corruption of all Europe .... *J.G. von Herder*
The Chinese are a practical and rational people......... *Charles de*
Montesquieu
However, their religion and philosophy advocates inaction that
has caused the Chinese to murder each other. They are guided
by rites, but are the greatest cheats in the world. They act only
through fear of being bastinadoed .... *Montesquieu*

F 030
CHINA'S FIRST ENCOUNTER WITH THE WEST
We possess all things............................ *The Qian Long Emperor*
The emperor was not impressed with our gifts ... *Lord McCartney*
The only thing they will buy from us is opium .... *British East India*
Company

Many man smoke, but .... *Fu Manchu*
Burn all the opium................................*Commissioner Lin*
Everyone in Canton then
became high for six weeks.................... *Governor of Guangzhou*

F 031

THE TAIPING REBELLION & MODERNIZATION IN CHINA
I am the younger brother of Jesus Christ, and my Taiping army
will destroy all the opium and all the foreign
devils living in China ....*Hong Xiuquan*
My army will defend Shanghai against
the Taipings...............................*General "Chinese" Gordon*

F 032

Nanjing has now been taken back from
the Taipings...................................... *Zeng Guofan*
China must adopt new programs of
self-strengthening .... *Chang Chih-tung*
Chinese backwardness must end and we must adopt many
western systems of technology (while keeping Chinese culture
intact) .... *Li Hung-chang*

F 033

Help us take Peking back from the Boxers
(righteous fists)...................................... *Empress Cixi*
First, we must cut off our queues and drive out the
evil Manchus...............................*Sun Chung-shan*
Out with Qing, restore Ming ....*Chinese revolutionary slogan*

G 001

CIVIL WAR AGAINST THE MANCHUS
When the revolution was successful, I received the
good news in Denver, Colorado where I was
staying at the Brown Palace Hotel ....*Sun Yat-sen*
I was the last Manchu emperor of China, and during this time,
the Japanese began to covet our natural resources
in Manchuria...................................*Henry Pu-yi*

G 002

CHINA'S WARLORD PERIOD

The Fallen Manchus were replaced by
Chinese warlords .... *Wu Beifu*
I was called the Dogmeat General, but it's not something I ate.
It's a form of gambling called pai gow (eating dog meat)... *Zhang Zongchang*
I did not betray the revolution, and stop calling me
bullet-head .... *Yuan Shih-k'ai*

G 003

THE NORTHERN EXPEDITION

I was the most successful warlord in China in the 1920s. We marched all the way from Guangdong province in the South to Hebei province in the North. This became known as the "Northern Expedition." We took Peking and renamed it Beiping (northern peace), and reunited China.................*Chiang Kai-shek*

G 004

THE RAPE OF NANKING

In 1937-38, the Japanese invaded China and committed some of the most terrible and inhuman atrocities at Nanjing. It is still known as the "Rape of Nanking" ....*Chiang Kai-shek*

G 005

I was called the "Old Marshal of Manchuria" and the "Tiger of Mukden" before I was assassinated by
the Japanese ....*Chang Tso-lin*
I inherited my father's warlord army and became known as "The Young Marshal." I later emigrated to Hawaii and lived there for
the rest of my life.................................... *Chang Hsueh-liang*
Hawaii is not a state of mind,
but a state of grace ....*Paul Thereaux*
I was the Chinese Ambassador to the United States
for a while... *Hu Shih*

G 006
THE LONG MARCH

While the war with the Japanese was still going on, we continued
to face heavy losses in the southern province of Hunan in
fighting Chiang Kai-shek's Kuomintang army (aka, Guomindong
in pinyin). We then fled northward and came into Shan Hsi
(Shanxi) province, where we stayed until the Japanese war was
over .... *Warlord Mao*
This became known as "The Long March" .... *Mao Zedong*
Following heavy losses to the Communists, we fled the mainland
and settled in Formosa, which had already been taken back from
the Japanese .... *Chiang Kai-shek*

G 007
MAO ZEDONG & THE PEOPLE'S REPUBLIC

Power comes from out of the barrel of a gun .... *Chairman Mao*
Dr. Kissinger, how do you get all those girls?.............. *Zhou Enlai*
Power is the greatest aphrodisiac...................................*Kissinger*
Hide your strength and bide your time .... *Deng Xiaoping*
When the enemy tires, advance.. *Sunzi*
I don't care what color the cat is,
so long as it catches mice...*Deng*

G 008
AFTER MAO

After Mao, we've embarked on a massive program of national
strengthening and building projects, including irrigation, sea
ports, highways, railroads, dams, and brand-new cities that some
of the best previous heads of government advocated for during
the late Qing Dynasty. Fifty of these cities remain empty and are
called "ghost cities." But someday, they all will be full
of people...*Hu Jintao & Jiang Zemin*

G 009
We also put into practice many modernization policies advocated
by the later Qing Dynasty heads of government; namely,
Zeng Guofan, Zhang Zhidong, and Li Hongzhang would be
pleased...*Jiang Zemin & Hu Jintao*

G 010

MARTIAL ARTS

For centuries, ancient martial arts practitioners in China have developed many different ways of self-defense, such as wushu, kung-fu, jujitsu, kung-pao, baijiu, falun gong,
tai-qi, and dofu ....*Chop Chop*
Specifically, we have built a new modern navy, and ships are now patrolling the nearby seas. Admiral Zheng He would be
pleased .... *Xi Jinping*

G 011

RAILROADS & FENG SHUI

Why should railroads have such bad feng shui?....... *Sun Yat-sen*
One belt, one railroad, good feng shui........................ *Xi Jinping*

G 012

One must spend a long time with mouth open waiting for roast
duck to fly in .... *Won Ton*
There's been a terrible traffic accident outside in front of this restaurant. Anyone want some freshly pressed
Peking duck? .... *Chiang kai-chef*
Fry me to the Moon .... *Ali Wong*
Chop Suey or Lo Mein with your Tsing Tao?.......... *Charlie Chow*
No, we use pinyin now. So bring me a nice
Qing Dao, Hsieh xie ....*Don Ho*

G 013

MODERN CHINESE ECONOMICS & POPULAR CULTURE

In ancient China, most traditional marriages were determined by the ancient Chinese Zodiac. Some birthdates are compatible,
some aren't .... *Chinese matchmakers*
A lot of Chinese restaurants in the U.S. buy these zodiac place
mats ....*Lee Chow*
Egg rolls with your roast beast? ....*Hop-Sing*
Wo bu dong, I'm just fresh off the boat .... *Eddie Huang*
Come and see my best Chinese motion pictures...... *Jackie Chan*
Watch my comedy monologue on late night talk
shows in America ....*Joe Wong*

G 014

WUSHU & KUNG FU CHAMPS

I'm a well-known film actor, producer, and martial arts
professional. I am also a retired Wushu champion...............*Jet Li*
I was Hollywood's blackest belt kung-fu, karate, and karaoke
master ....*Bruce Lee*

G 015

ALIBABA & BEI-DA

I founded the Alibaba tech-group in China
and I'm very, very rich..*Jack Ma*
Just me and my basketball .... *Yao Ming*
Just me and my yoyo.. *Yo yo Ma*
The best university in China today is still Bei-da ....*Xi Jinping*

G 016

HINDUSTANI LANDSCAPES & CASTE MORES

Hindus are tame, servile, intimidated, and living in stupid
debasement...*Henry T. Buckle*
Hindu mythology is disgusting and trivial. Hindus will not
step on ants, but are indifferent when people
starve to death...*George W.F. Hegel*
Brahmans are especially immoral, avaricious, and deceitful.
But most Hindus are gentle, courteous,
temperate, and chaste..*G.W.F. Hegel*

G 017

BRAHMINS & GANISHA

The Brahmins in India build extremely expensive temples with
the money of the poor, sweating, low caste laborers. Inside these
temples are erotic paintings and sculptures that would disturb
the harmony of any museums in the world, such as
women copulating with elephants
(like with Ganesha).................................... *Hendrick W. van Loon*

G 018

HIGH AND LOW CASTE HINDUS

Practice peace and nonviolence to all people and adopt the new names for Untouchables: Harijans (Children of God) or Dalits (Oppressed Ones). Between WWI and WWII, I sought to raise up the lower castes and outcastes; I also helped create the non-violent Home Rule movement in India.............. *Mahatma Gandhi*
Before and during WWII, we Indian nationalists promoted the Quit India Movement and practiced non-violent resistance against the British... *Gandhi*
After WWII, the nearly bankrupt British departed and we became free... *Nehru*

G 019

SHUDRAS, DALITS, & UNTOUCHABLES

As a member of the Indian Parliament for years, I have always worked to end the inhuman depressed status of Shudras (low caste Hindus in Indian society), the low social standing of tribal groups (mostly in the Deccan), and all "scheduled outcastes," who prefer to be called Dalits (the oppressed), who must no longer be called "untouchables," which is an abomination (just like the n-word in America and Britain).................. *Jagjivan Ram*

G 020

MODERN INDIA'S WEALTHY & FAMOUS

In India today, less well-off Brahmins are in demand as waiters, cooks, and dishwashers in restaurants because they are ritually pure and, thus, can cook, carry, and hand out food, water, ghee (melted clarified butter), Pimm's cups, big macs (really, with mutton), to everyone, regardless of caste ..... *Hindu Michelin Guide*

G 021

THE PATELS

We are a tribal or lower caste group living for years in Gujarat and, before that, in many other parts of north and western India. Many of us have emigrated to the UK and US. A lot of us have bought inexpensive motels all over America, and have been running them while living in them. Some Indians who have emigrated into the US have changed their names to Patel...*New arrivals*

G 022
INDIRA GHANDI

I am currently the richest man in India ....*Mukesh Ambani*
If you run your car over a man in the street, stop and give the victim some money. If you run over a cow, drive away as fast as you can.......................................*Modern urban saying*
Since home rule began in India, all politics are caste politics. The Congress Party, for example, is a coalition of Brahmins and Pariahs (Untouchables) ....*Indira Ghandi*

G 023
BHARATA JANATA

Today's Bharata Janata Party is for middle and lower caste Hindus (Shudras), who are also working to spread Hindutva, or "Hinduness" "Saffron" (Hindu) nationalism throughout all of India, and out into the Indian Ocean, as well, and out into the rest of the world...*Narendra Modi*
For many years I have been working with and representing India's Untouchable and oppressed communities in India's parliament...*B.R. Ambedkar*

G 024
There is today a newly growing awareness in India that there is an on-going Dalit political revolution among educated Dalits since the 1990s in northern India, particularly in Uttar Pradesh. Activists are challenging the dominant position of higher caste Hindus in the UP and elsewhere in northern India. But not much in small rural and marginal communities. These efforts represent something new in modern India.........*Craig, Pat, & Roger Jeffery*

G 025

KAYASTHAS & VEGETARIANISM

In modern India's state of West Bengal, the Kayasthas are a lower caste group, who are regarded locally as the equals of Brahmins. They perform the work of scribes, accountants, keepers of public records, and do not follow high caste dietary restrictions.......................................*N.K. Sengupta & T.J. Hopkins*
Vegetarianism is for rabbits....................*Most Bengali Kayasthas*

G 026

MODERN INDIAN BUSINESSES & SOCIAL CUSTOMS

I've appeared on many TV shows dealing with
medical topics .... *Dr. Sanjay Gupta*
I'm the best cricket player in all of India....................... *Virat Kohli*
I'm the all-time top leading actor in Bollywood today ....*Amitabh Bachchan*

G 027

BANNERJEES, MUKHRAJEES, CHATTERJEES, & SINGHS

In India, to form a successful business or a government committee or any other kind of collective professional endeavor, at least four different people must be made part of the team. Ideally, three of them must be named Bannerjee, Mukhrajee, and Chatterjee, and the fourth must be a Singh .... *Mukesh Ambani*

G 028

The first three are Bengali Brahmins, who are very smart (above) and can create elegant and highly intelligent
business plans .... *Pawan Munjal*
But many of the highest caste Hindus are vegetarians and consequently are lethargic, weak, and tend to avoid unnecessary physical exertion, and spend much time in contemplation of one's navels .... *Hindustan Times*

G 029

And so, the committee needs a strong person of action to command, organize, and put the plan into operation

(i.e., a vigorous, meat-eating, strong Sikh
named Singh) ....*Kalanithi Maran*
I'm the best Bollywood actress and
I'm also Miss India ....*Madhuri Dixit*

G 030
HINDU MATRIMONIAL PRACTICES
Indian matrimonial ads used to appear daily in most Indian
newspapers like the Hindustan Times, Indian Express, and
others. Now everything is online. For example, questions ask
about caste, community, and sub-castes, such as Jat, Agarwalj,
Khatri, Rajput, Brahmin, Nair, or Anglo-Indians. Occasionally,
questions are about low caste individuals, such as: Scheduled
caste? Shudra? Or "Caste no bar" (where a member of a higher
caste or jati will consider a lower caste spouse)? Complexion
(fair or not)? Income? Education? Languages? Slim? Rich?
Once married? Never married? Beautiful? Quiet? Smart? Family
owns a liquor store, or a BMW, an airplane?........... *Azimu Premji*

G 031
Different Gothra/Gotra? A Gotra is a family that has a direct and
unbroken male descent from a particular ancient or distant
ancestor (a kind of clan with patrilineal surnames). Usually, a
couple must have a different Gothra if they are to be married.
They usually must be from the same varna (large caste group) or
subcaste (jati). Traditionally, people of the same Gothra could
not marry, but today and in cities it is usually
allowed .... *Om Prakash & Sunil Munjal*

G 032
NUKES & WESTERN SCIENCE
Following an underground nuclear detonation by Pakistan in
1998, we followed their provocation with two underground
explosions of our own .... *Atal Bihari Vajpayee*

G 033

Many Hindustanis have a great contempt for the West. Yet they cannot create and maintain a modern state without western knowledge and culture .... *V.S. Naipaul*
Most foreigners, when they think of India, tend to think only of fire-walkers, snake charmers, naked sadhus,
and the rope trick .... *Brijmohan Munjab*
I became a world figure at the World's Fair in Chicago ...... *Swami Vivekananda*

G 034

HINDU GODS & GODDESSES

India is sometimes called the land of ten-thousand gods. Some of the favorites include Sita (goddess of chaste womanhood), Agni (fire), Varuna (wind), Ganesha (remover of obstacles and the patron of students), Kali (goddess of destruction), Lakshmi (goddess of wealth, good luck, and well-being), Indra (king of the heavens, lightning, and rain), Saraswati (goddess of learning), and Hanuman (the monkey god) .... The *Vedas & The Ramayana*

H 001

ANCIENT & MODERN SAYINGS

Now where did those two go? .... *King Minos*
Fly as high as you want................... *Jonathon Livingston Seagull*
OMG, I'm about to crash into the sea................................. *Icarus*
I told you not to fly too close to the sun .... *Daedelus*
All is fire and instability.. *Heraclitus*
Now you have fire .... *Prometheus*
Keep the bonfires burning .... *Zarathustra*
All is geography.. *Claudius Ptolemy*
All is Nirvana .... *Siddhartha*
All are map projections.. *Mercator*
Everything is on my maps .... *Strabo*
All is preventing starvation .... *Nehru*

H 002

All is quantification	*Pythagoras*
All is Sophistry	*Protagoras*
All is statistical	*Gauss*
All is storytelling	*Homer*
All is geometric	*Euclid*
All is moderation	*Euripides*
All is fertility	*Cybal*
All is the moon	*Armstrong*
All is vanity	*Narcissus*
All is shipping	*Onassis*
All is triangular	*Pascal*
All is existential	*Kierkegaard*
All is dance	*Zorba*
All is law	*Lycurgus*
All is flying	*Earhart*
All is battle	*Leonidas*
All is lying	*Trumpski*
All are rocks	*Petrocles*
All is war	*Mars*
All is questioning	*Socrates*
All is justice	*Justinian*
All is strength	*Hercules*

H 003

All is gravity	*Newton*
All is gluttony	*Trimalchio*
All is relative	*Einstein*
All is sleep	*Morpheus*
All is wandering	*Odysseus*
All is reform	*Solon*
All is illusion	*Plato*
All is matter	*Aristotle*
All is golden	*Midas*
All are eggs	*Ovid*
All is deliverance	*Mahavira*
All is nirvana	*Bodhisattwas*
All is moksha	*Hindu Rishis*
All is free love	*The Baghwan*

H 004

All world scriptures are true ....*Bahai*
All is my ashram in Oregon ....*Rajneesh*
All is non-violence ....*Brahmins and Jains*
All is free love..*Baktivedanta*
All is obfuscation .... *Sarah Hukkabee*
All is dancing at airports ....*Hairy Krishnas*
All is living long... *Methuselah*
All is staying young ....*Peter Pan*
All is jumping off this bridge... *Horatio*
All is revolt and freedom....................................*Spartacus*
All is our freedom ....*Nat Turner*
All is our freedom .... *Denmark Vesey*

H 005

All is mine.. *Cyrus*
All is more ....*Xerxes*
All was mine.. *Darius*
All is now mine...*Alexander*
All is duty.. *Cincinnatus*
All is oratory .... *Cicero*
All is living well ....*Seneca*
All is freedom from grief and joy ....*Zeno*
All is history.. *Herodotus*
All is searching for eternal life.....................................*Gilgamesh*
All is tragedy .... *Sophocles*
All is comedy..*Bennie Hill*
All is drama .... *Aeschylus*
All is more f*#k% comedy.....................................*George Carlin*
All is grass..*Cheech & Chong*
All is chess..*Bobby Fisher*

H 006

ANCIENT ROMAN SAYINGS & STATEMENTS

Anno urbis conditae ....*Romulus*
Ab urbe condita...*Titus Livy*
Delenda est Romae ....*Tarquin*
In omnibus Aeneid ....*Virgil*

Delenda est Carthago..Cato
Delenda Romae est.. Hannibal
I've taken Spain and Sicily............. Hamilcar Barca (of Carthage)
I took elephants through
the Alps .... Hasdrubal Barca (of Carthage)
I did not fiddle while Rome burned.. Nero

H 007
GRECO ROMANS

All virtuous Greeks and Romans may go to Mt. Parnassos after
they die... Dionysian priests
I put down the Jewish revolt in Judea ....Vespasian
We tried but failed to pass new land and
social reform laws..Gracchi Brothers
When in Rome, don't do as the Romans do..............St. Ambrose

H 008
OF VINO

In vino veritas .... Pliny the Elder
In vino beatitudes .... Ben Franklin
In vino ingenuity...Aristophanes
Vino, vedi, vici...Caesar
Vino from aqua converti...Jesus
Vino, viagra, valium .... Hefner
Vino pluribus...Dionysus
Vino, vino, vino ....Bacchus
Vino, alter ego, libido ....Freud
Vino, toga, toga ....Belushi
Vino bonum lasts into aeternity.. Cicero
Vino, time, and rain brings sleep...Ovid
Vino, olive oil, vendetta.................................. Don Vito Corleone
Vino is no more.. Eliot Ness
Vino into aqua converti ....Wrong Jesus
Vino is back..................................... Mondavi, Krug, Carlo Rossi

H 009
LATIN PHRASES IN ENGLISH

Deus ex machina...Sophocles

Status quo.. *Warren G. Harding*
In Hoc Signo Vinces...*Constantine*
Quid pro quo .... *Luca Brazzi*
Carpe diem .... *Horace*
Habeas corpus...*Perry Mason*
Corpus delicti .... *Agatha Christie*
Mea culpa .... *Yoko Ono*
Caveat emptor ....*Charles Ponzi*
Lese majesty..*Henry Tudor*
Lex Talionis... *Sargon I*
Vox Populi.. *Voice of the people*
Pax Romana .... *Marcus Aurelius*
Pontifex Maximus..*Big bridge-fixer*
Tabula Rasa.. *Zeno, Avicenna*
Modus Operendi..*Sgt. Joe Friday*

H 010

Excreto ergo sum..*Descartes*
Esse est excretti.. *George Berkeley*
Cum laude..*Egg Head*
Magna cum laude...*High Egg Head*
Summa cum laude ....*Highest Egg Head*
Best with bourbon ....*Highest Egg Nog*
Magnum opus ....*Will & Ariel Durant*
Magna carpa..*Beached Whale*
Magna crapo ....*El Chapo Guzman*
Magna charta ....*King John the Bad*
Annus Horribilis .... *Queen Elizabeth*
Persona non Grata..*Nightclub Bouncer*

H 011

MORE LATIN PHRASES IN ENGLISH

Three 57 magnum..*Dirty Harry*
Per diem..*Room & bored*
Maximum flatus...*Wind in his hair*
Déjà vu...*This has happened before*
Vuja day...........*This has never happened before (George Carlin)*

H 012
Natalis Sol Invicti, winter solstice (25 Dec.).......*Priests of Mithras*
In nomine patris, et filii, et spiritus sancti..........*Pontifex Maximus*
In nomine patris, et filii, et spiritus salami...................*Tony Totino*
In nomine patris, et filii, et flying pepperoni.................*Red Baron*
In nomine patris, et filli, et spiritus fasciitis ....*Mussolini*
In nomine lobos, et lupus, et spiritus coyotes............*Dances with coyotes*
In nomine canis, et lupus, et hombres lobos..............*Dances with werewolves*

H 013
All good Romans and Greeks may dance forever in the Elysian
Fields..*Zorba*
Poseidonius's assertions that people can live in the hot and wet
equatorial zones in southern Africa and elsewhere are
unbelievable ....*Strabo*
I recorded where everything is or was on the map following
Caesar's assassination. Those interested have an account of
known lands, and especially those that were of some importance
in the Roman World..*Strabo*

H 014
The map of Europe by Eratosthenes
has errors .... *Strabo of Amnesia*
My writings about Iberia, Gaul, and Italy are drawn in
part from Polybius, Posidoneus, and the Greek
scholar Artimedorus....................................... *Strabo Romanicus*
I have travelled to Egypt, Kush, Tuscany, Corinth,
Rome, and Anatolia, and up the Nile, and
into Ethiopia.. *Strabo Geographicus*
All world maps drawn in Europe are
upside down .... *Abu Abdullah al-Idrisi*

H 015
Why should I not sack Rome? ....*Attila the Hun*
Because it isn't nice, and God will dry
up your schmeckle...*Pope Leo I*

What did his Holiness say to Attila?...........*Bishop to the Cardinal*
Only God knows,
but it looks like it worked ....*Cardinal to the Bishop*
Read my book on Attila the Hun's management secrets ...... *Wes Roberts*

H 016
The empire is now too large and must be split
up into pieces..*Diocletian*
We defeated Attila and his Ogres at Chalons..... *Flavius Aetius & Theodoric*
Italy is a great place to visit .... *Gothic tourist brochures*
All roads now lead to nowhere .... *Alaric the Visigoth*

H 017
ANCIENT HOUSE SHOPPING
We love Spain and we'll stay for a while.................... *Genseric of the Vandals & Alans*
When evil and wicked Greco-Romans die, they will spend the
rest of eternity in Hades ....*High Priests of Rome & Athens*

H 018
All are new clothes... *The Emperor*
All is living long... *Methuselah*
All are no clothes... *Bettie Page*
All is staying young ....*Peter Pan*
All is vulgarity .... *Redd Foxx*
All is nothing cheap ....*Stormy Daniels*

H 019
EVIL & GOOD
All men are born depraved and damned ....*Augustine*
All unbaptized infants are damned at birth...........................*Calvin*
All men are born good and free ....*Pelagius*
All men are free on Facebook ....*Mark Zuckerberg*
All is fortune telling.. *Madam Zenobia*
All is forgery .... *Mr. Eight-Eighty*
All is staying alive.. *John Travolta*

H 020
THE POOR & THE HUNGRY
The poor will always be with us ....*Matthew*
The peasants are poor and hungry and
taxed too much .... *Wat Tyler*
Please, sir, can I have some more?............................*Oliver Twist*
Let them eat pork and beans ....*Rowen Atkinson*
Why was I not told the people in
East London were starving? ....*Edward VII*
We erected a monument thanking King Edward
for his help..*Jews of Whitechapel*

H 021
Let them eat gruel..*Ebenezer Scrooge*
Let them eat bon bons .... *Marie Antoinette*
Let them eat dogs and cats.. *Kim Il-sung*
Let them eat their young ....*Jonathan Swift*
Let them eat money.. *Scrooge McDuck*
Let them eat dope..................................*Virgil "The Turk" Sollozzo*

H 022
Being poor is no sin ....*George Herbert*
Feed the hungry ....*Isaiah*
Feed the poor ....*Jesus*
God must love poor people, he made so many of them.........*Abe
Lincoln*
Damn the poor. Let them do what I did .... *Cornelius Vanderbilt*

H 023
KARMA & REBIRTH
All people who behaved badly in past lives are reborn poor and
and into low castes. It's called Karma ....*Krishna to Arjuna*
You reap what you sow .... *Galatians*

H 024

THE POOR

You can't do much for the poor, they just aren't in with any of the
right people ....*Will Cuppy*
Religion keeps the poor from murdering the rich .... *Napoleon*
The poor are already damned at birth .... *John Calvin*
I owe the poor nothing..*J.P. Morgan*
Screw the poor.. *Ayn Rand*
F__k the poor... *Richard Nixon*

H 025

HEAVEN & HELL

St. Peter, don't you call me cause I can't go,
I owe my soul to the company stoe ....*Tennessee Ernie Ford*
I hear you knockin', but you can't come in ....*Fats Domino*
I am the keeper of the Pearly Gates ....*St. Peter*
I keep track of who's naughty and nice......................*St. Nicholas*

H 026

HEAVEN

All Dogs go to heaven .... *Don Bluth*
All Vikings go to Valhalla..................................... *Ragnar Lodbrok*
All Giants go to San Francisco .... *Megasthenes*
All Barbers go to haircut heaven .... *Willy Moore*

H 027

HARRY POLLITT & CHARLETON HESTON

Let me speak with comrade God............. *I'm Harry Pollitt, please*
We will show you where to go ....*Heavenly Cherubs*
But we won't let Charlton Heston in......*Heavenly Assistant Angel*
They couldn't get the gun from his cold dead hand ...... *Jim Carry*

H 028

THE RIVER STYX

Hi, I'm Karen, I'm your hostess, and I'm here to make your
voyage over the river Styx a pleasant one .... *Charon*
(pronounced "Karon")
I painted from horrific dreams of what Hell looks
like.. *Hieronymus Bosch*
Wrong place, you are coming with me .... *The Fallen Angel*

H 029

Most people hate listening to other people sing. Yet they look
forward to cloud heaven where everyone is singing
and never stop..*Mark Twain*
Bad historians are consigned to missing-document
heaven.. *Titus Livy*
Bad linguists will go to deaf-mute heaven............ *Noam Chomski*
Bad naturalists will go to the ends of the earth...... *Alexander von*
Humboldt
I have published many articles on how language began, but
many of my colleagues don't agree. They argue that because my
theories cannot be falsified, then they are not science........*Noam*
Chompski

H 030

DANTE & OSIRIS

This is my underworld. Who the Hell are you? .... *Osiris*
Abandon all hope, ye who enter here ....*Dante*
Follow me through The Gates of Hell.................................... *Pluto*
Well, I'll be damned .... *Faust*
That you are .... *Mephistopheles*

H 031

Stand back, I've just been made First People's Commissar of
Soviet Hell ....*Harry Pollitt*
No, go back into Hell, go back, go back.........................*Cerberus*
More noise, fire, and brimstone .... *The Evil One*
None of this for you... *Demon Rum*
Why do people in Hell always want ice water?...........*Old Scratch*

H 032

TIMELY INNOVATIONS & OBSERVATIONS

It's round ....*Eratosthenes*
It falls ....*Newton*
It's circular...*Copernicus*
It's elliptical...*Kepler*
It moves ....*Galileo*
It pumps ....*Wm. Harvey*
It talks ....*Alex. G. Bell*
It makes everyone happy ....*Dago Red*
It will go..*James Watt*
It computes ....*Jobs & The Woz*
It speaks..*Thomas Edison*
It flies ....*Orville & Wilbur*
It should fly..*Leonardo*
It will cure infections ....*Fleming*
It will keep the pox away ....*Jenner*
It's in the water...*John Snow*
It flew ....*Howard Hughes*
It's alive ....*Frankenstein*
It wasn't enough..*Rommel*
It's all gone kaput ....*Adolph Galland*
It was plenty...*Montgomery*
It all worked out fine ....*George Patton*
It's just over the horizon ....*Columbus*
It all worked here too...*Georgy Zhukov*

H 033

FRAUDULENT CLAIMS: IGNORANCE, FRAUD, ENVIRONMENTALISM, & NONSENSE

Historians say my book on the ancient Kings of Britain are absolutely false. But what do they know? ....*Geoffrey of Monmouth*

All journalism is fake news media......*Donald "The Mouth" Trump*
Hot climates produce stupid and weak people. Cold climates produce intelligent and vigorous people ......*Ellsworth Huntington*
Plutonic aethers cause bloating in corpses..........*Lucius Varenus*

Those whom the gods wish to destroy are first
made blind ....*King Ougodugo*

H 034
EVIL HUMORS
Evil humors and miasma create most illnesses..............*Medieval
physicians*
The ancient pyramids were full of grain and
green cheese... *Secretary Ben Carson*
Why must financial crooks go to the worst level of hell? ....*Bernie
Madoff*

H 035
TREATMENTS BY BLEEDING
Bleeding can cure illnesses ....*Medieval barbers*
The Barnacle Goose originates in the North Sea...........*Geraldus
Cambrensis*
Sometimes it's off and sometimes it's on .... *Onandoffsthenes*
The sun goes around the Earth ....*Pope Urban VIII*
If you don't agree, we have methods to make
you believe ....*Pope Guilty X*

H 036
COLD CLIMATES PRODUCE COLD PEOPLE
People living toward the North Pole have no culture and have
been negligible factors in history...............*Ellen Churchill Semple*
The people of northern Europe are energetic, provident, serious,
and cautious. These traits developed from several climate and
topographic influences, including proximity to oceans, drainage
systems, natural resources, population density, and seasonal
variety..*Ellen C. Semple*

H 037
MONGOLS, TURKS, & HUNS
The Kipchak Mongols (later Turks), who live near the Kazakh
Turks, are the most wicked. They are all lazy and live by thievery
and banditry...*Hadud al-Alam*

In the north, the lawless and merciless Khirgiz live like wild beasts. The tribes living to their east are merciless man-eaters. The Turks and Turkomans are arrogant, quarrelsome, malicious, and malevolent. They all are lazy and live by thievery and banditry .... *Hadud al-Alam*

H 038
TURKS CANNOT THINK
Turks cannot think due to an excess of blood and humors in their bodies that weigh down their minds............................*Jean Bodin*
Kazakhstan is most wonderful land on Earth. I visit
Kazakh village. I dance and have most fun.
It very dry there ....*Sacha Baron Borat*

H 039
HUNS & MONGOLS
The original ancient Huns came from the Mongolian steppes north of China. They later absorbed many peoples from the Central Asian steppes ....*Pythias*
The Huns were eventually defeated by an army of Romans and Germans ....*Priscus*

H 040
MESOPOTAMIA IS VERY RICH
Iraq is the most prosperous country
in the world.. *Hadud al-Alam*
The 14 provinces of Rum (Constantinople & Byzantium) have amenities beyond description .... *Hadud al-Alam*

H 041
Some Asiatics are good, but most are not..................*Hippocrates*
All non-Greeks are barbarians. Europeans living to the west of the Bosporus are more courageous and less cowardly than those living to the east of the Bosporus.................*Hippocampus*

H 042
People are always asking, "What does the word Bosporus mean?" It's a Thracian word meaning

"cow crossing" .... *Spartacus*
No, it's a Greek phrase that translates into Latin
as "caca de toro".. *Antonitus*
And into English as "bulls__t" .... *Dr. Johnson*

J 001

DIFFERENT CLIMATES PRODUCE DIFFERENT KINDS OF PEOPLE

A climate that is always the same, as is the case east of the Bosporus, fosters indolence, whereas climates that change periodically bring about laborious exertions that encourage bravery. People who live on thin, ill-watered soils are hardy, industrious, and well-braced, but are haughty........... *Hippocrates*
Soft regions produce soft men .... *Herodotus*

J 002

The Kartvelians (Kartulians) in the western Caucasus country of Georgia next to the Black Sea have poor shapes. They are tall, have gross bodily habits, speak with rough voices, and lack stamina... *Hippocrates*

J 003

SCYTHIANS ARE GROSS & FLABBY

The Scythians (Iranians) living north of the Black Sea are wild and unequal, as are all the central Asian Indo-Scythians (who are gross, fleshy, flabby, and sluggish). Scythian men are largely impotent because they wear trousers and spend too much time on their horses.. *Herodotus*

J 004

The cold, fatigue, and the trousers Scythians wear causes them to lose all sexual desires. Scythian women are indolent and fat, and their bellies are cold and soft. Their wombs are plugged up with fat, which keeps the birth rate down .... *Hippocrates*

J 005

Khorasan (northeast Iran) is a vast region with much wealth and many amenities. It is near the center of the inhabited world. It

has a salubrious climate and its people are strongly built and
healthy .... *Hadud al-Alam*

J 006
PRESTOR JOHN
It is said I created and ruled a mystical Eastern Rite, Christian
kingdom in central Asia (Russian Turkistan) during
the Middle Ages ....*Prestor John*
Many officials and scholars argue this ancient kingdom is real
and that Prestor John was a Nestorian
(Syrian Christian) ....*Hugh of Gebal*

J 007
GREEKS VS. BARBARIANS
All non-Greeks are barbarians. Europeans living to the west of
the Bosporus are more courageous and less cowardly than
those living to the east of the Bosporus. Climates that are always
the same, as is the case east of the Bosporus, fosters indolence,
whereas climates that change periodically bring about laborious
exertions that encourage courage and action.............*Hippocrates*
People who live on thin, ill-watered soils are hard and
industrious, but are haughty. All Asiatics (living east of the
Aegean) are feeble and gentler than Europeans and are less
warlike... *Hippodrome*

J 008
Only fools are stupid enough to prefer war over peace. During
peacetime, sons bury their fathers. During wartime, fathers bury
their sons .... *Herodotus*
Aristotle once said the face of a chameleon reminded him of a
baboon. But then, Aristotle wasn't very handsome himself..... *Will*
Cuppy

J 009
Plants and animals that acquire certain characteristics during
their lifetimes, like cutting off their tails, can pass tailessness on
to their offspring .... *Trofim Lysenko*
All men are created unequal... *George III*

Cold fusion will work ....*Pons & Fleischman*

J 010
HOT CLIMATES MAKE PEOPLE VIOLENT & STUPID
Hot climates make people violent, stupid, slow,
and indolent......................................*Ellen Churchill Semple*
Cold climates make people vigorous, smart,
and industrious ....*Ellsworth Huntington*
Global warming is real and is caused by humans .... *Phil Jones &*
Michael Mann
No, it really isn't ....*Robert Balling, Patrick Michaels, et al.*
Some races are stupider than others ....*Herrnstein and Murray*
Unfortunately, this just may be true.................... *Jordon Peterson*
It just might be, heaven help us ....*Robert Plomin*

J 011
PEOPLE IN HOT CLIMATES ARE INDOLENT & LAZY
People in hot climates are like old men. They lack curiosity and
are passive and indolent. They also lack enterprise and
generosity. Monkery has developed in hot countries where men
contemplate their fingernails rather than
lead active lives ....*Charles de Montesquieu*
Mediterranean peoples are cold, dry, swarthy, small,
and clear-voiced .... *E.C. Semple*

J 012
FRAUDS & FALSEHOODS
There is a vast hidden continent named Mu, located beneath the
middle of the Pacific Ocean ....*James Churchward*
There is also a lost continent (Lemuria) under
the Indian Ocean ....*Kumari Kandum*
Atlantis is a special island located in the
mid-Atlantic Ocean .... *Plato of Hellas*

J 013
MORE FRAUDS
Stressing mouse cells turns them
into stem cells...*Hiroku Obokata*

It's called tobacco and it will aid in digestion.... *Sir Walter Raleigh*
It stinks...*Vernon Wormer*
Piltdown man is real ....*Charles Dawson*

J 014

CAUCASIANS HAVE EVOLVED HIGHER THAN OTHER RACES

The Caucasoid race evolved into *Homo sapiens* earlier than Mongoloids, Congoids, Capoids, Cossacks, Malays, Australoids, Baboons, and New World Amerinds................. *Carleton S. Coon*

J 015

When Adam delved and Eve spanned, who was then
the gentleman? .... *John Balls*
All men are created equal .... *Thomas Jefferson*
All men are condemned to be free.....................................*Sartre*
Touch not the angry cat without a glove .....*Chief of Clan Chattan*
All men are equal before cats...................................*Claude Balls*
In ancient Egypt, many deceased cats were embalmed
by their owners and laid to rest in tombs where there
were lots of dead mice ....*Bastet, goddess of cats*

J 016

FISHES & THE DEEP BLUE SEA

I am the ruler of the ocean ....*Poseidon*
I am the overseer of the seven seas............................... *Neptune*
Tharr she blows...*Capt. Ahab*
I am the Prince of Whales .... *Moby Dick*
All men are equal before fish... *Hoover*
All fish rot from the head down .... *Dukakis*
O'Sama now sleeps with the fishes .... *O'Bama*
And joy to the world, and joy to the fishes
in the deep blue sea.................................... *Three Dog Night*

The Northern Pike is the meanest of all freshwater fishes
because of heredity and unfortunate social conditions in the
water .... *Will Cuppy*

J 017

SINGING IN THE RAIN

I'm just singing in the rain ....*Gene Kelly*
Raindrops keep falling on my head.............................*Goeff Love*
It's raining it's pouring, the old
man is snoring ....*Rude neighbor kids*

J 018

**RELIGIONS OF THE BURNED-OVER DISTRICT IN UPSTATE
NEW YORK**

Mormonism was one of many sects that appeared during the
"Great Awakening," aka, the "Burned Over-District" in western
New York during the 19th century. These included
Swedenburglers, Shakers, Quakers, Bakers, Fakers, and many
other religious sects and books written at this time and place by
con artists and self-proclaimed prophets, some of whom actually
believed in everything they said, such as Jemima Wilkinson and
many others......................................*Whitney Cross, John Martin,*
Mike McKenzie, et al.
Some Seventh-Day Adventists left our new church after the
"Great Disappointment" when the predicted end of time did not
materialize…And then everyone strolled down the hill and went
home .... *Ellen White*

J 019

HALLOWEEN

Our All-American holiday originated in 19th century in Ireland as
a harvest and New Year's festival called Samhain (pronounced
sa-ween).. *John Rhys*
In the 9th century CE, the Church converted it
into All Saints Day ....*James Frazer*
Here I am, what kind of fun
would you like? ....*Elvira, Mistress of the Dark*
And here I am...............................*Morticia of the Addams Family*

I'm here...*Vampira of the Coffin Show*
I'm also here .... *Lilly of the Munsters*

J 020
NEW RELIGIOUS BELIEFS, CULTS, BOOKS, & TRACTS
The Book of Oahspe, a New Bible, is absolutely true...........*John Newbrough*
I wrote several religious tracts, including the Oberlin or Honolulu Manuscript, my Conneaut Creek Manuscript, and my "Manuscript Found"...*Soloman Spalding*
Once upon a time, in Upstate New York, an angel gave me a story, written on metal plates (that no one ever saw), about the origin of the Mound Builders and certain Levantine peoples. This became known as the Book of Mormon ....*Joseph Smith*

J 021
Joseph Smith plagiarized a great deal from my manuscripts...*Soloman Spalding*
I became a spiritual healer who rediscovered ancient health and healing secrets and wrote a book about primitive bible healing......................................*Mary Baker Eddy*
Mary Eddy stole my healing secrets and wrote them down as hers...*Phineas Quimby*

J 022
JEWS INTO THE NEW WORLD
Many people in Utah believe that ancient Hebrews sailed across the ocean, settled in America, and built pyramids and earthen mounds .... *The Book of Mormonism*
We're on a mission from God .... *The Blues Brothers*
Rama Lama Ding Dong.. *Hare Krishnas*

J 023
HEAVEN'S GATE
Marshall Applewhite, following the writings of Robert A. Heinline and Arthur C. Clark, fabricated a millennial religious cult called Heaven's Gate. It featured extraterrestrials, and with various teachings, claimed to bring its followers to a "higher evolutionary

level." The cult members (20 or 30) waited for the comet Hale-Bopp to take them away. They sold all their possessions and waited, and waited, and waited. When no comet came, everyone took barbiturates, alcohol, and put plastic bags over their heads and died.........*Robert Hecht, Evan Thomas, John Hall, Catherine Wessinger, Newsweek, & The NY Post*

J 024
SCIENTOLOGY
Scientology requires all members to give up all their families, wealth, friends, and periodically submit to
"audit screenings" ....*John Travolta*
I did all of that s__t and was a member for many years .... *Tom Cruise*
Phrenology can reveal people's moral qualities and intelligence by measuring bumps on their heads .... *Geo. & Andrew Combe*

J 025
JEHOVAH'S WITNESSES
Jehovah's witnesses believe that only 144,000 of their members will survive "The Coming of the Great Rapture" at the end of time, where lions, bears, lambs, goats, chickens, skunks, fleas, elephants, mango worms, and bot flies will coexist next to each other in perfect harmony...............*Charles Taze Russell and The Watchtower*

J 026
I founded Eckankar, the
only true Path of Spiritual Freedom........................ *Paul Twitchell*
This religion opens up knowledge of past lives, dreams, soul travel, and enlightenment, which will lead disciples down the path to becoming elders and leading Eck Masters....... *Sri Harold Klump*

J 027
For $25.00, I can ordain anyone who wants to be a minister in my Modesto, California-based
Universal Life Church .... *Kirby Hensley*

When I started to sell theology doctorates in California,
the state authorities forced me to move my ministry
to Arizona ....*The Rev. Hensley*

J 028

EVIL PSYCHOPATHS

All is murdering and genocide .... *Timur, Pol Pot, Idi Amin,*
Hitler, Stalin, Nero, Torquemada, Genghis Khan,
Caligula, Himmler, Tojo Hideki, Ted Bundy,
John Chivington, Tomoyuki Yamashita,
John Wayne Gacy, and the Whitechapel Slasher

J 029

TARTARUS, HELL, HADES, & RETRIBUTION

Everything here is crime and punishment ...... *Fyodor Dostoevsky*
You all are staying here forever ....*Angra Mainyu*

J 030

Time's up, and forever starts now .... *Satan*
Here I am, straight from Brazil. Would any of you like to
read my famous book, "*Mein Putz*"? .... *Der Furor*
First, you are going to the de-lousing showers
down below .... *Der Teufel*
All is escape ....*Houdini*

J 031

Then we will toss you into Tartarus, a pit of perpetual torment
beneath Hades for the most wicked ....*The Down-Under*
Welcome Committee
Tell them to stop whining...*Beelzebub*
How long must I stay here? .... *Jack the Ripper*
Look it up in my Devil's Dictionary .... *Ambrose Bierce*

J 032
Time to turn up the thermostats to 666 degrees................ *Lucifer*
This place is hotter than Vulcan's dick .... *Titus Pullo*
It's hotter than Hell down here .... *Anton LaVey*
What did you expect? .... *Pluto*
I think he wants a little professional courtesy .... *The Devil's*
Advocate

J 033
NOTABLE SOCIOLOGISTS
Max Weber, C. Wright Mills, Georg Simmel, Robert Park, John
Dewey, Thorstein Veblin, Auguste Compte, Robert Merton,
Emile Durkheim, Karl Manheim, Pitirim Sorokin, C. Wright Mills,
W.E.B. duBois, John Stuart Mill, Johann Pestalozzi, Talcott
Parsons, Hannah Arendt .... *Louis Coser, Robert Nisbet, et al.*

J 034
HISTORY & HISTORIANS
All is ancient Greek history ....*Herodotus*
All are historical biographies... *Plutarch*
Historians should follow new topics in historical analysis,
such as environmental and social histories...... *Giambattista Vico*

J 035
All is historiography... *Ibn Khaldun*
All is natural history.. *von Humboldt*
All is universal history .... *von Ranke*
All is challenge and response .... *Arnold Toynbee*
All are universal histories................................. *Will & Ariel Durant*
All are new environmental, economic, cultural, and social
histories ....*Fernand Braudel*

J 036
All is to see that the Guns of August, which started WWI, was the
result of mobilizations brought about by
secret alliances..*Barbara Tuchman*

All is my "Beard Thesis," arguing that the U.S. Constitution was mostly created by the wealthy Founding Fathers as a way to preserve their personal wealth and property......*Charles A. Beard*

K 001

GEOGRAPHY & GEOGRAPHERS
In the beginning was The Textbook........................ *Harm J. Deblij*
All are rural French landscapes....................... *Vidal de la Blache*
All is spatial differentiation............................. *Richard Hartshorne*
All is a better library index for geography books ... *Preston James*
All is historical and cultural geography .... *Richard Nostrand*
All is cultural and historical geography .... *Donald Meinig*

K 002

NOTABLE GEOGRAPHERS
In the beginning was Sauer and
William Morris Davis... *Geoffrey Martin*
All is Central Place geometry ....*Walter Christaller*
All is my hexagonal urban land use model .... *August Losch*
After this war, we will have lebensraum and will settle multitudes of superior Aryan-German families into our new eastern empire in accordance with the hexagonal Christaller and Loschian landscape models. I also introduced the Swastika into the Nazi ideology ....*General Karl Haushofer*
I exposed this Nazi Geographic strategy of
world conquest... *Derwent Whittlesey*

K 003

All is anarchist geography .... *Élisée Reclus*
All are feral landscapes... *Ellie Irons*
All is theoretical geography .... *William Bunge*
All is the Isolated State land use model..................... *von Thunen*
All is the urban concentric ring model..............................*Burgess*
All is the urban sector model ....*Hoyt & Bogue*
All is the reverse Burgess model .... *Schnore*

K 004
All is the principle of least effort .... *G.K. Zipf*
All is the retail gravity model .... *William Reilly*
All is the multiple nuclei model............................ *Harris & Ullman*
Nearby things are more similar than
things at a distance..*Waldo Tobler ;-)*
All are cardinal neighbors and mental map analysis .... *Elliott*

K 005

ANTHROPOLOGY & ANTHROPOLOGISTS
I once wrote a tourist brochure about
my trip to Mexico ....*Edward B. Tylor*
Some of my Samoan girls may have misled me about
their sexual practices in the western Pacific......... *Margaret Mead*
Read my book on chrysanthemums...................*Ruth Benedict ;-)*
All my former graduate stoonts are Boasians..............*Franz Boas*
We took good care of Ishi of the Yana .... *Alfred Kroeber*
All is ethno-geo-musicology..................................... *Alan Lomax*
All is just one damn cannibal after another ....*Michael
Rockefeller*

K 006

IBN BATTUTA ON SOUTHEAST ASIANS
The people of Java and Sumatra are black, wild, naked
man-eaters ....*Hadud al-Alam*
We visited these people living in a land called Sunaridwan
(Sumatra). Near this land, I witnessed people in a territory
called Barahnaka, occupied by today's
Andaman Islanders.. *Ibn Battuta*

K 007
The Barahnakarese are a vile race. They have no religion,
neither that of the Hindus, nor of any other. They live in houses
made of reeds along the sea shore. The men are like us but their

mouths are like dogs (cynocephhalus). The men and women
wear leaves to cover up their private parts .... *Ibn Battuta*
Among the people of Barahnakar live some Muslims from Bengal
and Sumatra, who live in separate villages................ *Ibn Battuta*

K 008
We've been hired as English teachers at the court of
King Mongut and Prince Chulalongkorn .... *Anna Leonowens*
& Julie Andrews

I was the best king of Siam for
a short time, etc., etc., etc. .... *Yul Brynner*
We are Siamese if you please, or if you don't please .....*Siamese*
feline twins

In Singapore, you may not spit
on my sidewalks...*Lee Kuan Yew*

K 009
NORTH & SOUTH VIETNAM
Good Morning Viet Nam!...................................*Adrian Cronhauer*
Follow the Ho Chi Min trail .... *Robin Williams*
Hoo dat don dar? ....*Cao Dai*
Come see my new liquor
and wine store in Los Angeles...........................*Nguyen Cao Ky*

K 010
GENOCIDE, ATROCITIES, & MISERY
Long ago, we built a large temple complex called Angkor Wat. It
was originally a Hindu temple dedicated to Vishnu, and then a
Buddhist temple .... *The Khmers*
The Khmer Rouge did horrible things in
Cambodia, so what? .... *Pol Pot*
All is genocide................................... *Genghis Khan, Tamerlane,*
Attila the Hun, Boku Haram
Hitler, Tojo, Cortez, Pizarro, Andrew Jackson,
Wm. F. Cody .... *UN Genocide Bureau*

K 011

All is suffering ....*Buddha*
All is genetics...*Mendel*
All is cubism ....*Picasso*
All is surreal...*Dali*
All is fantasy ....*Disney*
All is bizarre...*Gaudi*
All is roaring...*MGM Lion*
All is darkness ....*Dracula*

K 012

All is illogical ....*Spock*
All is love ....*St. Valentine*
All is sculpture ....*Michelangelo*
All is rubber ....*Michelin*
All is beer...*Michelob*
All are Oreos..*Nabisco*
All are nukes...*The Seven*
All are sunsets ....*Monet*

K 013

All is winning..*NY Yankees*
All is losing ....*St. Louis Browns*
All is travel ....*Ibn Battuta*
All is tradition ....*Tevya of Anatevka*
All is random..*Heisenberg*
All is human sacrifice ....*Aztec priests*
All is kindness..*Eleanor Roosevelt*
All are homeless ....*Streets of San Francisco*

K 014

PREDICTIONS

I predict there will be rain......................................*Nostradamus*
I predict that there will soon be snow ....*Edgar Cayce*
I predicted the stock market would
crash and I got out...*Joseph Kennedy*
The Caldera is going to erupt soon .....*Yellowstone Park Rangers*

K 015

Open this box and you'll be sorry .... Pandora
The sky seems to be falling, and no one believes me ..... Chicken
Little
Nobody believes me any more either .... Cassandra
Just the facts, Ma'am .... Joe Friday
I was just getting ready to say that myself .... Dick Tracy
A cigar is usually just a cigar .... Freud

K 016

NUMERICAL & SCIENTIFIC INNOVATIONS

I invented the printing press .... Gutenberg
I invented the wireless telegraph .... Marconi
I invented algebra... Al-Khwarizmi
I invented algebra.. Diophantus
I invented trigonometry... Hipparchus
I invented the calculus...Newton
I invented the calculus.. Leibniz
I invented the calculus...Ramanujan
All is uniform .... Lyell
All is adrift .... Wegner

K 017

ALL IS & ALL ARE

All is preservation... Isaac Walton
All is a good landing .... Lucky Lindy
All is natural beauty... John Muir
All is organic geopolitic..Frederich Ratzel
All is rustica .... Vivaldi
All is silent.. Rachel Carson
All is elementary... Sherlock
All is in the Jungle ....Frank Buck
All is natural selection...Darwin
All is binomial .... Galton
All is natural selection.. Wallace
All is revenge ....Clemenceau

K 018

All is victory ....*Patton*
All is on Amazon..*Jeff Bezos*
All are quanta ....*Max Plank*
All are haplogroups.................................*Svante Pääbo*
All are guns & shooting...*NRA*
All is alternate news.. *TYT*
All is boring..*PBS*
All is inaction and too long ....*MLB*
All is too much action..*NBA*
All are too many head injuries................................ *NFL*
All is Chipped beef on toast ....*SOS*
All is an excellent lunch ....*BLT*
All are inspections .... *IG*
No Bucks, no Buck Rogers .... *NASA*

K 019

BEWARE OF WHAT MIGHT HAPPEN

Beware of Greeks bearing gifts...........................*Laocoon*
Beware the Helots & Perioikoi ....*Leonidas*
Beware the Gordian Knot ....*Phrygian Gordium*
Stupe the Gordian Knot .... *Iskander of Macedon*
Beware the Sword of Damocles.............................. *Cicero*

K 020

Beware the Military and
Industrial Complex.................................... *Dwight D. Eisenhower*
Beware the Ides of March...........................*The Augur Spurinna*
Beware of those who have studied only
one book...*Thomas Aquinas*
Beware the Slaves... *Spartacus*
Beware the Teutoburger Forest................................... *Arminius*
Beware the sword Excalibur .... *Merlin*

K 021

Beware the Great Pox... *Montezuma*
Beware the headless horseman .... *Ichabod Crane*
Beware the horse latitudes.. *Magellan*
Beware the Bermuda Triangle...................................*von Daniken*
Beware the Jabberwock .... *Lewis Carroll*
Beware the Morlocks..*H.G. Wells*
Beware the Kryptonite .... *Jor-El*

K 022

SOUTH SEA ISLANDERS

About 3400 years ago, we left the Solomon Islands and travelled
more than 2,000 miles eastward over the ocean and settled on
Tonga and Samoa. After 300 more years, we settled Tahiti,
Hawaii, and Aotearoa..................................*Polynesian seafarers*
A thousand years ago, we settled Madagascar...........*Malagasys*
from South Borneo

Bali Hai's your favorite island,
come to me, come to me..................................... *The Sea Witch*
Come see my raft Kon Tiki .... *Thor Heyerdahl*

K 023

Beware the fire and lava.. *Pele*
Beware the Ki'eki'e winds.....................................*Kamehameha*
Beware the Sandwich Isle Luaus .... *Capt. Cook*
Beware the Moais of Rapa Nui...............................*The Kahunas*
Beware the sweating disease.......................................*Malama*

K 024

ITALY & ITALIANS

Scholars in the west must start studying Greco-Roman and
Arabic math, science, and astronomy. There is so much to learn.
Here also is the decimal numeral system along with Arabic
(Hindu) numerals. And this device is called an abacus........*Pope
Sylvester II*
Paint according to reality and nature, and help jump-start the
Italian Renaissance....................................... *Giotto di Bondone*

K 025

MARCO POLO'S JOURNEY TO CHINA

I was born in 1254. Our journey to Cathay lasted from 1271 to 1295. We commenced traveling from Venice to Turkey and passed toward the Far East through eastern Turkey along the ancient Silk Road to Cathay..........*Maffeo, Marco, & Niccolo Polo*

K 026

The land route took us through Armenia, Persia, Bactria, and the Pamir Mountains through central Asia, where we crossed lands inhabited by Mohammedans, Zoroastrians, Buddhists, Nestorians, and Manichaeans. We crossed the Central Asian deserts, and then went on to Shangdu (Xanadu) and Dadu (Beijing) where the court of the Great Khan was in residence...................................*Marco, Maffeo, & Niccolo*

K 027

We continued east through Gansu province. After following the Silk Road through Gansu province in western China, we arrived at the court of the Great Khan in the year 1274 or 1275 ....*The Polos*

In 1274 or 1275, we arrived in Shangdu (the Mongol northern summer residence). I was 20 years old in 1274 when we entered China... *Marco*

K 028

MARCO POLO IN CHINA, CHUNGUO, CATHAY, KITAI, & CIPANGO

Once in Cathay (the Mongol word for China or Chunguo), I learned some Chinese, and the Great Khan gave me a "passport," which enabled me to travel freely throughout Cathay (Kitai). During that time, I learned about an island nation to the east called Cipango (Jih pen-guo in Chinese), meaning "sun-rise kingdom." The Chinese also called it the land of hairy people. Interestingly, the Chinese eat spaghetti just like us............ *Marco Polo*

K 029
MARCO POLO GOING HOME TO ITALY
We spent 16 or 17 years in Cathay. Seventeen years later in
1283, we travelled westward back toward Europe, going through
Burma, Tibet, and India via the Indian Ocean. Then we went on
to the Gulf of Hormuz along the south
coast of Persia ....*Marco Polo*

K 030
I wrote down the story of Marco Polo's journey to Cathay
before he died in 1324.....................................*Rustichello da Pisa*
It's safer to be feared than loved ....*Machiavelli*
Here is something nice to drink ....*Lucrezia Borgia*
Thanks, but no thanks.....................................*Giovanni de Medici*
I discovered sunspots, the rings of Saturn, the moons of Jupiter,
many stars, and a whole lot of other heavenly objects ......*Galileo*
Gannymede

K 031
ILLUSTRIOUS & SOME NOT-SO-ILLUSTRIOUS POPES
I stayed in my apartment and studied science......*Pope Sylvester*
I ruled the Vatican for three years ....*Pope Innocent XIII*
I never visited the Vatican & stayed in Avignon ...... *Pope Guilty II*
We did not see any of the Nazi
atrocities in WWII .... *Pope Pius XII*
The Church must open up and modernize........... *Pope John XXIII*
The Pill is a no-no .... *Pope Paul VI*
The first non-Italian pope in 500 years .... *Pope John Paul II*
All people have the right to change
their religion ....*Pope John Paul II*
I just couldn't take it any more .... *Pope Benedict XVI*
Evolution and the Big Bang are real .... *Pope Francisco*

K 032
THE ITALIAN STALLIONS
When the moon hits your eye
lika big pizza pie, at's amore .... *Dean Martin*
Three coins in the fountain .... *The Four Aces*

Best canned spaghetti with meatballs in da south Bronx ......*Chef Boyardee*
Stop calling me the chicken of the sea...... *Capt. Franco Schittino*
Ain't gonna be no rematch.......................................*Apollo Creed*
There's gotta be a rematch..................................... *Rocky Balboa*
Beware the Five Families............................... *Don Vito Corleone*
Beware the real Five Families............................ *Carmine Persico*

K 033

THE HEAT THEORY ON HUMAN CULTURE & HISTORY

The people of southern Italy, feeling the relaxation of
hot climates, are indolent, irresponsible,
and improvident.......................................*Ellen Churchill Semple*
Mediterranean peoples are cold, dry, hard, bald, weak, swarthy,
small, and clear-voiced .... *Jean Bodin*

K 034

IN MODERATE TEMPERATURES, VOICES BECOME SWEET & MELODIOUS

In countries where the temperatures are moderate, one's voice
becomes sweet and melodious, as is true among the
Italians and the French .... *John Bodin*
There is a steady stream of Italians to Argentina, which
will make that country great .... *Hendrick Willem van Loon*

K 035

The Southern Europeans (of France, Iberia, and the Balkans)
are the product of the intermingling of races, which perpetuated
disharmony. The civilizations of Italy attained the grade of
beauty, but not of rationality...........................*George W.F. Hegel*
Yeah, and don't ask us for any more money
for your wars... *The Doge of Genoa*

K 036

ITALIAN AMERICANS

Don't you just love old Italian opera? ....*Enrico Caruso*
Make him an offer he can't refuse.................... *Don Vito Corleone*
See? It's just business ....*Michael Corleone*

We're bigger than U.S. Steel ....Meyer Lansky
Stop the car, I gotta take a leak...........................Fat Clemenza
The movie was as good as my book ....Mario Puzo

K 037
Best Pizza from out of old Italy ....Chef di Giorno
Tax evasion? Mama Mia! ....Al Capone
Faciitis will make Italy great again ....Mussolini
That's what Trump keeps saying about America .... Anderson
Cooper

L 001
GERMANIC TRIBES IN MEDIEVAL SPAIN
We have been here since the beginning
of time .... *The Basques of Euscaria*
We have been here for many centuries.............. *The Celtiberians*
We love Spain. And we'll stay a while .... *The Roman
Legionnaires*
We are coming here to live in sunny Spain............. *The Visigoths*
We will settle in Catalonia .... *The Goths and Alans*
We will settle in Andalusia....................................... *The Vandals*
We will settle in Galicia............................*The Sueves and Gauls*

L 002
MOORS IN IBERIA
We conquered the Germanic kingdoms of Spain and built
Cordova, the most beautiful city in the world .... *Tariq ibn Ziad*
We are now changing the name "Pillars of Hercules" to Jebal al-
Tariq (later called Gibraltar), and then we will teach you
Spaniards Arabic.. *Tariq the Moor*

L 003
GERMANS IN IBERIA
The Reconquista begins in Asturias .... *Chanson de Roland*
I'm the 1st Adelantado, and we beat back the
Moors at Cordova....................................... *Pelagius of Asturias*
I am now the Adelantado, and I will defeat the
Moors in battle .... *Rodrigo Diaz de Bivar*

We are winning. Estoy montando en mi caballo muerto......*El Cid Campeador*
Yes, good, and you will strike terror among the Moors...... *Sophia Loren*

L 004
SEPHARDIC JEWS IN MOORISH SPAIN
During our Diaspora, thousands of us settled in tolerant Moorish Spain .... *Jews of Spain*
Teach a man to fish and he might eat
nothing but fish forever .... *Hillel*
Learning to say "I don't know" is the first
step to true wisdom.....................................*Moses Maimonides*
All Jewish dead will enter and remain in Sheol, a dark place in the shadowy underworld. After death, all Jews will go there regardless of whether they were virtuous or villains
during their lifetimes.........................*Medieval Talmudic scholars*

L 005
JEWS IN SPAIN
Under the Islamic Moors, the Jewish population in Spain experienced several "golden ages" under several Arab rulers, who followed the Koranic teaching that dictates tolerance of Jews (and Christians) as ahl-al kitab (people of the book) Isaac ben Albalia, Soloman bin Ezra, Moses ben Enoch, Judah Halevi, and many others.......*Misc. Medieval Jewish scholars and writers*

L 006
BENJAMIN de TUDELA'S JOURNEY
I was born and lived in the northern city of Tudela (in the kingdom of Pamplona), near to and directly south of the Basque country of Navarre. During the twelfth century (1159–1163), I travelled through southern Europe, the Near East, and the Mediterranean .... *Benjamin ben Jonah de Tudela*

L 007
In Spain, I travelled to Barcelona, then to Narbonne, then to Arles and Marseille in France. In Italy, I visited Genoa, which

was surrounded by a great wall, and the city had no king or ruler.
Instead they appoint judges to settle disputes and function as
administrators. I went on to Pisa, Rome, and Naples .... *Benjamin
Tudela*

L 008

In Rome were many beautiful buildings. One of these was a
large church that they call St. Peters. There are also eighty
palaces there that were built by eighty different rulers called
Imperators, starting with Tarquinius (of Tuscany) down
to Tiberius and Nero, who lived there at the time of
Jesus the Nazarene and then went on to Salonika, and
Constantinople .... *Benjamin of Tudela*

L 009

In Tyre and Antioch, there were Jewish glass-makers, and
Jewish ship-owners. Jewish workmen were employed by the
ship-owners and were domiciled among the Druzes there. I went
on to Mesopotamia and journeyed through Mosul, Baghdad, and
Basra. In Baghdad, I encountered several different Jewish sects,
namely the Karaites of Constantinople, Askelon, and Damascus.
There were also sects in Cyprus where the beginning of the
Sabbath was held on Saturday mornings instead of Friday
evenings.. *Benjamin Tudela*

L010

Continuing eastward, I went through Tyre, Damascus, and
Jerusalem in the Levant. Traveling on to Baghdad, I observed
the grave of Ezekiel the prophet, where there were periodic
ceremonies carried out by the Jews of the area. I also learned at
this time of the Pseudo-Messiah David Alroy .... *Benjamin
de Tudela*

L 011

I then travelled around the Arabian Peninsula to the south and
then the west and spent some time in Alexandria, Cairo, the
Fayum, and Darmietta. On the way back to Spain, I stopped in

Sicily and visited Messina and Palermo. Arriving back in Spain, I went through Granada, Cordoba, and Toledo.............. *Benjamin de Tudela*

L 012
IBERIAN OCEANIC EXPLORERS
I sailed down the west coast of Africa and then came back because I was afraid the heat might burn up
my ship's sails ....*Henry the Navigator*
We will fund your expedition ....*Isabella & Ferdinand*
In fourteen hundred and ninety-two,
I did sail the ocean blue... *Columbus*

L 013
I have returned from over the Ocean Sea, and the
Indies are ours...*Cristobal Colon*
I sailed around southern Africa and then on to India ..... *Vasco da Gama*
I will call it the Pacific Ocean.................. *Vasco Nunez de Balboa*

L 014
MAGELLAN'S JOURNEY
I was not the first to sail around the world. Because I was detained permanently in the Philippines along the way, but my ship made it back to Spain and became the first ship
to sail around the world...*Magellan*
All non-Catholics in Spain and the
Indies must be expelled .... *Torquemada*

L 015
SPAIN & THE SPANIARDS
Africa begins at the Pyrenees.......................................*Napoleon*
I can't see in the distance un molino de viento......... *Don Quixote*
Don't worry, I'll paint a picture of it for you ....*Picasso*
I loved them all ....*Don Juan*
So did I .... *Cassanova*
Que será, será...*Doris Day*

L 016

The French lined up our villagers and shot them all .... *El Greco*
The Germans bombed our villages................................. *Picasso*
I looked a lot better than Franco did
in the Bull Ring..*Evita Perón*
The Spanish Mackerel is misnamed. It's not really Spanish ... *Will*
Cuppy

L 017

COLD CLIMATES & HUMAN CULTURE

The Slavs north of the Black Sea are primitives living in the
trees. Russians are evil-tempered, intractable, arrogant,
quarrelsome, and warlike .... *The Hadud al-Alam*
Russians exhibit unsystematic and desultory work habits and are
benumbed by the sloth of the far north. They have been
subjected to the retarding effects of East and Central Asia and
the melancholy of the Slavs................................. *Ellen C. Semple*

L 018

RUSSIA & RUSSIANS

Russians are mostly agricultural slaves. Many people in Moscow
readily sell themselves into slavery because their liberties are not
worth keeping. It is necessary to flay a Muscovite alive to make
him to feel anything. The Russian soul is not
sensitive to pain .... *Montesquieu*
I should know, having spent some time in the
Gulag Archipelago...*Solzhenitsyn*

L 019

THE MUZHIKS OF RUSSIA

The muzhiks (serfs) of Russia are touched by melancholy and
exhibit unsystematic and desultory work habits and are
benumbed by the sloth of the far north ..... *Ellen Churchill Semple*

L 020

CLIMATIC INFLUENCE ON HUMAN CULTURE & PHYSIQUES

Climatic forces produce well-formed and ill-formed people. Well-
formed peoples do not feel the compressing cold of Northern
Russia or the dry winds of Mongolia. Neither do they feel the
burning heat of deserts or the wet violent changes in the
American climate ....*Johann Gottfried von Herder*

L 021

RUSSIA & THE CZARS

We brought Christianity to all the Russias and invented
the Glagolitic (Cyrillic) alphabet so all Slavs now
can read ....*Saints Cyril & Methodius*
I was the first Russian tsar....................... *Rurik of the Varangians*
I was the most feared tsar of all the Russias.......................... *Ivan*
aka, John Terrible
Burn your kaftans and cut off your beards ....*Peter the Great*
Now watch me as I build a modern sailing ship................*Санкт-*
Петербург

L 022

CATHERINE THE GREAT, CZARINA OF ALL THE RUSSIAS

I am bringing in hundreds of families from Germany who will
build new agricultural villages along the middle Volga that will
increase agricultural production in Russia. I also established The
Pale of Settlement (a line in western Russia), which defined
where Jews from eastern Europe could build and live
in shtetls (small Jewish agricultural settlements in
western Russia)... *Catherine the Great*
Scratch a Russian find a Tatar....................... *Marquis de Cuisine*
Come listen to some of my piano recitals.... *Sergei Rachmaninoff*
In 1867, I sold Alaska to the United States
for plenty of rubles ....*Czar Alexander II*

L 023

I wrote 130 poems between 1814 and 1817 and then spent
twenty years in the south of Russia. After that, many of my

works were deemed "inappropriate" and
seditious by the Czar.. *Alexander Pushkin*
I am freeing all the serfs .... *Czar Alexander II*
Czar Alex has been assassinated .... *St. Petersburg*
Court Heralds
No good turn ever goes unpunished............. *Gogol & Dostoevsky*
YO-o Oh-ho.. *Volga Boatmen*

L 024
I can heal the Czardine ....*Rasputin*
I was the last Russian Czar..*Nicholis II*
It takes a village ....*Hillary Clinton*
No, it really doesn't take a village ....*Potemkin*
Starting wars is entirely the work of rulers ....*Tolstoy*

L 025
Russians are hardy, vigorous, and patient, but extremely rude,
ignorant, and barbarous ....*Jesse Olney*
Many years ago, I was going to become a priest.................*Stalin*
Now tell me, how many divisions does the pope have?....... *Josef*
Dzhugashvili

L 026
RUSSIANS, WARS, & THE REVOLUTION
Does anyone know what Hegel meant by the negation of the
negation? ....*Marx*
Work is the curse of the laboring class ....*Engels*
What is not to be done ....*Lenin*
Yes, this is more just...*Zhivago*
Oh, no they shot the Czar and his family...........................*Kulaks*
That means there is no turning back ....*Party apparatchicks*
Comrade Trotsky must be liquidated ....*Stalin*

M 001
We defeated the Nazi supermen at Stalingrad and Kursk, and
drove them all back into the snow to die............. *Marshal Zukhov*
Just like Napoleon...*Mother Russia*

M 002
I was the best dancer in the Bolshoi Ballet at Moscow.....*Nijinsky*
Russia is a riddle, wrapped in a mystery,
inside an enigma ....*Winston Churchill*
We've avoided conflict with the Anglo Saxons
and America ....*Molotov*
Stalin was a monster ....*Nikita Khruschev*
In 1994, I won an Olympic Gold medal in ice
skating from the Ukraine.. *Oskana Baiul*

M 003
First Russian into outer space .... *Yuri Gagarin*
If we let them, will they leave? ....*Gorbachev*
More vodka!.. *Boris Yeltson*
Don't I look dashing riding bareback in the afternoon?.... *Vladimir*
Putin

M 004
VLADIMIR PUTIN
We've got all kinds of compromising dirt on Trumpski and we're
blackmailing him. Just watch him grovel. He wants to build some
hotels and golf resorts in Russia after he leaves office, and he
needs our approval and funding .... *Vladimir Putin*
See how well-conditioned he is?............... *Ivan Petrovitch Pavlov*
I moved Crimea into the Ukraine with only
my signature.. *Khruschev*
I put the Crimea back into Russia with only my signature ....*Putin*

M 005
POLAND & THE POLES
The nobles of Poland are brave, hardy, and active, but they are
illiterate, haughty, and extremely fond of dress. Polish peasants
are ignorant, poor improvident, and drunk (who believe that only
what they drink is theirs) ....*J. Olney*
Please record that I've taken into account and have always kept
my concern for the welfare of the Polish people................ *Ignace*
Paderewski

M 006

I spent the greater part of my adult life in Paris writing piano
compositions and concertos and giving piano lessons to gifted
pupils .... *Frederic Chopin*
I discovered radium and then my fingers started to glow and fall
off and then I died of a new malady, called
radiation poisoning .... *Marie Sklodowska Curie*

M 007

During the first weeks of WWII, when the Germans invaded
Poland, we charged Nazi tanks on horseback trying to get close
enough to fire the anti-tank weapons we
carried into battle..................................... *Polish Cavalry Soldiers*
I was a National League All Star for
four seasons .... *Ted Kluszewski*

M 008

CENTRAL ASIAN NOMADS & ANATOLIAN TURKS
In Central Asia, the lawless and merciless Khirgiz Turks live like
wild beasts. The tribes living to the east are merciless man-
eaters. The Central Asian nomadic Turks are arrogant,
quarrelsome, malicious, and malevolent............... *Hadad al Alam*

M 009

All Anatolians (living east of the Aegean) are feeble and gentler
than Europeans and are less warlike.........................*Hippocrates*
Turks are rapacious and extravagant ....*Jean Bodin*
Turks are uncongenial and alien ....*Ellen Churchill Semple*

M 010

Turks are not suited to engage in contemplation because blood
and humors weigh down their minds ....*Jean Bodin*
Turks are a terrible people who threaten to overwhelm all of
Europe in a barbarian invasion............................. *Georg Wilhelm
Frederich Hegel*

M 011

In Constantinople and Algiers, the rulers have large seraglios,
but not with many women in them..........*Charles de Montesquieu*
The same thing exists in Algeria and Morocco........*G.W.F. Hegel*

M 012

TURKISH WARS & CONQUEST

In 1453, we took Constantinople, and renamed
it Istanbul... *Mehmed II*
Now you can't go back to Constantinople ....*Nat Simon*
I have the world's largest turban .... *Suleiman the Magnificent*
After taking most of the Balkans, we were
unable to take Vienna and were beaten back
by the Infidels ....*Suleiman the Lesser Magnificent*
We lost the naval Battle of Lepanto .... *Admiral Lala*
Kara Mustapha Pasha

M 013

I financed the Battle of Lepanto, where we beat the Turkish
antichrists ....*Pope Pius V*
Come and see the wonderful Turkish Baths in Istanbul .... *Jean*
Ingress
Reading secular books will distract Turks from reading
the Koran... *The Grand Muffler*

M 014

YOUNG TURKS & MODERNIZATION

After our miserable efforts in the Great War, we must modernize
Turkey. Burn your fez's and cut off your beards....*Mustafa Kemal*
Our school children can't read the Arabic alphabet, so now we
are teaching them to read Turkish in the Latin alphabet....*Ataturk*
In Istanbul, there are few bookstores because nobody
there reads ....*Dale S. Elliott*

M 015

MODERN AUSTRIA

The nobles of Austria are ignorant, haughty, and oppressive,
while the lower classes are active, moral,

and industrious.. *Jesse Olney*
We beat off the Turks at the siege of Vienna......*John III Sobieski*
And we defeated the Turkish fleet at the
Battle of Lepanto ....*John of Austria*
The Pope ordered me to stop studying
garden peas .... *Gregor Mendel*
Napoleon is gone and Europe is now safe
from democracy .... *Metternich*
I'd like to pay a nice friendly visit to Serbia ....*Franz Ferdinand*
Edelweiss, edelweiss .... *Trapp Family Singers*
The skiing in Innsbruck, Austria is A-OK................. *Picabo Street*

M 016

AUSTRIANS & OSTERREICH

We composed beautiful band music and waltzes about
Osterreich (Austria)..*Johann Strauss,*
the elder & the younger
I was a top Austrian composer .... *Franz Schubert*
I wrote beautiful music and long symphonies ....*Gustav Mahler*
I composed lots of chamber music in Austria ...... *Joseph Hayden*
I composed many symphonies and operas in Salzburg.....*Mozart*
So did I as the court composer for Emperor Josef II.........*Antonio*
Salieri
In 1866, we lost a terrible war with the Prussians...... *Franz Josef*

M 017

I am the manufacturer of the best side arms
in the world... *Gaston Glock*
We are both famous Austrian Economists............... *Otto Neurath*
& Joseph Schumpeter
I designed the Volkswagen Beetle and the
Mercedes-Benz ....*Ferdinand Porsch*
We are the best Austrian
actors in Hollywood .... *Maximillian Schell & Romy Schneider*
I go back to Austria occasionally ....*Arnold Schwarzenegger*

M 018
GERMANS & DEUTSCHLAND
I settled thousands of Roman Jews to my new
city of Cologne..*Agrappina*
For many years, I ruled my German domains from the western
town of Aachen. In the end, my empire will be split up equally
among my three sons .... *Karl der Grosse*
Ich haben ein few suggestions............................... *Martin Luther*

M 019
Germans and their habits of carousing can never be
changed by any laws .... *Jean Bodin*
Toujours l'audace ....*Frederick der Grosse*
The World as Will .... *Shoupenhaur*
What doesn't kill me makes me stronger ....*Fredrick Nietzsche*

M 020
Germany is the foremost country in the world.......*Georg Wilhelm*
Friedrich Hegel
Germany is the center of Europe and is a bulwark of science
against the barbarism of ecclesiastical tyranny. Germans have
founded all the modern nations of Europe, and it is good that the
strong, noble, handsome, chaste, and generous Germans took
over the Roman world instead of the
Huns or Bulgarians..........................*Johann Gottfried von Herder*
The Nordic race is predominant in all
of Europe.. *Madison Grant & Gobineau*
Bulgarians are the worst of all.. *Voltaire*

M 021
Germanic countries in Europe are also great......................*Hegel*
In Prussia, the higher classes were generally well-informed and
polite, but extremely fond of dress. The lower classes are
ignorant, degraded, and superstitious.......................*Jesse Olney*
Germany is the fatherland of thought and a font of
intellect and innovation in the art and sciences, and
civilizations .... *Roswell C. Smith*
Germans lack astuteness and cunning .... *Jean Bodin*

M 022
Originally, Germans were savages, but also with a decided
sense of beauty.................................*Hendrick Willem van Loon*
Ich bin der beste...............................*Wolfgang Amadeus Mozart*

M 023
PRUSSIAN GLORY
In 1886, we won a glorious victory over the Austrian Empire in
the Seven Weeks' War....................................*Otto von Bismark*
I composed the famous Prussian Glory March...... *Johann Piefke*
Come and listen to my accordion rendition of Prussian
Gloria on YouTube and Roku............................ *Jackson Parodi*
Deutschland uber alles.. *Bismarck*
Let us now build a magnificent railroad from
Berlin to Baghdad.. *Kaiser Wilhelm II*

M 024
Thesis, antithesis, sisyphus.................... *Johann Gottfried Hegel*
Sturm und Drang...............................*Johann Wolfgang Goethe*
Diplomacy without arms is like a band
without instruments .... *Frederich der Grosse*
Ich vass die founder of Daimler-Benz................. *Gottlieb Daimler*
Ich bin der world's beste architect ......*Ludwig Mies van der Rohe*
Everything has ein end, but only die wurst has zwei............. *Lara*
Harker

M 025
DEUTCHLAND ISS NUMERO EINO
In the 1930s, the Nazis claimed we were
really Aryans .... *Ainu of Japan*
Die Valkyries sind Deutschland .... *Wagner*
Religion is the opium of the people.. *Karl*
Say da magic woid and win 100 rubles .... *Groucho*
Die Valkyries sind Deutschland .... *R. Wilhelm Wagner*
Ich bin der beste Kaiserstrudel
in Deutschland .... *Kaiser Wilhelm II*
Ich bin der best flying weinerschnitzel ....*Hermann Goering*
Ich bin der rote baron, 80 kaput & gefallen ......*Manfred Richtofen*

How about some mock combat?..........................*Waldo Pepper*
Jawohl! .... *Ernst (Udet) Kessler*

M 026
Whenever Ich hear das word Kulture,
Ich reach for mein revolver ....*Goering*
You ain't nothing but a schweinhund.........................*Elvis*

M 027
Ich habe only ein ball ....*Schmecklegruber*
Ich haben zwei, but eine ist schmall............................. *Goering*
Ich haben zwei, but eine iss similar..............................*Himmler*
Und ich nicht haben anything at all .... *Goebbels*
Und Ich never had any to begin with............................*Axis Sally*
Ich vass die furst und die last in das Luftwaffe ....*Adolf Galland*
Ich bin der beste gestupen wustenfux................... *Erwin Rommel*
Ich hate all diss +@%# snow..............................*Heinz Guderian*

M 028
Ve are going to name our new V-2 rocket
"das fier-geschpittin-geschnorten" .... *Albert Speer*
In German und English, Ich learned to count down, und Ich
learning Chinese, says ....*Wherner von Braun*
Ve hid your car keys, Capitan ....*Katzenjammer Kids*

M 029
During der Grosse War, ve engaged die British at Jutland.
We lost ein battleship, ein battle cruiser,
und nine other ships ....*Admiral Scheer*

M 030
THE COLLAPSE OF NAZI GERMANY
Mein 6th Wehrmacht ist kaput und
vie are surrendering...................................... *Field Marshal Paulus*
Der Bismarck is listing to port, pull das plug.........*Admiral Lutjens*
Der Schornhorst has capsized
and is going down...................................... *Kapitan Fritz Hintze*

Das Boot ist home, und vie are safe now .... *Captain-Lieutenant Lehm*

You are ordering me to do what? .... *Irwen Rommel*

M 031

Der Graf Spee ist doomed, pull den plug......... *Admiral Langsdorf*

Any port in a storm .... *Popeye der Sailor Mensch*

Vere doss Ich signen?.. *Admiral Donuts*

On the dotted line.................................... *General Eisenhower*

M 032

We will now begin trying German Nazis for crimes
against humanity .... *Harry Truman*

We will now control all of East Germany and most of eastern
Europe and create for them beautiful worker paradises....... *Josef Stalin*

We make our own car right here in East Germany.
Go, Little Trabant .... *Erich Honecker*

I was the 1988 Olympic Gold Ice skating winner
from East Germany .... *Katrina Witt*

M 033

This wall will keep everyone in .... *Erich Honecker*

Mr. Gorbachev, tear down this wall .... *Ronald Reagan*

The Berlin Wall is coming down, und we will welcome all East
Germans into our new reunited Germany. Also, the East
German Mark will be exchanged equally for the West
German Deutsch Mark .... *Helmut Kohl*

After many years, It now takes zwei
hands to hold ein Vopper .... *Der Burger Koenig*

M 034

THE ANCIENT GAULS

Veni Vitae Vici... *Julius Caesar*

We lost everything.. *Vercingetorix*

Not to worry, every month a comic book is printed in Paris that
shows how I won most of our battles
against the Romans .... *Asterix the Gaul*

I am watching over our
Gaulish towns and villages ....*Magestix the Gaul*

M 035
THE EARLIEST FRENCH
We will settle down here in
Gaul if nobody minds..............................*Merovech of the Franks*
I will also deal with the schmuck who smashed
my vase at Soissons...*Merovech*
In seven thirty-two at Tours,
I myself defeated the Moors................................. *Charles Martel*
I will divide my great Carolingian Empire among
my three sons.. *Charlemagne*

M 036
LES HERETIQUES
Medieval heretics include the Gnostic Catheters and the
Albigensians in southern France and northern Italy .... *Vatican*
Archives
I sent an army to southern France and called it the Albigensian
Crusade. All of the heretics were slaughtered. Jesus would be
pleased..*Pope Guilty III*

M 037
And God Created Woman, and we put her in a film .... *Roger*
Vadim
Here I am, and in several years, I will become Marianne, the
national personification of the French Goddess of Liberty and all
France ....*Brigitte Bardot*

M 038
LES LOIS
The best laws come from areas between the fortieth and fiftieth
parallels. This zone also produces the best rulers, the most
equitable judges, the most versatile orators, and cleverest
merchants.. *Jean Bodin*

M 039

LES EGOUTS

The sewers of Paris aren't as bad as they say, but they are really just Less Miserable .... *Jean Valjean*

Liberté, Egalité, Sororité...*Marianne*

Marianne at the barricades was my best painting............ *Eugene Delacroix*

N 001

LES HISTOIRES

History is a collection of lies commonly agreed upon..............................*Voltaire and Napoleon* In France, the nobility is marked by superior ability and virtue. France has been increasing in power for centuries because of the goodness of its laws. We are vain, but it's good and has led us to work more efficiently.................... *Charles de Montesquieu*

N 002

FRENCH NOTABLES OF THE REVOLUTION

Arrete cure' et ecraser l'infame...*Voltaire*

Of noble sausages ....*Rousseau*

L'etat, c'est moi .... *Louis XIV*

Apres moi le deluge .... *Louis XV*

Apres moi le reign de terror.. *Louis XVI*

Off with their heads .... *Robespierre*

Arrete la guillotine! ....*Danton*

I'm now working for the revolution ....*Comte de Mirabeau*

A Marat .... *Jaques-Louie David*

N 003

LATER FRENCH NOTABLES

Je suis pas merde in a silk stocking .... *Tallyrand*

Oh, oui…yes you are.. *Napoleon I*

L'empire, c'est grand ....*Napoleon III*

J'accuse ....*Emile Zola*

I can put everyone to sleep ....*Franz Mesmer*

I will call them germs.. *Pasteur*

N 004
MODERN FRENCH NOTABLES
A bas la Peste .... *Camus*
Vive les Boches... *Petain*
Je suis la France .... *de Gaulle*
Je ne vinaigrette rien .... *Edith Piaf*
Je suis le hunchback de Notre Dame .... *Lon Chaney*
Thank heaven for little girls .... *Maurice Chevalier*

N 005
The French are mostly hot-headed and lack the whimsical
originality of the English...........................*Johann Gottfried Hegel*
Come see our painting
of the Burglars of Calais .... *Rodin & Moeglin*

N 006
The rural French are insular and provincial and they have the
hideous habit of scraping, filching, and rooking on every
necessity of life. The French are the most selfish and self-
centered in the world .... *Hendrick Willem van Loon*
We will not go to just anywhere .... *Medecins Avec Frontieres*

N 007
LES DANSERS EN FRANCE
An American in Paris .... *George Gershwin*
Sur le Pont d'Avignon on y dance ....*Fred Astaire*
You didn't dance alone. You also danced with me.... *Leslie "Gigi"*
Caron
Non, nous ne danse pas..............*Moulin Rouge dancers on strike*
Yes oui can.. *Emmanuel Macron*

N 008
I am the pope of French Cuisine.............................. *Paul Bocuse*
I'm getting rid of my motor scooter...................*Francois Hollande*

N 009
Belgian Waffles are good for you.............*Krusteaz Baking Mixes*
Has anyone found my ear yet? .... *Vincent van Gogh*

What am I going to do with the Congo?....................*King Leopold*
Belgian draft horses are the strongest in the world.............*Horse*
breeders

N 010
SCANDINAVIANS
Something is rotten in Denmark .... *Marcellus*
Scandinavians are honest, grave, hospitable, hardy, industrious,
moral, patient, and persevering................................*Jesse Olney*
We frequently vacationed along on the east
coast of England ....*Eric Bloodaxe*

N 011
Denmark and England are now One .... *Cnut the Great*
The Little Mermaid lives on in Copenhagen.......... *Hans Christian*
Anderson
Oboes sound like clarinets with sore throats .... *Victor Borge*
I spent a few months communing with nature in
New Mexico .... *Niels Bohr*

N 012
SCANDINAVIA & SWEDES
Scandinavians are honest, grave, hospitable, hardy,
industrious, moral, patient, and persevering.............*Jesse Olney*
We Swedes tend not to speak to anybody till we
are introduced ....*Marshal Bernadotte*

N 013
NORWAY & NORWEGIANS
Norway is a highly respected little nation where they
catch a lot of fish .... *Ellen C. Semple*
I took the first Norse settlers to Iceland in the
year 874 CE...*Ingolfur Arnasson*
At that time, Irish monks were already living in
Iceland ....*Carl Sauer*

N 014

ANCIENT NORWEGIAN EXPLORERS

I left Norway and settled in Iceland ....*Eric the Rouge*
During the 10th Century, I left Norway and settled in Iceland. A
few years later, during the Medieval Warm Period (about the
year 1000 CE), I traveled to Greenland. Then 30 of us sailed on
to Vinland. We built a small settlement there at L'Anse aux
Meadows on the Northeastern tip of Newfoundland, but
it lasted only a few years ....*Leif Ericson*

N 015

MODERN NORWEGIAN EXPLORERS

I was a Norwegian explorer and have my name on two glacier-
covered land areas on the opposite ends of the earth. I was the
first explorer to cross the Greenland ice cap on skis .... *Fridtjof
Nansen*
I led the first expedition to the South Pole......... *Roald Amundsen*

N 016

FINNS, LAPPS, SAAMI, & THE FROZEN NORTH

People living toward the North Pole have no culture and have
been negligible factors in history...............*Ellen Churchill Semple*
Lapland is cold, gloomy, and barren, and the people
who live there are miserable, ignorant, and superstitious..... *Ellen
Churchill Semple*

N 017

When the Lapps sit around a campfire, they squat on their heels
and eat their food from the ground
with their fingers ....*Jesse Olney*
Lapps are a harmless people living in tents and
rude huts made of dirt and stone .... *Roswell C. Smith*

N 018

LAPLAND IS COLD & BARREN

Lapland is cold and barren, and the people who live there are
miserable, ignorant, and superstitious ....*Jesse Olney*
Baltic peoples are alternately warm, wet, hairy, soft-fleshed,

and deep-voiced..*Jean Bodin*

N 019

We are the reindeer herders of Lapland. We live in northern
Sweden, Finland, Norway, and the Russian Kola Peninsula. We
still follow our traditional occupation that began many centuries
ago and we prefer to be called by our ancient self-designation;
namely, Saami (or Sami).......................................*Saami Elders*

N 020

During WWII, we Finns beat off the Russians. Their military skills
were not the best. After several months of battle, they finally
broke through, and we lost the Winter War.......*General Carl Emil
Mannerheim*

N 021

THE NETHERLANDS & THE DUTCH

The Dutch are lusty, tough-fisted, and practical.....*Ellen Churchill
Semple*

We've come to fish for the herring fish that swim in this beautiful
sea...*Wankin, Blankin, & Nod*
I can't get my finger out of this x+*p#!]$ dike ....*Hans Brinker*

N 022

TULIP BULBS

Everyone will get rich buying and selling these nice
Dutch tulip bulbs. Aren't they pretty? (1634-1637)......*Amsterdam
stock brokers*

We still grow tulips today...Two billion
in 2017 alone ....*Dutch tulip farmers*
The Dutch are honest, grave, hospitable, hardy, industrious,
moral, patient, and persevering...............................*Jesse Olney*

N 023

Come see our annual Tulip Festival in Holland......*Wooden Shoe
Tulip Farm*

De Vliegende Hollander will fly on forever....*Royal Dutch Airlines*
I discovered the Tappan Zee in New Netherlands,

and the river I named after myself..........................Henry Hudson

N 024
THE MANHATTAN PURCHASE
We bought Manhattan Island from the Indians for 24 guilders
worth of worthless trinkets .... *Peter Minuit*
Then we built the city of New Amsterdam on the southern tip our
new Island .... *Peter Stuyvesant*

N 025
Then British warships then came and gently persuaded us to
lower our flag and let them take over our city, which they
renamed New York..................................... *Governor Stuyvesant*
We still have a nice little Dutch village here in
Sleepy Hollow... *Katrina Van Tassel*
Everything here is now organized, tidy, and
spic & span.. *Dutch Cleanser Girl*
Come to Holland, Michigan, which is populated
mostly by Dutch..................................... *Chamber of Commerce*

P 001
IRELAND & THE IRISH
Other people have a nationality,
but the Irish have a psychosis..............................*Brendan Behan*
All snakes begone .... *St. Patrick*
I sailed across the Atlantic to America
in a nice Irish curragh .... *St. Brendan*
I sailed across the Atlantic in a Welsh coracle
to America ....*Prince Madoc*
After death, Tir na nOg (land of eternal youth) is a small
island to the west that awaits for virtuous and sober
Irishmen to enter...*Ancient Irish Druids*

P 002
CU CHUCHULAINN & FINN MacCUMMAIL
I had many adventures, and then was killed in battle after tying
myself to a standing stone ....*Cu Chuchulainn (koo-kullan)*

After many experiences and quests, I went into a cave and went
to sleep, and someday I'll come back to
defend Ireland............................*Finn MacCummail (finn mc-kool)*
The idleness and levity of the Irish is the result of low
wages and not the result of being
Celtic or Catholic......................................*Henry Thomas Buckle*
The Irish love fairy stories and have a big sense of the
unreal..*Hendrick van Loon*

P 003
We are all settling in Dublin and are calling our neighborhood
Ostmantown (on the north bank of the Liffey).........*Norse Vikings*
There goes the neighborhood ....*King Dermot*
MacMurrough of Leinster
Now the Normans are also settling here in Dublin. What in the
hell should I do? So I married off my daughter Eva
to Richard Strong-Bow de Claire. Now we are
all Normans...*Dermait Mac Murchada*

P 004
THE BLACK IRISH
Are Black Irish really black? Are they really Irish? They have
black hair and dark eyes. Some people say they were
shipwrecked sailors going home to Spain after the defeat of their
Armada in the late 1500s. Others say they are the descendants
of Irishmen and free Africans in the American South. In 1521
along the coast of South Carolina, Spanish explorers observed a
small group of farming villagers whom they described as being
Irish and called them the Duhaire people. The sightings were
recorded in the book "De Orbe Novo" by ....*Peter Martyr*
d'Angiera
Today, in America, the Black Irish live mostly in South Bend,
Indiana (employed by the Fighting Irish) or in the Boston
neighborhoods of Roxbury and living in Harlem, working for the
Globetroppers ....*NBA, NCAA, NFL*

P 005
THE POTATO FAMINE
In Ireland the potato blight left nothing for anyone to eat. Perhaps
the Irish should start eating their children..............*Jonathon Swift*
Too many Irishmen die of the damp, the dark,
and the drink...*Frank McCourt*

P 006
Work is the curse of the drinking class......................*Oscar Wilde*
bejayzzus/wtf/byob/omg/ob-gyn/yuk ....*James Joyce*
If ya sees a head, hit it..*Paddy O'Roark*
In Dublin, I'm the dish with the fish.......................... *Molly Malone*
In Dublin, I'm the floozie in the jacuzzi ....*Anna Livia*

P 007
As a boy, I joined the Royal Bengal Infantry as a cadet and saw
combat against the Afghans in India. Afterwards, I was promoted
to administrator in the western Indian state of Punjab and forged
alliances with the Afghans and the Sikhs................... *"Irish" John
Nicholson*

P 008
ANCIENT BRITONS
We are here to make Briton part of the
Roman Empire.. *Suetonius*
Not without a fight, gobshita....................................... *Boadicea*
Remember the Battle of Mons Graupius, where the Picts under
Calgacus fought off the Romans under Julius Agricola .....*Tacitus*

P 009
HADRIAN'S WALL
This wall might keep some of the marauding Picts at bay, but
more importantly, it will also now mark the northern border of
our Roman Empire ....*Hadrian*

Remember the Battle of Mons Badon, where the Britons fought off the invading Saxons .... *The Venerable Bede*

P 010
BEOWULF
I can't stand all this noise .... *Grendel*
Come hear my classical rendition of Beowulf .... *Julian Glover*
We've come to teach you people Anglish .... *Hengist & Horsa*
These cakes taste horrible .... *Alfred of Wessex*

P 011
FATHER URE THU THEE ART IN HEOFONUM
Fæder ure þu þe eart on heofonum....................... *Offa of Mercia*
Get back, back I say!.. *Canute the Dane*
I'm riding my horse through the town....................... *Lady Godgifu*
Sorry, but I am watching you .... *Peeping Tom*
Put your clothes back on, wife............................ *Leofric the Dane*

P 012
THE NORMANS
The Bayeaux Tapestry, which commemorates the battle at Hastings, is accepted by most as an authority on many details of life at the time and on the finer points of history in the eleventh century. For example, horses in those days had green legs, blue bodies, yellow manes, and red heads, and all the people were double-jointed, and, thus, not like people today............ *Will Cuppy*

P 013
KINGS & QUEENS OF ENGLAND
By the Saxons he conquered, he was hated and cursed, and then he became William the First .... *Eleanor & Herbert Farjeon*
I harried the North and made the first census, which we called the Domesday Book, in which we counted all people and what they owned and owed in taxes .... *William the First*

P 014

Now that we're here, we will teach all of you to speak French. Swine will become pork, sheep will become mutton, calf will become veal, chickens will become poultry, cattle will become beef, and a drink will become a beverage. Wine will remain wine, and deer will become venison.................. *Guillaume of Normandy*

P 015

It is said that Henry the First died one night of eating too many lampreys. Then his blood vessel burst, and that was the end of Henry the First...................................... *Eleanor & Herb Farjeon*
Stephen and Matilda always fought with each other over who was first and over who was in charge .... *Henry Fitz Empress*
Henry II passed many new laws and one day accidentally said "Who will rid me of this pesky priest?" And then one of his knights struck Thomas Becket down............................. *Farjeans*

P 016

KING JOHN
John, John, bad King John, disgraced the throne
he sat upon.. *Eleanor & Herb Farjean*
I spent most of my reign out of town and out of England on crusades..*Richard I*
Henry III was unfit to rule, so Simon Montfort went and made Parliament .... *The Farjeans*

P 017

EDWARDS & GEOFFREY
I defenestrated the foul wretch.................... *Edward I Longshanks*
Oh no! Piers Gaveston was my best and only friend..... *Edward II*
To Canterbury they wende,
the blissful martir for to seke .... *Geoffrey Chaucer*
You may call me Bubbles .... *The Wife of Bath*

P 018

EDWARDS & HENRYS

It's often said we defeated the French with our archers and
bowmen at Crecy (possibly not true) ....*Edward III*
Henry IV Bolingbroke, what will you do?
Your kingdom has broken and split into two .... *Herbert &*
Eleanore Farjeans
We will remember we were all here on Saint Crispin's Day, and
now, once more onto the beach ....*Henry V*
I never understood what the Wars of the Roses
were all about...*Henry VI*
They say I murdered my brother by drowning him in a
barrel of wine .... *Edward IV*

P 019

CROOK-BACKED DICK

Everyone calls me crook-backed Dick. Then they said I
murdered my two nephews. And later, at the Battle of Bosworth,
I fell off my horse and was killed and hastily buried in a nearby
parking lot. Then, after several centuries, I was dug up and put
on public display.. *Richard III*

P 020

THE TUDORS

I put an end to the pretenders, Lambert Simmel and
Perkin Warbeck...*Henry VII*
Bluff King Hal was full of beans,
he married half a dozen queens ....*H. & E. Farjeans*
I fell off my horse while jousting, and was never the same.
Eventually, I weighed 28 stone (392 lbs.) ....*Henry VIII*
I tried to bring Catholicism back and was unable to
produce an heir .... *Queen Mary*
I was executed by the Queen for intriguing with
Catholic Spain... *Mary Queen of Scots*

P 021

All the world's a stage (in London).............. *William Shakespeare*
Hackney Theater (in London) was a great

place to start .... *Charlie Chaplin*
Ding dong, Bard of Avon calling...Hello, I'm broke and I'm selling
some of my play scripts door to door .... *Wm. Shakespeare*
I don't like wars, they have uncertain outcomes, but we did
destroy the Spanish Armada rather nicely, didn't we?....*Elizabeth*
The Great
I've just returned from Virginia .... *Sir Walter Raleigh*
I just got back from California .... *Sir Francis Drake*

P 022

THE HOUSE OF STUART

It's called tobacco and it will aid digestion .... *Sir Walter Raleigh*
Get rid of that stinking weed .... *James Stuart I & VI*
Here's my new book dedicated to your Majesty ... *Edward Gibbon*
Scribble, scribble, scribble, eh Mr. Gibbon? .... *King James I*

P 023

I lost my head in London town .... *Charles I Stuart*
We defeated the Royalists and have imposed our rule...
No smiling and no bowling, no football, no beer, wine,
or spirits, no fornication, no fun .... *Oliver I Cromwell*
I never told anyone I was Catholic
until just before I died.. *Charles II Stuart*

P 024

THE HOUSE OF ORANGE

Yes, we are Dutch Protestants,
and we will come .... *Mary and Wm. of Orange*
It's a long way to Tipperary .... *William of Orange*
Whom the gods wish to destroy, they first take
away their sanity.. *King Lear*
Get out of my way, and get me to France, now!.. *James II Stuart,*
the Old Pretender
I was the last English king to lead troops into battle,
and we defeated the Jacobites in the "15"
at the Battle of the Boyne .... *William III of England*
Queen Anne is dead....................... *Eleanore & Herbert Farjeans*

P 025

THE HOUSE OF HANOVER
George, George, in England they
want you for their king today.
Say you will with heart and soul,
and George, delighted, said Jawohl ....*George I*
Just what I need, another Jacobite uprising...................*George II*
This second George his army sends, to Scotland damp and
sodden, and smashed the young pretender's claims,
at the battle of Culloden ....*The Farjeans*

P 026

MORE GEORGES
We lost everything at the "45"................... *Charles Edward Stuart*
I lost America, and I am no longer insane.....................*George III*
Yo ho ho, me hearties! Hark the sailors sing. With a bottle of rum
for Will-i-um, the Fourth, our Sailor King....................... *Eleanore*
& Herbert Farjeans

I am the grandmother of most of the
royal households in Europe..*Victoria*

P 027

RULE BRITANNIA, BRITANNIA RULES THE WAVES
We destroyed the Spaniards at Trafalgar, which kept Napoleon
at home and stuck in Paris ....*Admiral Nelson*
Britannia rules the waves .... *James Thomson & Thomas Ame*
Oh, I've seen Nappy's back before................*Duke of Wellington*

P 028

Patriotism is the last refuge of the scoundrel..... *Samuel Johnson*
The pigeons up here are a bit messy ....*Lord Nelson*
We have the world's best roast beef and dark ale .... *John Bull*
The British are very whimsical and original.......................*Johann*
Gottfried Hegel

P 029

Are you going to Scarborough Fair?............... *Simon & Garfunkel*

Which road will you be taking? .... *Dick Turpin*
Going through Nottingham?
Stop and chat for a while ....*Robbing Hood*
Come see England's first Puritan congregation at
Scrooby in Nottinghamshire before we move to
Leiden in Holland.. *Thomas Blossom*

P 030
The English are prone to suicide, due to a distemper complicated
by scurvy, which makes them whimsical, impatient,
cold, and phlegmatic..............................*Charles de Montesquieu*
The most powerful agents influencing the human species include
climate, food, soil, and nature in general. From these
conditions, Britain and France are the two greatest
countries on earth..................................... *Henry Thomas Buckle*

P 031
In Britain and France, it is not necessary to examine the history
of any other nation on earth, except for only these two nations
that stand out for scrutiny: namely,
America and Germany............................... *Henry Thomas Buckle*
Britain is a rich overpopulated island
off the Dutch coast...................................*Hendrick Wm. Van Loon*

P 032
ENGLISH WRITERS & OCKHAM'S RAZOR
Eliminate unnecessary entities in seeking what is sufficient, and
what is not sufficient in analysis and/or proof. And, where two
explanations compete with each other, the shorter one with
fewer explanatory variables is better...............*William of Ockham*
World population will multiply faster
than the world's food supply .... *Thomas Malthus*
I discovered Uranus...*William Herschel*
Only the fittest survive .... *Herbert Spencer*
Britain must abolish the slave trade .... *William Wilberforce*
Britain really does have some kind
of a constitution ....*Walter Bagehot*
What is now proved was once only imagined.......... *William Blake*

P 033

SCOTLAND & THE SCOTS

All the rich are good and are going to Calvinist heaven, while the poor are evil and are already destined for damnation, so we owe them nothing. Let them eat oats and sawdust. My views on the doctrine of free will, predestination, and damnation are free, obscure, and complex .... *John Knox*

P 034

Whenever men of business get together, they immediately begin to conspire against the public good .... *Adam Smith*
Human happiness consists in action, pleasure,
and indolence .... *David Hume*
I never got the chance to prove that
my demon was real .... *James Clerk Maxwell*

Q 001

ON SCOTTISH TARTANS

I entertained at my manor house "two experts" (the brothers Sobieskis) on the setts of "ancient" tartans in the Scottish Highlands. They claimed to be closely related to Prince Charles Stewart, the "young pretender" .... *Sir Walter Scott*
They later proved to be frauds and their
"tartans" were bogus .... *The Royal Celtic Society*

Q 002

He who wears the tartan honors the Chief, whether he's Scottish or not .... *The Chiefs*
At Culloden, the Clansmen wore various tartans and mixed them all up together. Several of them appeared in a re-enactment painting by David Morier while they were in a British prison in London where they were interned after
the "Forty-five" uprising .... *Celtic Society*

Q 003

There are many infamous clan feuds in Scotland, and the Campbells and the MacDonalds at Glencoe were some of the worst .... *Robert Bain & George Fraser*

That damn German in London
took away my family name...........................*Rob Roy MacGregor*
Ya canna be both grand and comfortable ....*Rabbie Burns*

Q 004
Here lies Andrew McPherson. He was a most peculiar person.
He was six-foot-two without his shoe, and he was slew at
Waterloo .... *Gravestone in Dumfries, Scotland*
Buy one of my Scottish walking sticks and
I'll sing you a song ....*Harry Lauder*

Q 005
THE HAGGIS
The Haggis is an ancient kind of Scottish casserole. But it seems
it is no longer the preferred side dish of Scots, unless one enjoys
liver, oats, pepper, lungs, kidneys, sweet breads, tripe, lips, ears,
tumors, bull dicks, sheep testicles, and lots of whiskey to wash
down the taste of decaying offal, grizzle, viscera, pig intestines,
wilted cabbage, turnips, groats, and leftovers, all boiled up inside
a football...*Aye, Hoot Mon*

Q 006
A new alternative, beside haggis (as a light novelty topping on a
Spud-You-Like baked potato) are deep-fried Mars Bars (which
seem now to be the choice of those who live north of the
Cheviots) ....*The Lord Lyon of Cuisine*

Q 007
KNOWLEDGE & EDUCATION
Knowledge is power...*Francis Bacon*
Knowledge is good ....*Emil Faber*
We don't need no edjukaition and we don't want no
thwaught control ....*Pink Floyd*
This is not your life, it's my life, so leave me alone.........*Billy Joel*

Q 008

SCIENTIFIC TRAVELERS

Read my travel book on finches in the Galapagos........... *Charles Darwin*
Read my travel book on the East Indies .... *Alfred Wallace*
Read my travel book on English-speaking
America.. *Alexis de Toqueville*
Read my travel books on the Pacific and Britain......*Paul Theroux*
Read my travel book to the center of the Earth.......... *Jules Verne*

Q 009

THE BRITISH EMPIRE

There's a lot of money to be made in India
(opium and tea)..*British East India Co.*
Also in Singapore, and China
(opium, jade, silk, and tea) ....*Jardine Matheson & Co.*
Also in the Caribbean
(sugar, rum, slaves) .... *British West Indian charter companies*
Also in Canada
(timber, furs, and Molson) ....*Hudson's Bay Company*
If we let in people of color from any of these
Commonwealth countries, there will be rivers of
blood in Britain .... *Enoch Powell*

Q 010

As a major contributor to the world rule of the British Empire, I
fought in the Crimean War and routed the Russians at
Sebastopol. I also fought in China against the Taipings and took
part in the pacification of natives near Capetown. I later fought
against the Mahdi in the Sudan .... *Charles "Chinese" Gordon*

Q 011

I was a cavalry Lieutenant in the 7th Hussars and fought against
the Afghans in India. At Omdurman, I took part in Britain's last
cavalry charge against an enemy of the British Empire (the
forces of the Mahdi) in the Sudan. I later saw action in the
Boer War.. *Winston Churchill*

Hackney Theater on Mare Street in London was a great
place to start a career..*Charlie Chaplin*
After Britain's wars, I went into politics and became the First Lord
of the Admiralty. In that and subsequent offices, I found I couldn't
live without brandy. In winning, I deserved it, and in defeat, I
needed it...*Winston Churchill*

Q 012
COME ON OUT TO AFRICA
Come out to Africa, young man, and help pick up the White
Man's Burden, and also help build
the Cape-to-Cairo Railroad.....................................*Cecil Rhodes*
Go west, young man... *Horace Greeley*

Q 013
Dr. Livingstone, I presume? ....*Henry M. Stanley*
Oh Bingo Bango Bongo,
I don't wanna leave the Congo.......................... *David Livingston*
Aba daba daba daba daba,
said the monkey to the Chimp .... *Debbie Reynolds*
Great Britain is the most important island on the
face of the earth. It's morning drumbeat never
ceases, and on it, the sun never sets................. *Roswell C. Smith*
"Mustn't grumble" is the
most common of English expressions..................... *Paul Theroux*

Q 014
THE HOUSE OF WINDSOR
Before World War I, as king, I kept the peace in
Europe, along with France and Germany...................*Edward VII*
I was the first to broadcast
all over Britain on the radio .... *George V*
I am the first and only king to end up as
Duke of Windsor...*Edward VIII*
I encouraged Boy Scouting in Britain, the
Commonwealth, and America...................................... *George VI*
I've now reigned longer than any
other British Monarch...*Elizabeth II*

Q 015

GREAT BRITAIN IN WORLD WAR ONE
At the Battle of Jutland (WWI), we lost fourteen ships.
Among these were a battleship and three
battle cruisers..*British Admiralty*
We will attack directly into the machine gun fire from the
trenches and we will win this war by attrition. But I will not be
there leading the charge................... *Field Marshal Douglas Haig*
Oh, it's Tommy this and Tommy that, and throw him out, the
brute, but he's the savior of his country when the
guns begin to shoot..*Rudyard Kipling*

Q 016

We all yearn to see again the great city of Cordova that existed
many centuries ago in Moorish Spain......................... *King Faisal*
Time to be great again .... *T.E. Lawrence*

Q 017

We've taken Aqaba and Damascus............... *Lawrence of Arabia*
The Turks are now on the run .... *Maj. Thomas Edward Lawrence*
What in blazes am I supposed to do with
Aqaba and Damascus?...................................... *General Allenby*
Gallipoli was a disaster. We'll not do that again..... *ANZAC troops*
We eventually abandoned the Battle of the Somme
north of Paris...*Gen.*
Douglas Haig

Q 018

I led an exploration journey into Antarctica...... *Ernest Shackleton*
So did we ....*Admiral Richard E. Byrd & Paul Siple*
At the time, I represented the Boy Scouts and the Geography
Department at Clark University. Later, I led my own
expedition to Antarctica ....*Paul Siple*

Q 019

EARLY OLYMPIC MEDAL WINNERS
I won an Olympic gold medal in
Paris in 1924 .... *Harold Abrahams*

So did I ....*Eric Liddell*
I also won a medal there.................................*Jackson Scholz*
I did too.. *Charles Paddock*
Chariots of Fire ....*Vangelis*

Q 020
MORE OLYMPIC TRACK STARS & SPEED RECORDS
I did too, in the 1912 Olympics, but the U.S. Olympic Committee
later took away my medals .... *Jim Thorpe*
I outran the Huns in Berlin in the 1936 Olympics. And then Hitler
refused to shake my hand. Then he got his ....*Jesse Owens*
I was one of England's flying aces in the Great War. I also held
the world's fastest land speed record on the
Bonneville Salt Flats .... *Malcolm Campbell*

Q 021
I won the Olympic decathlon in 1960 .... *Rafer Johnson*
I outran all of them at the 1984 Olympic sprints .... *Flo-Jo*
Griffith Joyner
I was the first to break the four-minute mile ....*Roger Bannister*
I broke it shortly after .... *John Landy*

Q 022
CHURCHILL & THE BRITISH ADMIRALTY
More punishment until morale improves .... *Capt. Bligh*
We must preserve the British Navy's most
cherished traditions..*British Admiralty*
What traditions? You must mean rum, sodomy,
and the lash.. *Churchill*
Mr. Churchill, if I were your wife I'd put poison
in your brandy..*Lady Plushbottom*
Madam, if I were your husband I'd drink it.........*Winston Churchill*
Women are like pianos. When they aren't
upright, they're grand... *Bennie Hill*

Q 023
Those who control the present control the past........ *Geo. Orwell,*
and vice versa

Peace in our time ....*Neville Chamberlain*
The Germans have invaded France, and
we must now act ....*British Parliament*
Our boys are in France and stuck at Dunkirk. All Navy ships, all
fishermen, and all small boat owners must go and rescue them
while they still can .... *The London Sun*
It was a noble and successful effort......*Parliament and Congress*

Q 024
THE BRITISH NAVY
The Hood has blown up in the
Denmark Strait.. *Captain John Leach*
of the nearby HMS Prince of Wales
All available ships must chase and sink
the Bismarck .... *British Admiralty*
We found that German battleship that's makin such a fuss,
We had to sink the Bismark cause the world depends on us…
We hit the decks a-runnin' and we spun the guns around
And when we found the Bismarck,
we fired and sent her down ....*Johnny Horton*
And never, never, ever, ever give up............... *Winston Churchill*

Q 025
THE UNITED KINGDOM DURING THE BATTLE OF BRITAIN
The Yanks have now come to Britain. And now they are
everywhere. They're all over-fed, over-paid, over-sexed,
and over here.. *London Times*
The Brits in England are under-fed, under-paid,
under-sexed, and under Eisenhower...................... *American GIs*

Q 026
The victory of the Battle of Britain was due to the Merlin engine,
radar, and the RAF fighter pilots. This was their finest hour. After
that was the Royal Navy, the American Merchant Marine supply
convoys, Alan Turing's decipherment of the Nazi Enigma code,

General Patton's phantom army, and the successful landing
force in Normandy consisting of American, British, and
Canadian invasion forces and lots of
Polish fighter pilots ....*Winston Churchill*

Q 027
On the Road to Mandalay where the flying fishes
play and the dawn comes up like thunder over
China across the bay.....................................*Popular WWII song*
Come ye back ye British soldier,
come ye back to Mandalay .... *Rudyard Kipling*
The Japanese have taken Singapore, and the
Prince of Wales is sunk .... *Lord Mountbatten*

Q 028
ANIMAL FARM
Once upon a time in England, there was a farm owned by a
drunken farmer and his wife. There was an animal revolution,
and the pigs became rulers, the horses kept quiet, the donkeys
objected to everything, and the dogs protected the pigs and the
ruling boar named Napoleon.................................. *George Orwell*
All animals are equal, but some animals are more
equal than others... *Nap. the Boar*
Why do some people think Pygmalion
is a story about hogs?............................... *George Bernard Shaw*
If we let these animals in, there will be rivers of blood........*Enoch
Powell*

Q 029
ANIMAL RANCH
Featuring: Lynden Bull, Lady Duck, Ho Chip Munk, Mutton
Luther King, Cow Ky, Flidel Casdroah, Richard Vixen, Von
Brown Cow, Owl Warren, Barry Toadwater, J. Edgar
Bloodhound, the Lovely Duckling, and the Dung Beetles, all
singing The Cattle Hymn of the Republic and
Flock of Ages........................ *Jack Newfield & Robert Grossman*

Q 030

BIG BROTHER

In 1984, Big Brother came to power and ruled Britain and kept
everyone happy and obedient. New words were coined, and old
words acquired new meanings. Big Brother ruled and kept track
of what everyone was saying ....*George Orwell*
War is peace. Freedom is slavery. Ignorance is truth ....*TV &*
radio messages
And I am watching you...*Big Brother*

Q 031

ALPHAS, BETAS, DELTAS, & SOMA

I will predict that many centuries from now, people will be chosen
to breed. Everyone in Britain will be decanted instead of born.
There will be Alphas, Betas, Gammas, and Deltas, who will take
their places in society according to their fitness, strength, docility,
and intelligence ....*Aldous Huxley*

Q 032

Alphas will rule, and Deltas (like Dalits, in India) will be followers
and menial workers. The lower ranks will be kept ignorant and
servile with the soothing drug soma .... *A. Huxley*
Oh, the things we do for England. Bond, James bond......... *Sean*
Connery

Q 033

THE ELOI & THE MORLOCKS

I have travelled into the future, and it is not what we want to
become. The human race has devolved into two different
species. The first are the Eloi (who look like us) and
second are the Morlocks (who don't)..........................*H.G. Wells*

Q 034

The Eloi live on the surface and are beautiful, ignorant, and
docile. The Morlocks are ogres who live underground. They
breed the Eloi up on the surface and then
eat them like chicken wings.....................................*H.G. Wells*

Q 035

SPEAKING OF PLANTS & ANIMALS

Talk to your garden plants ....*Prince Jughead*
Speak with the animals... *St. Francis*
Talk to the animals ....*Dr. Dolittle*
Come on Dovah, come on boy, move yer bloomin arse!...... *Eliza Doolittle*
And don't eat your animals .... *The Vegan Legion*
And stay away from Bodega Bay and all those birds ....*Alfred Hitchcock*

Q 036

THE FALKLANDS WAR

Argentina has invaded the Falkland Islands, and we are
responding. Just don't bomb the Argentine mainland..... *Margaret Thatcher*
Don't cry for me, Argentina ....*British Marines singing while boarding the QE2 troop ship bound for the Falklands*
They're called Los Islas Malvinas, cabrones....... *General Galtieri*

Q 037

WORLD GEOPOLITICS

Those who control the seas control the world .... *Themistocles*
Those who control the seas control world trade ..... *Carthaginians*
Those who control the shipping lanes rule the seas........ *Onassis*
Those who control the high ground control the wars.........*Lyndon Johnson*

Q 038

Those who control the heartland control the world.......*Mackinder*
Those who control the rimland control the world........... *Spykman*
Those who control the past control the future .... *George Orwell*
Those who control the media rule the past .... *George Soros*
Those who control the news
control the masses ....*Rupert Murdoch*
Those who have the money
can control anything they want ....*The Koch Brothers*

R 001
WALTZING MATILDA
You'll come a-Waltzing Matilda with me .... *Banjo Patterson*
Tie me kangaroo down, sport...................................*Rolph Harris*
All were impressed when Australia's first mass-produced car
rolled off the assembly line 70 years ago. The top model
was the Holden V-8......................................*James A. Holden*

R 002
AUSTRALIA & AUSTRALIANS
We still have possession of the Ashes .... *The Botany*
Bay Growlers

Please send us more of those
nice ten-pound Poms .... *Australian Immigration Office*
Some us went back to England,
but then a lot of us came back for good...................*Aussie Poms*
The Australian Book of Etiquette is a
very slim volume ....*Paul Theroux*
When a kangaroo puts it's paws on
your shoulders, it's time to leave ....*Will Cuppy*
Any roo meat in Big Macs here? ....*Australian meat &*
carrion inspectors
Oh no, not yet, I hope...*Skippy*

R 003
All dingoes go to dingo heaven ....*Dame Edna*
And I do hope all those rabbits will stay
behind this fence.. *Alexander Crawford*

R 004
AUSTRALIAN ABORIGINES
Before the dreaming time,
there was Uluru... *Australian Aborigines*
I was once the tennis Sunshine Super Girl
from Down Under...*Evonne Gooligong*
The didgeridoo has been our
people's instrument for 40,000 years...................*Djalu Gurruwiwi*
I was the last of the Tasmanian Aborigines .... *Twi Truganini*

R 005

MAORIS, MOAS, & KIWIS OF NEW ZEALAND
I was the first European explorer to see New Zealand (aka,
Aotearoa)... *Abel Tasman*
The Polynesian natives of New Zealand are well-formed and
have uncommon sagacity. Long ago, they had been
cannibals, but they gave up their old practice of
consuming "long pig" .... *J. Olney*
Many years ago, there were many, many Kiwi birds
in Aotearoa ....*Maori Haka dancers*
There were also giant birds there, called Moas. The Maoris
wiped them all out by setting grass and forest fires. Then they
ate them until they were no more........................*Dr. Anna J. Lang*

R 006

A century ago, many Kiwis (New Zealanders) began to consider
joining up with Australia as a seventh or eighth state. Today,
more Australians than Kiwis support the proposal. Many Kiwis
(over 450k) live in Australia......................................*Peter Slipper*

R 007

**WE, THE KHOI & SAN, ARE THE EARLIEST IN SOUTHERN
AFRICA**
We were the first peoples to live in Southern Africa. Most of the
fossilized bones of early modern humans that have been found
around here in recent years are those of our ancestors. In the
distant past, we were the only humans in this land ....*San
Bushmen*
We've also been told that our genetic make-ups are the most
complex and varied in the entire world........................*San People*
My father is of Swiss and German ancestry, and my mother is a
South African Xhosa and part Khoi.......................... *Trevor Noah*

R 008

As our ancestors knew, we also know how to survive and live in
the Kalahari and on the Namibian deserts. In recent times,
however, most of our people (especially the young)

have moved away to the cities and have forgotten about our traditional gathering way of life........ *N!xau of the !kung Bushmen*

R 009

Others prefer to remain and receive free food and materials supplied by the South African and Namibian governments. Forty years ago, movie-makers came and made a movie about us called "The Gods Must be Crazy".................................*Jamie Uys*

R 010

THE GODS MUST BE CRAZY

One of us, N!xau, starred in that movie. The ! is a letter denoting one of several click sounds that are common among some South African languages, such as Khoi and San, and several Bantu languages (Xhosas, Zulu). Other click marks besides ! are ~ ; ≠ '..........................*Wilhelm and Dorothea Bleek*

R 011

In addition to the Khoisan people, there are also the Sotho and the Swazi people here who speak click languages.
Another click language is spoken by the Hadza people in Tanzania (who are genetically unrelated to the Koi, San, or anyone else)... *M. Ruhlen*

R 012

COMING OF THE BANTUS

Then the Bantus came, followed by the Portuguese, the Dutch, the Malays, the English, and the Germans. We've been called Bushmen and Hottentots by outsiders for several centuries.............*Koi San people (or just San) or Khoikoi*

R 013

The Khoikhoi (formerly known as Hottentots) were gradually driven out of the north. They relocated, and some were absorbed by the great southward migrations of the Bantu peoples, originally from southeast Nigeria and the Cameroons starting around the first century of the Common Era...............*Roderick J. Mcintosh*

R 014

ZIMBABWA

In ancient Zimbabwa, there was built a great stone structure ca.
1050 CE (11th to 12th century CE) called the Great Zimbabwe. It
was the capital of the Shona kingdom. The first people to inhabit
the area around this structure were the Khoisan, San (aka,
Khoikhoi) people (aka, Bushmen and Hottentots)......... *Robert K.*
Hitchcock

R 015

TIMBUKTU

In the eleventh century CE, the city of Timbuktu was founded
several miles north of the great bend of the middle Niger River
by the Berbers (aka, Tuaregs), who came south from the
Maghreb (also called the Barbary Coast). Timbuktu is located in
modern day Mali. Over the centuries, along with the coming of
Islam, Timbuktu became a well-known center of Islamic
scholarship .... *John Hunwick*

R 016

BOKU HARAM

In the last 20th decade, Boku Haram outlaws came to South
Sudan and northern Nigeria and kidnapped young girls from
schools and enslaved them and even married some of them and
then made others concubines. After these atrocities occurred,
the gangs came to Timbuktu and destroyed many of the high-
rise stone towers that stored many thousands of irreplaceable
historical documents, books, and manuscripts............*al-Jazeera,*
Reuters, AP, Time, & Newsweek

R 017

EUROPEAN EXPLORERS IN SOUTH AFRICA

Centuries ago, I was the first European to discover the Cape of
South Africa... *Bartholomeu Dias*
I also sighted the Cape and named it
Taboa de caba...................................... *Antonio de Saldanha*
Next, the Dutch East India Co. came.
And we founded Capetown............................. *Jan van Riebeeck*

R 018

THE DUTCH EAST INDIA COMPANY

We met and were the first to welcome van Riebeeck
and his Dutch tourists to southern Africa.
(They never left.)... *The Khoisan people*
We brought many Dutch and French Huguenots
to the Cape ....*Dutch Recruiting agents*
Many Malays were brought in to South Africa
from Java .... *Dutch East India Co.*

R 019

The hot climate in southern Africa has changed skillful Dutch
traders into crude pastoral Boers .... *Ellen Churchill Semple*
It takes ca. 13.54 Kruger Rands to equal one
US Dollar.. *XE Currency Converter*

R 020

After the first explorations, Dutch Reformed migrants, Protestant
French, and some Swiss settlers came to South Africa in great
numbers and settled along the southern coast..... *Geert de Beers*

R 021

BOERS & ZULUS

As the Dutch settlers spread to the east and north, they came in
contact with several powerful and populous Zulu kingdoms.
Many skirmishes ensued, and several major battles were fought
between the Zulus and the Boers (a descriptive title assumed by
the Dutch migrants meaning "farmers")........ *Jan Gerritze Bantjes*

R 022

After two centuries, the Boer style of speaking Dutch gradually
evolved into Afrikaans, a separate language from the Dutch
spoken in the Netherlands...................................... *Bart de Boer*
Migrants from Germany settled in what is now Namibia and their
descendants still live there in small transplanted German
villages. Many of these settlements were mining towns, and
some of the mines are still in operation .... *Kaiser Wilhelm II*

R 023

Originally, the Namib Desert and surrounding areas were claimed by Germany. After WWI, Germany lost its overseas territories, which were seized and turned over to the victors. SW Africa and Tanganyika were given to Britain ..... *Woodrow Wilson, Clemenceau, & David Lloyd George*

R 024

As the Dutch expanded outward from our first settlements in South Africa, the British began to take an interest in the region, and many Brits began to settle in the Capetown area. As the British presence expanded, we Dutch began our great covered wagon Voortrekker movement into the high veldt north of Cape Colony ....*Piet Retief*

R 025

In Natal, we expanded into the interior and came into contact with the Zulus. A battle was fought at Blood River. We circled our wagons into a lager and drove away the Zulu attackers...*Andries Pretorius*

R 026

I later became an ally of the Boer Trekkers....*Zulu Chief Dingane* A few years later in Natal, we demolished one British regiment and then were driven back by another company of British soldiers occupying a small outpost at Roark's Drift..............*Chief Catshwayo*

R 027

BOERTREKKERS & THE ORANGE FREE STATE

Becoming aware of the greater British presence in Cape Colony and disliking British policies toward the Bantus and slavery, the Boer community decided to leave and migrate deeply into the interior of the high veldt and create two new separate countries. We took our covered wagons deep into the interior, crossed the Orange River, and founded the Orange Free State ....*Josias Philip Hoffman*

R 028
THE TRANSVAAL
Those who continued farther north crossed over the Vaal River and founded the Transvaal. The two became known as the two Boer Republics...*Martinus Pretorius*
The two were later absorbed into the South African Republics ....*Paul Kruger*

R 029
THE WHITEWATERSRAND
At the same time, isolated deposits of gold, copper, and diamonds were discovered. Soon, extensive gold deposits were discovered in the Whitwatersrand district of the Transvaal, and gold seekers from all over the world arrived in South Africa. Relations with the newcomers turned violent, and the British annexed the South African Republic ....*Jan Christian Smuts*

R 030
THE BOER WAR
The Boer War followed, which lasted for three years..*Louis Botha*
I saw action in the Boer War, was captured, and later escaped... *Winston Churchill*
The British defeated the South African Boers, and they became part of the British Empire. But after so much bloodshed, Britain became skeptical about the need to do so .....*British newspapers and Parliament*

R 031
BOY SCOUTING
During the Boer War, I discovered how little British officers and men knew how to fight and survive in the great outdoors. So, after the war, I founded the Boy Scouts, emphasizing marksmanship, camping, woodcraft, hiking, mountain climbing, trapping, fire-starting, campfire cooking, outdoor survival, athletics and personal fitness, swimming and life-saving, wall-scaling, and other skills necessary for fighting wars in the great

outdoors. The movement spread throughout Britain, the British
Commonwealth, and America.............. *Lt. General Baden Powell*

R 032
APARTHEID
Over many decades, hundreds of thousands of Bantu laborers
were hired to work in the gold and diamond mines, lasting up
until after WWII, when Apartheid was instituted as a means to
segregate Black African natives from the White African
Europeans living in South Africa. Violence ensued. Eventually,
Apartheid was abolished, and Bantus *et al.* were granted the
vote .... *Desmond Tutu & Nelson Mandela*

R 033
BRITISH EAST AFRICA COMPANY
Before WWI, the British East Africa Company enlisted agents to
go to East Africa and create a presence there for the British
Empire. And later, to have dominion over goods and resources
to exploit and enrich Britain............................ *William MacKinnon*

R 034
We established the East Africa Protectorate, primarily to keep
the Germans out and also to help the commercial interests of the
Crown. At the time, this included Kenya, Uganda,
and Zanzibar..*Lord Delamere*

R 035
EAST AFRICA & THE MAU MAUS
We also encouraged white settlement in the region. These
settlements came to be known collectively
as the White Highlands in Kenya ....*Arthur Henry Harding*
And this was portrayed in the film
"Out of Africa" ....*Meryl Streep & Robert Redford*
Over the years, a resistant movement evolved
against the British called Mau Mau. We eventually
prevailed, and the British went home .... *Kwami Nkruma*

R 036

I was president for life ....*Idi Amin*
I was president for life .... *John-Bedel Bokasa*
I was president for life .... *Robert Mugabe*
Zimbabwe's currency has become worthless ....*Banknote*
street peddlers

R 037

THE CARIBBEAN

We rebelled against the French in Haiti
and we won .... *Toussaint Louverture*
Voodoo is real and keeps my people in line while my Tonton
Macoutes will keep the peace .... *Papa Doc Duvalier*
Santeria is also real and is quite useful .... *Baby Doc Duvalier*
After being kicked out of office, I relocated to France ... *Baby Doc*

R 038

My main Caribbean pirate and privateer port and harbor is
Kingston, Jamaica, where some very
good rum is distilled ....*Captain Sir Henry Morgan*
The rum there is excellent and it is
named after him ....*Capt. Jack* Sparrow
Work, work, work Senora, work your body line-a........ *Beetlejuice*

R 039

Come mister tally man, tally me banana.
Daylight come and I wan go home .... *Harry Belafonte*
We have the best baseball players in the world......... *Dominicans*
What a hell of a way to end a career .... *Usain Bolt*

R 040

NORTH AMERICAN INDIANS

In the beginning there was Gitche Manitou, who existed
everywhere and rules over everything.......... *Northern Chichimec*
tribal shamans
In the beginning was Tawa, who raised up all peoples from the
many underworlds down below and scattered them to the four
wind ....*Spider Grandmother*

After death, the spirits of skillful warriors and hunters can spend
eternity in the Happy Hunting Ground...................... *Many Horses
of the Lakota Sioux*

S 001

In Central America, many of us built open enclosures in our cities
as rubber ball courts, which were used for athletic contests
between nearby tribes and cities. The losing sides had to flee
before the winning sides confiscated all their clothes and any
other wealth or food they might be carrying .... *Mayan umpires
& officials*

S 002

NORTH AMERICAN INDIAN MOUND BUILDERS

For hundreds of years in the eastern woodlands of North
America, there were the Adena peoples (who lived ca. 1000 BC
to ca. 200 BC), Hopewell peoples (ca. 100 BC to ca. 500 CE),
and Mississippian peoples (ca. 100 BC or 800 CE to ca. 1600
CE), who built large burial, ceremonial, residential, and extended
effigy formations and meanders (birds, snakes), mostly east of
the Missouri in the Ohio watersheds and the watersheds of the
Great Lakes, beginning from ca. 3500 BC to ca. 1500 CE. West
of the Mississippi, there were mound-building complexes by
people who had lived there for hundreds or maybe several
thousand years........... *Constance Richards, Robt. Preucel, et al.*

S 003

During this time, there were large trading networks mostly in
eastern America, where art objects, pottery, jewelry, sea shells,
beads, precious stones, copper earrings, and other objects of
value were exchanged...................................... *Tim O'Neil, et al.*

S 004

CAHOKIA MOUNDS

The largest of these was a major settlement complex inhabited
by 20,000 to 40,000 people living east of the Mississippi and a
bit north of the Ohio River. This great settlement declined and

disappeared, most likely from excessive hunting, gathering, shrinkage of the forests, and much pollution ...... *The Great Chief of Cahokia Mounds*

S 005

NATCHEZ MOUNDS

Many years ago, there were between 4,000 and 6,000 of us living in our settlement complex on the banks of the southern Mississippi. One day, a band of "white" soldiers came by, and when they left, most of our people died of the spotted and/or sweating disease...........*The "Great Sun" of the Natchez Mounds*

S 006

MANDANS & SMALLPOX

During the 1500s and 1600s, the Mandan Indians living in the vicinity of what is now St. Louis suffered many smallpox epidemics, likely brought from French and American fur trappers. Later, in 1763 after the end of the last French and Indian Wars, dispossessed French families founded St. Louis, and many French followed from Canada, France, and the American Old Northwest. They settled on both sides of the Mississippi River. All those people probably brought diseases, as did others arriving on steamboats from New Orleans and Louisville ....*George Catlin, Ken Burns, & Tim O'Neil*

S 007

One day in the 1790s, a white man named John T. Evans came into one of our villages and asked if there were any blond-haired Welshmen living among the Mandans. I said, "No," and asked him if he knew anything about the terrible diseases we were dying of. He said, "No," and left.........................*Chief Four-bears of the Mandans*

S 008

The last epidemic occurred during the 1830s. It was a much worse outbreak of smallpox than the original ones that had decimated almost the entire population of Mandans who were living there. By the time Americans arrived in large numbers, the

remnants of the Mandans who had abandoned St. Louis and its
surrounding hinterland moved northward and settled along the
upper Missouri River in what is now North Dakota..........*Lewis &*
Clark

S 009

There were so many residential, ceremonial, and burial mounds
that St. Louis was called the "Mound City" for many years. As the
Americans moved into the vicinity, the mounds began to be
destroyed, such that few remained .......................*R.G. Robinson*
The last one, called "Big Mound," was levelled in 1869..........*Tim
O'Neil*

S 010
EARLIEST SPANISH LAND EXPLORERS

We never found the fountain of youth .... *Hernando de Soto*
We were never able find any of the seven
cities of Cibola ....*Cabeza de Vaca*
My expedition didn't find anything either (just desert)....*Coronado*

S 011

We'll construct a road through California and call it the El
Camino Real, and we'll establish missions along it that the
Indians will build as they learn to love Jesus.........*Junipero Serra*
We've come to teach you Spanish, and all about Jesus.....*Cortez
& Pizarro*
We've been expecting you, Lord Quetzalcoatl...........*Montezuma*
Please go away and leave us alone.............................*Atahualpa*

S 012
MEXICAN & MIDDLE-AMERICAN INDIANS

After the beginning, the Mayan Long Count calendar was
created ....*Mayan sages*
Long ago, there were the Zapotecs (people of the clouds) and
the closely related Mixtecs (people of the rain), who were raised
up to the surface in the Valley of Oaxaca from underground
caverns and then went to work building the city of
Monte Alban .... *Mixtec and Zapotec chroniclers*

S 013

THE NAHUATL PEOPLE (AZTECS)

In the beginning was our Nahuatl creator god in the form of the
feathered serpent, Quetzalcoatl .... *Sacredots of Teotihuacan*
After an obscure beginning, there also was our hermaphrodite
god Ometecuhtli-Omecihuatl, along with the sun god
Huitzilopochtli (who sent us south from our original northern
homeland). We called our place of origin Aztlan, meaning "the
white country." It was near some large bodies of water and
certain kinds of plants.
This original homeland may have been near the lower Colorado,
while others say it was in Utah. Of note is their language, which
is related to the Ute people of modern Utah. Modern linguists
classify their language as a part of the great Uto-Aztecan
linguistic phylum...........................*John W. Powell, Edward Sapir,*
& Benjamin Whorf

S 014

We travelled south to Lake Texcoco in the Valley of Anahuac
(now Mexico City), where we saw an omen from our god
Huitzilopochtli. He told us to settle where we saw
an eagle perched on a cactus, shaking a snake
in its beak... *The Aztecs*

S 015

After a while, we soon overcame all the tribes living
around the lake ....*Aztec chroniclers*
We began to call the semi-nomadic tribes immediately to the
north of us Chichimecs (dog people). We gradually referred to
any tribes farther north as Chichimecs, whether they were
nomadic or not, and captured them for human sacrifice
rituals .... *Henry Ibarguen & Fernand de Alva*

S 016

Of note, it is interesting to be aware of the location of Lake
Texcoco as the place where corn (maize) was first
domesticated... *Montezuma*
How would you like your nachos and tacos? .... *Aztec chefs*

S 017
THE QUECHUA PEOPLE (INCAS)
After the beginning, the sun god Inti raised up our ancestors out
of Lake Titicaca and onto the flat surface of the Peruvian
Altiplano... *Inca sacerdotes*
We also live today on the Altiplano .... *Aymara people*
Today, there are also some Quechua people living in the
mountains of Ecuador... *National Census*

S 018
Today, the descendants of the Incas are indolent and lazy,
wandering aimlessly on the streets of Cuzco with nothing to do
except to occasionally participate in meaningless
revolutions .... *Hendrick*
Willem van Loon

S 019
Goodness of heart and general innocence are leading
characteristics of all American Indians. They are industrious,
neat, brave, and active. On the other hand, the Indians of Tierra
del Fuego are diminutive, ugly, and have an odor that is
unendurable .... *Johann G. von Herder*
In Anglo-America, the only good Indian was a dead Indian. In
colonial Hispanic America, the only good Indian was a
working Indian .... *Henry Ibarguen*

S 020
THE AURACANIAN PEOPLE
For centuries, we Araucanian Indians of southern Chile were
able to keep the Incas and other northerners away from our
lands. The Incas attempted several times to take our territory
south of the Rio Biobío, but they were unsuccessful, and we beat
them off many times. After a long time, we were finally subdued
by the Spaniards and we become part of Chile.......... *Araucanian*
tribal leaders

S 021

FIRST ENGLISH SETTLERS IN AMERICA

We were the first Europeans to set foot on the Newfoundland coast ....*English fishermen*

We should now make an attempt at founding English colonies in America. These should be in higher latitudes with cooler climates instead of the hot, tropical settlements founded by the sluggish, sleepy, and violent Spaniards............................ *Queen Elizabeth*

S 022

ROANOKE ISLAND SETTLEMENT

In 1585, I founded a colony on Roanoke Island in Albemarle Sound and returned to England. Then there was a little skuffle with the Spanish Armada in 1588.............................. *W. Raleigh*

In 1590, we came back with supplies, but everyone was gone.. *Governor John White*

What happened to them and where did they go?
We still don't know .... *Missing Persons Bureau*

S 023

JAMESTOWN COLONY

We incorporated a trading company in London in order to establish a colony on the American shore. In December 1606, our flotilla of three ships—the Godspeed, the Susan Constant, and the Discovery—left London. After 144 days at sea (almost four months), we spotted land in May of 1607. We established our first settlement there and named it Jamestown after our king. Then came starvation and death for many of us.............. *Captain John Smith*

S 024

POCAHONTAS

I was one of the earliest to make contact with the English..*Pocahontas*

I established a rule that if you don't work, you don't eat. This put the "high-born" men to work. Eighty percent of the original settlers died of hunger... *James Smith*

I think people in Britain will find tobacco rather
appealing...*Sir Walter Raleigh*
But we will need some hired help
to make it work ....*Sir W. Raleigh*

S 025
OF PLYMOUTH PLANTATION
After 65 days on the ocean, in September of 1620, we arrived in
the New World. We founded our settlement and called it
Plymouth. Before we knew anything about the land around our
new settlement, an Indian walked in and introduced himself. He
said his name was Samoset of the Abanaki and that a few years
earlier he had learned fairly good English
from British fishermen...................................... *William Bradford*

S 026
SAMOSET & SQUANTO
Samoset said he could help us become acclimated if we could
help his tribe against their enemies living north of
Plymouth ....*William Brewster*
Later Samoset returned with another Indian named Squanto, the
last of the Patuxet tribe. Squanto spoke better English than
Samoset, and he said he had learned English from fishermen.
He told us about how a great illness had killed all of the people
living in his village.............*"Mourt's Relation" by Edward Winslow*

S 027
One day, Squanto came to our village and showed us how to
grow crops here by burying a fish with the seeds. He spoke very
good English. Several years earlier, he had been captured by
English sailors and sold as a slave in Spain. Later, he escaped
and spent some time in England where he had
learned good English ....*Wm. Brewster*

S 028

MASSASOIT

Later, Squanto came with an Indian chief and a retinue of
followers and introduced the chief as Massasoit of the local
Wampanoag. After much discussion, he volunteered to help
us build our settlement if we could help him with his tribe's
enemies, and for a while, these Indians were our friends
and allies... *Edward Winslow*

S 029

KING PHILIP'S WAR & THE GREAT SWAMP FIGHT

Later, many Indians started to die of diseases. And more Indians
died in our wars of extermination, such as the Great Swamp
Fight in 1675 during King Philip's War. This happened when the
Narragansetts living to the west were burned up in their
dwellings and slaughtered with gunfire by men of Plymouth. "And
great was the stinke thereof." .... *Returning Militiamen*
of Plymouth

S 030

AMERICAN PROTESTANT SETTLERS

It is good that America was settled by good Protestants, and has
become known for freedom, civil, order, and
prosperity .... *Georg W.F. Hegel*
American democracy is alive and well..... *Alexis de de Toqueville*
All witches in New England are being rounded up
and burned. And witches in Pennsylvania must be
rounded up too.. *Cotton Mather*
We have no laws here forbidding witches to fly around on
broomsticks, so get thy sorry ass out of Pennsylvania and go
home... *William Penn*

S 031

NATIVE AMERICAN DIPLOMACY

After many years of conflict with the English, French, and the
Spaniards, we have seen many new settlements built by white
people coming from out of the great eastern ocean. We have

seen them become more and more numerous, and we have
come to realize that all of us must unify and live peacefully
among ourselves and come together as a fighting force so we
will lose no more land ....*Hiawatha of the Iroquois*
We must unite and keep all our combined territories and
warriors, otherwise we all will die....... *Tecumseh of the Shawnee*
With the help of British regulars, we annihilated the
Yamassees and drove the survivors out of South Carolina and
into Florida.. ....*Gov. Charles Craven*

S 032
THE GREAT PUEBLO REVOLT
Many years ago, Spaniards invaded our pueblos and took away
our lands. We, the people of the upper Rio Grande, revolted
against these Spaniards, and drove all them out and kept them
away for twelve years. Our rebellion included warriors from 14
different pueblos and tribes, including Acoma, Tesuque, Tano,
Keres, Taos, Apaches, and seven more ...... *Popé of the Pueblos*

S 033
MEXICANS & LATINOS
My name Jose Jimenez...*Bill Dana*
Awright, you can have #*^@! Tejas ....*Santa Anna*
I was the first Indio president of Mexico ....*Benito Juarez*
We don't need no steenking badges........................ *Pancho Villa*
Vaya con carne.. *Cantinflas*
All the world loves Gordo Lopez .... *Gus Arriola*
I was a Mexican guerilla leader during
the California gold rush.......................................*Juaquin Murrieta*

S 034
LATINOS & MEXICANOS
You're in Hernando's Hideaway, Ole'...................*Mariachi Bleyer*
Trump can take his stinking wall and
shove it up his gazebo .... *Felipe Calderon*
We're never gonna to pay for Trump's
loco caca wall .... *Andres Lopez Obrador*
Las wall de los Americanos is

mierdo de Circo.. *Enrique Penya Nieto*
El Trumpski ought to shut his *^x%>+@! mouth....... *Vincinte Fox*
Besa mi colo, Trumpo ....*Ernestro Zedillo*

S 035
We were the Magnificent Seven, who did a good deed to the
people living in a Mexican village .... *Yul Brynner as Chris,*
also Steve McQueen, Chas. Bronson, James Coburn, Robert
Vaughn, Horst Bucholz, & Eli Wallach (as the head bandito)

S 036
JUAN & EVITA PERÓN
I am now Comandante of Argentina .... *Juan Perón*
No llores por mi, Argentina...............................*Eva Duarte Perón*
All of my llamas are numero uno .... *Bruno of the Argentine*
These llamas are not your llamas......... *Don Diego de la Pampas*
We came to the Argentine so we could found a
Welsh-speaking settlement along the Chubut River
in southern Patagonia ....*Michael D. Jones*

S 037
THE ARGENTINE DIRTY WAR & THE MALVINAS WAR
In 1976, we cracked down on left-wing dissident students and
anti-government guerillas. We loaded them into airplanes, and
after 100 miles, kicked them out into the Atlantic, which came to
be known as the "death flights"................*Argentine Military Junta*

S 038
In order to deflect attention away from what became known as
the "Dirty War," we tried in 1982 to take the Isles Malvinas Isles
away from the British, but our ships and airplanes were
destroyed, and we failed .... *Gen. Leopoldo Galtieri*

S 039
After Argentina lost the Malvinas War, we mothers of the missing
students began marching around the Plaza de Mayo in Buenos
Aires and demanding an account of what happened to our
disappeared children....................................*Argentine Mothers*

S 040
Hugo Chávez is dead. Now come to Venezuela and see a great
state implode, crash, and burn...........................*Nicholas Maduro*
Come to Colombia and I'll show you some
good coffee beans...*Juan Valdez*
Tall and tanned and young and lovely, the girl from Iponema
goes walking, and all the old men go "Aahhh"..........*Joao Gilberto*
Pele is a national treasure ....*Brazilian soccer fans*

S 041
In South America, the higher classes are generally well-educated
and wealthy, but they are dissolute in their morals. The lower
classes are ignorant, superstitious, and rude.............*Jesse Olney*
How are things in Guacamole?..............................*Pedro O'Reilly*
Don't ask .... *General Juan Bodega Garcia y Vega*

T 001
ESKIMOS, INNUITS, NUNAVUT, & NUUK
Eskimos have been in northern Alaska, Canada, and Greenland
for several thousand years. We have made the territory of
Nunavut for the Innuit .... *Canadian Parliament*
Come to Nuuk, our new
Innuit town in Danish Greenland .... *Innuit people*

T 002
People living toward the poles have been negligible factors in
history. Many people have called the Innuits (Eskimos) lethargic
and gloomy. But the cheerful and genial Eskimos
have overcome this cold and poverty of their
environment...*Ellen Churchill Semple*
When I went there, I actually found the Eskimos to be quite
happy and cheerful .... *Franz Boas*

T 003
In 1909, the two of us explored and made it to the North Pole.
Along the way, we fathered Inuit children by our four "country
wives" .... *Robert Peary & Matt Henson*

A decade later, the two of us revisited our Eskimo village
to see how our children were (not
all survived)............................*Matthew Henson & Robert Peary*

T 004
FRENCH CANADA
In the early 1500s, French fishermen from Brittany and
Normandy fished along the coast of Newfoundland and explored
the lower St. Lawrence River..............................*French Archives*
From 1534 to 1541, I brought in many French settlers from
France and planted them in Quebec and Acadia.........*Champlain*
I founded the fur trapping industry
in French Canada.. *Verendrye*
I claimed all the territories west of the
Appalachians for France ....*La Salle*

T 005
THE CANADIAN METIS
During the 17th and 18th Centuries, the policy of France and
French Canada was that French fur trappers and those of other
occupations were encouraged to marry Indian wives, and it was
expected that their children would grow up to be "little
Frenchmen." Thus, sending women from France was not
necessary. Instead, the "little Frenchies" grew up to be "little
Indians." In time, we came to be known in Canada as Metis
(pronounced May-teez) ....*Louis Riel*
In Spanish America, Metis were called Mestizos (part Spanish
and part Indian). Most of us Metis today live in
Manitoba ....*David Chartrand*

T 006
During the 1700s, there were several French and Indian Wars in
America... *Louis XIV*
When the French lost the last of the French and Indian Wars with
the British in 1763, most French Acadians were exiled to
Louisiana, where they became known as Cajuns. Acadia was
renamed Nova Scotia... *Evangeline*

Some stayed and were hidden by neighboring British families,
and some hid out in the mountains .... *Nova Scotia highway,*
border-crossing, and rest stop
museum curator and tour guide

T 007
FROM VINCENNES TO SAINT LOUIS
After the last war with the British, many French people living
west of the Appalachians crossed the Mississippi and founded
the city of St. Louis (in what had remained French territory). With
my family, I went to St. Louis from Vincennes in Indiana, which
had been the largest frontier town in the former French western
interior (with about 3,000 people). Before that, we were from
Rivier des Prairies in Montreal ....*Amable Huge*

T 008
After Napoleon sold the Louisiana Territory to the U.S. in 1803,
most of us, for a while, continued to speak French. Then after a
generation or two, my grandchildren began to speak write, and
think in English. Many of us took English first names, and some
of us anglicized our French surnames ....*Edward Euge*
(orig. Huge)

T 009
BRITISH CANADA & THE GRAND BANKS
Since the middle 1400s, we were catching codfish all over the
Grand Banks and fishing off the coast of
Newfoundland...*Basque fishermen*
By the later 20th Century, codfish on the Grand Banks died
out and disappeared. The Grand Banks food chain also
went kaput..*Canadian fishermen*
We've been fishing on the Grand Banks
since the 1400s ....*Basque & English fishermen*
So have we.................... *Portuguese, Dutch, & French fishermen*
I claimed Newfoundland for
England in 1583... *Sir Humphrey Gilbert*
Newfoundland and Labrador were first settled by the British
during the early 1600s .... *Elisabeth Tudor & James Stuart*

T 010

After the wars with the French, Canadian authorities and the
British government set up procedures whereby immigrants,
alone or with families, were given land in Upper Canada. During
the 19th century, hundreds of thousands of European immigrants
moved to Ontario, the Prairie Provinces, and
British Columbia ....*RCMP Immigration authorities*

T 011

Don't build houses on top of the muskeg .... *RCMP*
building inspectors
If you don't build us a railroad into British Columbia, we will
approach the Americans, who will, and then we'll join
the U.S. .... *Vancouver businessmen*
We must build an alternative seaport to the Pacific and name it
after Prince Rupert of the Rhine, the first Governor of the
Hudson's Bay Company territory .... *BC Provincial Authorities*
In the year of ninety-two, tens of thousands of men from all over
rushed to the Yukon gold fields of Alaska.
Where the river is winding, Big nuggets they're a finding.
Way up North, Way up North, north to Alaska,
go north the rush is on. And see that old white mountain,
just a little south-east of Nome .... *Johnny Horton*
A few stayed on in Dawson and White Horse on the Yukon River
after the gold played out .... *Muktuk Marston & the Sons of the*
Tundra

T 012

At one time, there were more Americans in Dawson than
Canadians. One day, on the fourth of July, all the Americans
held a 4th of July parade .... *RCMP*
I will not and did not cremate Sam McGee .... *Robert Service*
When the gold played out, most people left the
Klondike. A few stayed .... *RCMP*
Mush, you Huskies .... *Sgt. Preston of the Yukon*

T 013

DEMISE OF THE GRAND BANKS
During the late 21st century, the Grand Banks experienced total
overfishing until all the codfish and all the food chain
disappeared. Also, stop killing so many
baby fur seals .... *Foreign non-Canadian activists*

T 014

CANADIAN HAT TRICKS
I scored hat-tricks well into my 50s ....*Gordie Howe*
Come to my restaurant in Toronto ....*Wayne Gretzky*
33 Stanley Cups pour Les Habs
de Montreal eh?...*Justin Trudeau*
OK guys, get out there and stay out of the penalty box.........*Paul
Newman*
What did he just say? ....*The Hanson Brothers*

T 015

Come and see beautiful Metropolitan Parry Sound... *John Candy*
Come see our Canadian sunsets.................*Heywood & Williams*
Don't know yet if the Canadian dollar or the British pound is
worth the same as the U.S. dollar? ....*The Economist*

T 016

EARLIEST INDIAN CONTACTS IN NEW ENGLAND
Sometime ago, I was taken to England by fishermen where I
learned English. After I came back, I told the new people at
Plymouth how to get a good crop by burying a fish with the
seeds of maize, beans, and squash......... *Squanto of the Patuxet*

T 017

We've settled here in this village we've called Plymouth
as friends...*William Brewster*
We celebrated our first Thanksgiving with some
of the Indians...*Edward Winslow*
Massasoit and the Wampanoag became our friends ....*William
Brewster*

T 018
We must all unite to keep
all our lands...*Tecumseh of the Shawnee*
The chief trait of American Indians is their passionless
disposition. They have also adopted brandy-drinking from the
Europeans, which has had a deadly effect ...... *Georg W.F. Hegel*
American Indians are industrious, neat,
brave, and active..*Johann von Herder*

T 019

THE AMERICAN REVOLUTION
We must hang together, or we will certainly
hang separately.. *Benjamin Franklin*
I'm sending an army to America to remind all
Loyalists of my love.. *George III*
The English are coming!
The English are coming!... *Paul Revere*
I taught the Continental Army how to drill and fight.
I also served as the first Inspector General of the revolutionary
forces .... *General Fredrich W. von Steuben*

T 020
With my army following, I crossed through the ice flows on the
Delaware River in a row boat and we caught the Hessians
sleeping at Trenton .... *George Washington*
I never said "I've just begun to fight".................. *John Paul Jones*

T 021
We followed the British troops marching southward through the
dense woods in North Carolina and we decimated them from
behind the trees as they marched along. I became known as the
"Savior of the South" and "The Fighting Quaker".............*General
Greene*

T 022
Patriot backcountry irregulars under Colonel William Campbell
defeated the Loyalist militia under Major Patrick Ferguson in
1780 at the Battle of King's Mountain in western
North Carolina .... *Frederick Hambright*

T 023
Take a look and see how Admiral Comte de Grasse's ships of
the line are keeping the British Royal Navy away
from Yorktown ....*Lafayette*
It's over. Play "The World Turned Upside Down" .... *General
Cornwallis*

T 024
They gave me a major general's commission in the British Army
and a yearly pension of 500 pounds .... *Benedict Arnold*
I shot Alexander Hamilton, a notorious pistol dueler ... *Aaron Burr*

T 025
WAR OF EIGHTEEN TWELVE
We built a large wooden fortress near today's Toledo on the
Maumee River and called it Ft. Meigs. British Regulars, backed
up by Indian warriors, laid siege to the fortress. Instead of
waiting, we went out and met the British and their Indian allies
near Tippecanoe Creek in what is now Indiana........ *Gov. William
Henry Harrison*
"Oh say can you see," sung to the tune of an old drinking
song called "To Anacrean in Heaven".............. *Francis Scott Key*
Three centuries later, it might be
"José, can you sí?" .... *Sung by
the Tijuana Trio*

T 026
BATTLE OF TIPPECANOE
We then defeated a large force of Tecumseh's Indian
confederation at Tippecanoe in Indiana. The Indians were led by
Tecumseh's brother, Tenskwatawa (aka, The Prophet), and were
armed with guns and ammunition by the British. The warriors ran

out of ammunition and had to retreat. We then burned down their
nearby village of Prophetstown where the Indians were
congregated. Then they all ran away................. *Wm. H. Harrison*
"Tippecanoe and Tyler too" later became the
slogan of my election.................................*Wm. Henry Harrison*

T 027
We should never have sacked Toronto. The British just burned
down the White House in return, and it wasn't even finished yet.
And then they carried off all the silver..................*James Madison*

T 028
We've met the enemy, and they are ours ......*Oliver Hazard Perry*
Napoleon wants to sell us all French territories
west of the Mississip................................... *Thomas Jefferson*
Quick, grab it all as fast as you can............................ *Uncle Sam*

T 029
BATTLE OF NEW ORLEANS
In 1814, we took a little trip, along with Colonel Jackson down
the mighty Mississip ....*Johnny Horton*
Our ship's cannons stopped the British
at New Orleans .... *Jean (John) Lafitte*

T 030
I invented an alphabet for the Cherokee language ....*Sequoia*
The Cherokee people may stay just where
they are... *Chief Justice John Marshall*
His decision, let him fx%#*+>]^ enforce it...........*Andrew Jackson*
Then we were evicted from our lands and set out along
the Trail of Tears. Several thousand of us died along
the way to Oklahoma....................................... *Cherokee Nation*
The Texas Rangers shot all our horses.................*Quana Parker*
of the Commanches

173

T 031

OLE MISS

Old Man River, he just keeps rolling along............*Paul Robeson*
This damn river goes on forever .... *Lewis & Clark*
The western ocean is just over the next mountain ......*Sacajawea*

T 032

REMEMBER THE ALAMO

Y'all can go to hell, I'm gonna Texas.....................*Davy Crockett,*
King of the Wild Frontier
We lost the Alamo, but we won Texas
at San Jacinto..*Sam Houston*
Fifty-four forty or fight..*James K. Polk*
I'd rather be right than president ....*Henry Clay*

T 033

THE CALIFORNIA GOLD RUSH

Gold is discovered at Sutter's Mill, and everyone can come to my
store in San Francisco and buy lots of supplies, including blue
jeans, boots, tobacco, whiskey, absinthe, condoms, glasses, and
gold-digging equipment ....*Samuel Brannon*
The tourist brochures didn't say there might be a little snow
blocking this pass .... *The Donner Party*
What's for supper?...*Alferd Packer*

T 034

BATTLE OF BULL RUN

Uncle Tom's Cabin was quite a book, eh?
And here we are ....*Northern Abolitionists*
I'm moldering in my grave... *John Brown*
Southern forces fired on Fort Sumter,
and Union forces withdrew.......................................*Abe Lincoln*
At Bull Run, all the Feds ran away, and we did too ..... *Spectators*
from Washington
We will call this the War of Northern Aggression..........*Jeff. Davis*
The South should call it what it really is: namely, the War to
Preserve Slavery ....*Edwin Stanton, Sec. of War*

T 035

BATTLE OF GETTYSBURG
Be there fustis with the mostest..................*General N.B. Forrest*
I graduated from West Point last in my class........*General Custer*
The British are threatening. But we only want one war
at a time .... *President Lincoln*
The Union line on Cemetery Ridge will break
in the middle...*Robert E. Lee*
Send my regrets to General Hancock.............. *General Armistead*

T 036

Let's go, Wolverines .... *George A. Custer*
We've run out of ammunition on Little Round Top.
BAYONETS!! .... *Joshua Chamberlain*
Some people said it didn't happen that way ....*Chamberlain*
They ain't coming .... *General Longstreet*
It's all my fault ....*Robert E. Lee*
General Pickett, you must look after your division .... *General Lee*
General Lee, I have no division .... *General Pickett*

T 037

The enemy is driven from our soil...................... *General Meade*
Hit 'em again and again.................................... *Ulysses S. Grant*
I made Georgia howl, and Atlanta went up
rather nicely ....*Wm. Tecumseh Sherman*

T 038

GRANT & LEE
I am here to surrender the
Army of Virginia.. *Gen. Robert E. Lee*
All officers and men are pardoned, and all soldiers can keep their
horses, which they will need for spring planting.
This war is over and all the rebels are now our
countrymen once again........................... *Gen. Ulysses S. Grant*

T 039

OH, CAPTAIN, MY CAPTAIN!
I spent most of my time in the early 60s
as a hospital volunteer.. *Walt Whitman*
An assassin has just shot the president,
and I wasn't there to prevent it................................*John Parker*
We caught all the culprits and hanged every one
of them .... *The Hunter Commission*

T 040

WHEN JOHNNY COMES MARCHING HOME
And we'll all go out when Jonny
comes marching home ....*Patrick Gilmore*
But you haven't an arm, you haven't a leg, you're a hopeless,
helpless, shapeless egg, and you'll have to sit with a bowl and
beg, and Johnny, I hardly knew ya....... *Anita Carter & Joan Baez*
The original Ku Klux Klan was a social fraternity dedicated to the
betterment of Southern Society .... *Nathan Bedford Forrest*

T 041

ALEXIS DE TOCQUEVILLE
I've travelled throughout most of America from 1860-1870, and it
is exhaustive to write everything down,
but I did my best ....*Alexis de Tocqueville*

U 001

I spent a great deal of time experimenting with peanuts. I
found many uses of peanut chemistry in the
American economy........................... *George Washington Carver*

U 002

THE GREAT AMERICAN FRONTIER
Out in the west Texas town of El Paso, I fell in love with a
Mexican girl at Rose's Cantina .... *Marty Robbins*
I'm an old cowhand from the Rio Grande.................. *Roy Rogers*
We're drifting along with the tumbling tumbleweeds......... *Sons of
the Pioneers*
Oh, don't forsake me, oh, my darling ....*Frankie Laine*

U 003

You've violated our gun ordinance. Now take your guns, get up
on your horses, and get out of Dodge .... *Wyatt Earp*
Where's the best place to stay in this town? ....*Doc Holliday*
You can stay in my Long Branch Saloon and boarding house.
We've got clean sheets, tidy rooms, a bar, a kitchen, gaming
tables, and the best whorehouse in Kansas .... *Miss Kitty*
I really did love that role ....*Amanda Blake*

U 004

I was a trapper and trail guide for many wagon trains moving
west .... *Kit Carson*
I shot 4,280 buffalo on the Great Plains ....*William F. Cody*
I ran off lots of cattle thieves in Wyoming and
shot all of them dead... *Tom Horn*
The last thing I need is more Indians..................... *Lt. Col. Custer*

U 005

THE BEAR RIVER MASSACRE OF 1863

With a force of 200 California volunteers under my command, we
attacked a Shoshoni winter encampment at the river in Cache
Valley in northeastern Utah. The Indians had rifles, and at the
start, they shot 23 of our soldiers .... *Col. Patrick Connor*
When we ran out of ammunition, the soldiers came in and wiped
out most of our people............*Chief Bear-Hunter of the Shoshoni*

U 006

THE SAND CREEK MASSACRE OF 1864

Stop shooting, we're friends ....*Black Kettle of the Arapahoe*
In 1864, we killed all the Indians in their encampment..........*John
Chivington*
I will fight no more ....*Chief Joseph of the Nez Perce*
Bury my heart at Wounded Knee .... *Spotted Elk of the Lakota*

U 007

THE BATTLE OF LITTLE BIGHORN IN 1876

The cavalry under Major Reno came too late. .... *Custer*

I killed Yellow Hair .... *Rain-in-his-face*
Yellow Hair shot himself .... *Sitting Bull*
Custer had it coming... *Crazy Horse*

U 008

THE GHOST DANCE

Join our Ghost Dance and wear these magic shirts. They will
ward off the bullets fired by soldiers........ *Wewoka of the Modocs*
I am the last of my people......................................*Ishi of the Yana*
We gave Ishi a nice bedroom in our building and a job for many
years until he died .... *Alfred Kroeber*
of the University of California

U 009

TELEGRAPH & TELEPHONE TECHNOLOGY

We finally completed the Trans-Atlantic telegraph
cable... *Cyrus W. Field*
I invented wireless telegraphy.........................*Guglielmo Marconi*
The original world oceanic distress
call in my earlier Morse Code was CQD:
(dah dit dah dit/...dah dah dit dah/...dah dit dit)............... *Samuel*
Morse

The new maritime oceanic distress call is now SOS:
(dit dit dit/ dah dah dah/ dit dit dit).................... *U.S. Coast Guard*
& Maritime Commission
Sorry, sir, but you've dialed the wrong number .... *Alexander*
Graham Bell

U 010

I once got sued for urinating out of my 2nd floor
office in Buffalo ....*Grover Cleveland*
Some people call me Jumbo.........................*President Cleveland*
I've got a few other things I'd like to call you .... *Benjamin*
Harrison

U 011

THE SPANISH AMERICAN WAR

Remember the Maine .... *Joseph Pulitzer*

You provide the ships, and I'll
provide the war.....................................*William Randolph Hearst*
Please don't make me sing anymore in public.......*Marion Davies*
In Cuba, I led our Rough Riders
up San Juan Hill...*Col. Leonard Wood*
I went up that hill too ....*Teddy Roosevelt*
It was a splendid little war ....*John Hay*
Stars and stripes forever ....*John Philip Sousa*

U 012

THE ALASKAN GOLD RUSH

In the early 1900s, gold was discovered in the Klondike region
along the upper Yukon River. Gold-seekers came from all over
the world. Those who had money sailed up the west coast of
America and got onto river steamers at St. Michael near the
mouth of the Yukon River. They then traveled up the river by
steamships. Those who had little money came on foot by land
from Skagway in Alaska up and over the steep Chilcoot
Pass into the gold rush towns of Dawson and
Whitehorse.................*Jack London & San Francisco newspapers*
And I went there to see what was happening
in the gold country..*Wyatt Earp*

U 013

NOTABLE AMERICAN NEWS REPORTERS

I was at various military camps in Cuba, the Boer War, and
Manchuria. And I was the only newspaper reporter allowed into
the British trenches during the Great War.........................*Richard
Harding Davis*
There's good news tonight on the radio.................*Gabriel Heater*
An optimist is someone who gets treed by a lion, but
enjoys the view..*Walter Winchell*

U 014

I was a world-class investigative newspaper correspondent. I
helped the Texas Rangers capture several Mexican bandits

along the Texas border. I was also present at many battlefields,
including the Greek insurrection against the Turks .... *Richard*
Harding Davis

U 015
In America, there are only three social classes, specifically: Land
Barons, Serfs, and Troubadours..................................... *O. Henry*
In recent years, others have added: captains of industries,
robber barons, foreigners, unbelievers,
and the poor .... *Modern academics, urban liberals,*
leftist revolutionaries, and many church leaders
Everyone loves my cartoons, except
Boss Tweed.. *Thomas Nast*
My constituents can't read, but it's them damn
pictures that gives me heartburn...............................*Boss Tweed*
The public be damned .... *William Henry Vanderbilt*

U 016
I founded the *New York Times*................. *Henry Jarvis Raymond*
I bought the *New York Times* for $75,000................. *Adolph Ochs*
I kept the *New York Times* going .... *Arthur Ochs Sulzberger*

U 017
E Pluribus Unum and we are the World .... *Uncle Sam*
I came in with Halley's Comet,
and I hope to go out with it too..................................... *Mark Twain*
This train will be a little late.....................................*Jesse James*
Banks are like pots of gold just waiting
to be emptied...*Butch Cassidy*
Use enough dynamite there, Butch?............... *The Sundance Kid*

U 018
WAY UP ABOVE & BEYOND
I drew pictures of what looked like "canals" on the planet Mars. I
also saw small irregularities in the orbits of the planets Uranus
and Neptune. It seemed that there might be another large planet
nearby, but I never found it ....*Percival Lowell*
Years later, I discovered the planet Pluto.......... *Clyde Tombaugh*

I discovered many asteroids, minor planets, and
comets at the Lowell Observatory, just north
of Flagstaff......................*Henry L. Giclas (orig. Gicquelais)*
I studied cosmic rays in the upper atmosphere and was the first
to ascend into the stratosphere in a balloon ....*Auguste Piccard*
I went a lot higher than that................*Jean-Luc Picard*

U 019
THE GREAT WAR TO END ALL WARS
Right after Franz Joseph was shot at Sarajevo, the Austrian
army mobilized and invaded Serbia where they were defeated.
The Austrians then retreated and went home. The Russians,
Germans, French, and British immediately mobilized, and the
Great War began. The French tried to get American
soldiers to replace French soldiers who were
killed in the trenches ....*Barbara Tuchman*
We will fight in France as independent units under
American command, and not as replacements
for dead Frenchmen......................*General Black Jack Pershing*

U 020
General Pershing shuns politics and does not talk for
publication..................................*Vanity Fair*
And he says we won't be back
till it's over over there ....*Irving Berlin*
And I wrote that "over there" song ....*George M. Cohan*

U 021
All my men are as clean as a whistle (no clap)......*Gen. Pershing*
Hands up, Huns, and now git! ....*Sgt. Alvin York*
I shot down 26 Fokkers ....*Eddie Rickenbacker*
I got a nasty whiff of poison gas over there ....*Christy Mathewson*
I was the best pilot in WWI and brought down
more enemy observation balloons than
anyone else...*Frank Luke*

U 022

As a war correspondent newspaper reporter, I tried to cover at
least one revolution each year. In the Great War, I lost my left
eye at Chateau Thierry ....*Floyd Gibbon*
I was the first civilian photographer to reach the western front
during the Great War ....*Merle LaVoy*

U 023

THE 11th HOUR OF THE 11th DAY OF THE 11th MONTH
Eleventh hour, eleventh day, eleventh month
of 1919 ....*Armistice Announcement*
Veterans of this armistice formed the
American Legion...................................... *Congress bill passage*
At Versaille, I couldn't interest anyone in my League of Nations. I
couldn't interest anyone in Congress either ....*Woodrow Wilson*

U 024

AFTER WORLD WAR ONE
Everything is just fine... *Calvin Coolidge*
A lot of us got rich during prohibition....................... *Joe Kennedy*
Mr. Coolidge, I have a wager that I can get you to say more than
three words at this banquet........................ *Madam Lilleth Astoria*
You lose .... *Silent Cal*

U 025

I won the Olympic decathlon in 1960 .... *Rafer Johnson*
I outran all of them at the 1984
Olympic sprints .... *Flo-Jo Griffith Joyner*
In the 1930s, I was America's best speed boat racer. I beat the
NY Central 20th Century Limited railroad train on a canal located
next to and paralleling the rail tracks (at the time the world's
fastest train). I was the first human to travel at over 100 miles per
hour on top of the water .... *Gar Wood*

U 026

This is a bank robbery, hands up ....*Bonnie & Clyde*
Because that's where the money is.......................... *Willie Sutton*

Dillinger now has a few more holes in him
than he used to ....*Melvin Purvis*
We shot Bonnie and Clyde through both sides of their stolen
Ford V-8 .... *Frank Hammer, et al.*

U 027

The daring young men in their flying machines, they go uppity,
up, up, and down ditty down, down .... *Ron Goodwin*
I was an air circus stunt flier with my Lockheed Vega.
During the 1930s, I held almost every airplane
speed record in the U.S... *Frank Hawks*
I won many air races during the 1920s
and 1930s ....*Jimmy Doolittle*
I was one hell of a great stunt flyer in my prime............*The Great*
Waldo Pepper

U 028

I won gold medals in the pentathalon and the decathalon in the
1912 Olympics. Later, they took away my medals because they
said I played minor league baseball in 1909 and 1910. In 1913,
after the Olympics, I played six seasons with the Giants, the
Reds, and the Braves..*Jim Thorpe*
Away, away with rum by gum...................................*Carrie Nation*
Americans do nothing but complain........................*Paul Theroux*
Please don't send me any more books.
I already have one... *Jean Harlow*

U 029

NEW YORK, NEW YORK

East side, west side, all around the town, boys and girls together
on the sidewalks of New York ....*Charles B. Lawler*
New York, New York. If I make it here,
I can make it anywhere ....*Kander & Ebb*
Come to my Ziegfeld Follies.............................. *Florenz Ziegfeld*
Come watch the New York Giants
at the Polo Grounds ....*Christie Mathewson*
New York, New York. The Bronx is up
and the Battery's down................................*Sinatra & Gene Kelly*

Hello, Dolly. You're looking swell, Dolly .... *Bette Midler*
Fan Dancing at Ziegfields and at the
Paradise Club .... *Fanny Bryce & Sally Rand*

U 030

THE MARX BROTHERS
I took my boys out of bellhop jobs and pushed them
onto the stage .... *Minnie Marx*
We're not related to Karl .... *Marx Brothers*
We all grew up in New York City .... *Gummo, Chico, & Zeppo*
I lost everything in the 1929 stock market crash .... *Groucho Marx*
Beep beep, sorry .... *Harpo Marx*

U 031

I was once the greatest black-faced stage personality ... *Al Jolson*
I was once the best hoofer on Broadway ...... *Bojangles Robinson*
I wrote and played "The Entertainer" on the piano ..... *Scott Joplin*
None of us ever had to prep for black-face .... *Paul*
Robeson

U 032

They say I'm among the best living embodiments of the culture
of Harvard College .... *Henry Cabot Lodge*
They say I'm among the worst living embodiments of the culture
of Yale College (boolla boolla) .... *Rudy Vallée*

U 033

State of Tennessee vs. John T. Scopes, aka The Monkey Trial,
in Dayton, TN. How many years did creation take? If not one
day, then maybe one week? One month? One Year? Or how
about 10,000 years? .... *Clarence Darrow vs.*
W.J. Bryan

U 034

Guilty, but the verdict was overturned by the Tennessee
Supreme Court on a technicality. Five days after the trial, William
Jennings Bryan died. He was my friend .... *H.L. Menken*
Not Guilty .... *Twelve Angry Men*

U 035
THE HINDENBURG
The Hindenburg has caught fire
and is going down .... *Herbert Morrison*
I told them not to fill that thing up with hydrogen.............. *Charles
Lindbergh*

U 036
I covered stories all over the world for many different newsreels
with my camera as a freelance photographer. Once I was
lowered into the Kileauea volcano and got some great pictures of
it in action...*Nick Cavaliere*
I met and wrote about T.E. Lawrence in Arabia....*Lowell Thomas*

U 037
MARTIANS IN NEW JERSEY
Martians have just landed near Grover's Mill
in New Jersey .... *Orson Welles*
Emperor Ming must be behind this........................ *Flash Gordon*

U 038
PEARL HARBOR
On December 7th 1941, the Empire of Japan deliberately
attacked the U.S. Fleet at Pearl Harbor, and this day will live in
infamy ....*Franklin D. Roosevelt*
I told them, but nobody would believe me......*Lt. Cmdr. Rochefort*
I told them, but I was told not to worry about it ....*Pvt. Elliott
(radar operator)*

U 039
YAMAMOTO
I planned this attack, but my heart wasn't into it. All we
accomplished was to awaken a sleeping giant, and fill him

with a terrible resolve....................................*Admiral Yamamoto*
I'm sending back my Japanese medals via special air mail
express. Right into the emperor's bedroom personally ......*Jimmy
Doolittle*

U 040
THE BATTLE OF MIDWAY
They will hit us again at Midway.............*Lt. Cmdr. Joel Rochefort*
We sank four Jap Carriers.........*Lt. Cmdr. Wade McClusky, et al.*

U 041
We lost everything at AF (Midway) ....*Admiral Nagumo*
We sank four carriers, one battle cruiser, hundreds of enemy
airplanes, several thousand pilots and sailors, and a lot of other
ordnance at the Battle of Midway.....................*Admiral Spruance*
Not a bad day's work, eh? ....*Admiral Nimitz*
Good work! We've shut down the Japanese Navy, and their
Army is next. And while we're at it, we'll also take
out Tokyo...*Admiral King*

U 042
As an Army Air Corps adjutant in 1945, I wrote many letters from
Yunnan in southern China to American families informing them
that their sons had been killed in action .... *Vernon G. Elliott*
I shot down 27 enemy planes in the Pacific and then spent a
year at the Tokyo Hilton.................................... *Pappy Boyington*
Later, I spent a few years at the Hanoi Hilton...........*John McCain*
I shall return... *Gen. MacArthur*
I'll be back..*Schwarzenegger*

U 043

PATTON & THE SPEECH

No poor dumb bastard ever won a war by dying for his country.
He did it by making the other poor dumb bastard die for his
country .... *George C. Scott as General Patton*
We're not going to hold any ground, let the Huns do that. And
we're going through them like crap through a goose. And, also,
there will be no battle fatigue in my command. It's a free pass for
yellow-bellies in the line of fire .... *General George S. Patton*

U 044

And when you're old and your balls are cold, and your grandsons
ask you what you did in the great world war two, you
won't have to tell them, well.....
I shoveled s__t in Alabama .... *George S. Patton*
Well, Pvt. Sad Sack did shovel s__t in Alabama..... *George Baker*

U 045

EL-ALAMEIN IN NORTH AFRICA

At El-Alamein, I drove Rommel's army westward and out
of Cyrenaica. And they never got all that oil they
were seeking.. *General Montgomery*
I later chased Rommel's sorry ass all the way out of
North Africa .... *George Patton*

U 046

NORMANDY LANDING ON D-DAY

OK, we'll go.................................. *General Dwight D. Eisenhower*
Omaha, Utah, Juno, Gold, and Sword Beaches
fell on D-Day. And we were the two Assault Commanders on that
first day, 6 June, 1944 .... *Capt. Edward Fritzche &*
Capt. Miles Imlay, both U.S. Coast Guard Officers
The war starts here .... *General Theodore Roosevelt, Jr.*
in Normandy

U 047

IN THE VALLEY OF THE SHADOW OF DEATH
Yea though I walk through the valley of the Shadow of Death, I
will fear no evil, for I'm the meanest SOB in the valley.....*General
Patton*

My Third Army liberated France and then on into western
Germany..*George S. Patton*
Willy and Joe also liberated France ....*Bill Mauldin*
Our 442nd Go for Broke regiment liberated Italy.....*Daniel Inouye*

U 048

You Americans are kaput and you
must surrender, mach schnell........................*General Manteuffel*
NUTS!.. *General McAuliffe, at Bastogne*
A man that eloquent deserves
to be relieved immediately .... *General Patton*

U 049

We kicked ass out of all Messerschmitts
and Focke Wulfs in Europe..............................*P 47 & P51 pilots*
We pulverized everything throughout Germany
during the day.. *B-17 crews*
And we blew up everything in Germany
at night.. *Lancaster bomber crews*
Berlin no longer exists, the Russians are just east of
the city, and all the top Nazis have fled,
taken cyanide, or a bullet............................ *U.S. Army Air Corps*

U 050

During World War II, I served in the Western Pacific and built
U.S. Army Air Corps runways and air bases on various
islands after the removal of Japanese forces stationed
on many of these islands ....*John Marshall,
U.S. Army Corps of Engineers*

U 051

Later, I ran a POW Camp in Casper, Wyoming. We had many
German and Italian prisoners. One day, the Germans scrub-
brushed a swastika on the mess hall floor. It took them a month
or two for all of them to do the same thing for the rest of the
entire mess hall floor in order to erase the swastika .... *J. S.*
Marshall

U 052

The Italian prisoners wanted tomatoes in their spaghetti,
so we put them to work on local vegetable
farms near Casper ....*John Stanley Marshall*
And I served in the U.S. Army Air Corps Weather Service in
Iceland during WWII as part of the European Theatre of
Operations (ETO)... *Warren S. Marshall*

U 053

JAPANESE & THE PHILIPPINES

The Japanese have taken Corregidor, and Roosevelt has
ordered me to escape in a PT boat and make it to Australia. The
Japanese went on and invaded the rest of the
Philippines, and I shall return ....*General MacArthur*
I'll be back .... *Schwarzenegger*

U 054

Later, after the amphibious landing at Leyte in the Philippines in
1944, we waded through the water and onto the beach where
the battle was fought. I said to General MacArthur,
"I can't swim."......................................*President Manuel Quezon*
Don't worry, everyone will see I can't walk on water........*Douglas*
MacArthur

U 055

THE MARINES & THE ARMY AIR CORPS

The Marines have taken Guadalcanal..........................*Roosevelt*
The Marines have taken Tarawa .... *Admiral Spruance*
We took back Guam in the western Pacific .... *U.S. Marines*

In 1945, on the island of Iwo Jima, I helped raise the U.S. flag on top of Mt. Suribachi..*Ira Hayes*
And I took the picture of that iconic ceremony........*Joe Rosenthal*
We then bombed everything in Japan that moved ....*Curtis LeMay*

U 056
THE BOMB
We made it, and it works .... *General Groves*
She's-a go Boom .... *Enrico Fermi*
Now I am become death,
destroyer of worlds .... *Oppenheimer (Bhagavad Gita)*
And then God said to me,
"Let there be annihilation." ....*Harry S. Truman*
Just me and my Enola Gay. It was a nice day's work............*Paul Tibbets*
We can build a bigger one .... *Edward Teller*

U 057
The great Pacific War has not turned out as we had planned. We must now endure the unendurable............. *His Majesty (Hirohito)*
Maybe I can get some sleep now............................... *Tokyo Rose*

V 001
THE KOREAN WAR
Yanks Battle Reds .... *1950 news headlines (not about baseball)*
We are defending the Puson Perimeter .... *Gen. "Bulldog" Walker*
Please get me off this boat headed for Korea ....*Rev. Pat Robertson*

V 002
We will land at Inchon, and we will prevail ..... *Douglas MacArthur*
We are now headed north to the Yalu................................. *MAC*
General MacArthur, you are relieved.
It's time to come home... *HST*
We'll settle for the 38th parallel......................... *Harry S. Truman*

V 003

Someday, Seoul will be the capital of all Korea ... *Syngman Rhee*
Would you like dog or cat with your kimchi? .... *Humjob Park*
How about some fish heads and rice instead? .... *Sandra Oh*
And how about some good Korean sake? .... *Sadeharu Oh*
Good Korean 200-proof vodka is much better .... *Kim Jong Il*

V 004

The homeless are penniless because they have
no religious faith .... *Mike Pence*
All the poor and downtrodden and their unbaptized
infants are damned .... *John Knox*
Greed is good .... *Gordon Gecko*
God loves rich people .... *Joel Osteen*
And camels can't navigate through the eyes of needles ..... *Jesus
of Nazareth*

V 005

GOOD DEEDS VS. GREAT WEALTH

Good deeds are not always rewarded, and generally only fervent
faith is rewarded. God selects people to be of the saved for
reasons known only by Her, or Him .... *Billy Graham*
Oh my god, my son has become a Christian .... *Madalyn
Murray O'Hair*

V 006

WEALTH, SALVATION, & PRESTIGE

Methodists are Baptists who can read .... *Rev. Maclean*
Episcopalians are Methodists who have money ...... *Father Guido*
Episcopalians have all the pageantry
and none of the guilt .... *Robin Williams*
Congregationalists and Unitarians are among
the richest .... *Kosmin & Keysar*

V 007

Episcopals and Presbyterians represent the Republicans Party
at prayer and the most well-off .... *Father Ernesto*
Lutherans, Jews, and Hindus are also among the

most well-off ....*Pew Research Center*
As are the nonreligious, Agnostics, and
Materialists ....*Richard Dawkins*
Pentecostalists, Fundamentalists, Evangelicals, Disciples,
Tongue-speakers, Snake-handlers, and Adventists
are the least well-off................................*Pew Research Center*

V 008
EARLY CALVINIST TEACHINGS
God favors merchants and businessmen and those who have
made a lot of money, and are thus worthy to be of the elect and
among the leaders of society ....*John Calvin*

V 009
Great wealth is a sign that someone has been elevated by God
to become one of the Elect, who will afterwards live in a shining
Emerald City, up on a hill, and can be gifted in the afterlife. This
is if one only truly loves God and Jesus.....................*John Calvin*

V 010
Wealthy Dutch Reformed, German Reformed, and French
Reformed (Christians) are saved .... *Uncle Zwingli*
All the poor and downtrodden and their unbaptized infants are
damned ....*John Calvin*
All non-Catholics in Spain and the Indies must
be eliminated .... *Torquemada*

V 011
ILLNESSES & FAITH
Illnesses are illusions that can be cured by faith, and intense
prayerizing. And everyone is welcome to come to Boston and
see my beautiful First Church of Christian Science on
Massachusetts Avenue.................................... *Mary Baker Eddy*
I've cured many sick, lame, blind, deaf, and
insane people .... *Amiee Semple McPherson*
Sick people are sick because they have strayed away
from Jesus... *V.P. Mike Pence*

V 012

I was pretty good as a child evangelist ....*Marjoe Gortner*
I once saw a 300-foot-tall apparition of Jesus Christ
in downtown Tulsa ....*Anal Roberts*

V 013

I got paid lots of money from Donald Trump for services
rendered.. *Stormy Daniel*
Jimmy Swaggart paid me a lot of money for
my services .... *Debbie Murphree*
I have sinned. Oh, how I have sinned.
Oh God, I'm a sinner .... *Jimmy Swaggart*
Here is some nice cool-aid that will help you find peace and
happiness...*Jim Jones*

V 014

Several thousand years ago, there were dinosaurs living
on Earth at the same time as
human beings .... *Jim & Tammy Bakker,*
                              Jerry Foulmouth, Pat Robertson, etc.
In Kentucky, I built a full-size wooden replica of Noah Zark, and
filled it up with cows, giraffes, ducks, roaches, crows, dinosaurs,
lobsters, worms, fleas, butterflies, ponies, muttons, cats,
dragons, and wild Indians....................................*Kenneth A. Ham*
Dinos? Hey, no way. And I ought to know .... *Trevor Noah*

V 015

Jesus has just asked me to buy a 54-million-dollar private jet
and use it to evangelize more heathens and
unbelievers with no layovers ....*Jesse Duplantis*
The Jet-set evangelists are in full swing ....*Marjoe Gortner*
Oh Lord, won't you buy me a Mercedes Benz? ....*Janis Joplin*
Be careful what you wish for, you just might get it ......*King Midas*
If you want to get rich, invent a new religion ....*L. Ron Hubbard*

I am not programmed to give judgments on these
distinctions...*Robbie the Robot*
Uhh uhuhhg uuuh .... *Chewbaca*
Beep beep *C-3PO*
Puttin' on the ritz...*Young Frankenstein*

V 016

One of our killer whales (aka, orcas) killed and ate one of our
best fish trainers. So we are now freeing all our dolphins and
orcas so they can swim freely and happily forever in
the ocean.. *Marine Fish-World Circus*
Free Willy ....*John Wayne Bobbitt*

V 017

NOT IN THE BACK OF THE BUS
We both refused to sit in the back of the bus ..... *Jackie Robinson
& Rosa Parks*

We integrated whites-only lunch counters in
Birmingham .... *Martin Luther King Jr.*
Segregation today, tomorrow, and forever..........*George Wallace*
Yeah, that's my biracial kid, but don't tell anyone.................*Strom
Thurmond*

V 018

Come on down to Dogpatch on Sadie
Hawkin's Day... *Li'l Abner & Daisey Mae*
Come on down to Hootin Holler... *Barney Google & Snuffy Smith*
Pa, I think it's gonna rain .... *Ma Kettle*
Fibber McGee, don't you dare open that closet........*Molly McGee*

V 019

Mr. Tracy, why don't you come over here and see our new house
at Sunny Dell Acres underneath the new highway overpass and
see our new little baby girl, Sparkle .........................*B.O. Plenty &
Gravel Gertie*

V 020

SEGREGATION IN DIXIE

We ain't never gonna allow any niggra stoonts to go to Little
Rock Central High School on my watch .... *Gov. Orville Faubus*
Ain't never gonna give up segregation in
the South.. *Sen. Jesse Helms*
Segregation is God's law............................*Gov. George Wallace*
& Senator Trent Lott

V 021

I will call up my Arkansas National Guard and order them to keep
these niggras outa our schools......................... *Governor Faubus*
If you do that, I will nationalize your National Guard and order
them to keep the peace while those kids go
inside and register...................................... *President Eisenhower*

V 022

Y'alls come on down to my whites-only restaurant in Atlanna and
git yourseles a free ax handle............................... *Lester Maddox*
We are not going to let Jim Crow come back into the
south again .... *Elbie Jay*
If we'd listened to Strom Thurmond back then, we wouldn't be
having all these race problems now .... *Sen. Trent Lott*
That's enough, you're out of office as of now ....*President*
George W. Bush

V 023

TO BE A KING

It's good to be king ....*Mel Brooks*
Every man a king .... *Huey Long*
Best royal grocery store in America........................ *King Soopers*
I'd like to forget I was once a king .... *Edward VIII*
In America, I'm no longer king...............................*King George III*
I was king for a little while...................................... *King Ralph*
I hate those +#!*^! little airplanes................................. *King Kong*
Holy macaroon, Andy.. *The Kingfish*
One of my seven sons can wear my
golden crown.. *The Alligator King*

V 024
I was the first to explore the Grand Canyon. I also translated
many American Indian languages, and grouped them
into phyla..*John Wesley Powell*
Everyone loves Brighty, our loveable burro of
the Grand Canyon ....*Margaret Henry*
Brighty the Burro is one of our major living
stars of attraction ....*Park Rangers*
Maybe you'd like some music from my
Grand Canyon Suite? ....*Ferde Grofé*

V 025
Come to our hotel in Oak Bluff, Mass .... *Chief of the Pequots*
Come to one of our casinos in northern
Minnesota... *Chief of the Chippewa*
Welcome to our new casino in
Washington ....*Chief of the Quinault*
Come to our new casino, hotel, and museum
in Idaho.. *Shoshone-Bannock*

V 026
Come to one of our many casinos in Florida...... *Seminole Nation*
Visit our casino in Oklahoma .... *Shawnee Nation*
We have several casinos in Oklahoma ....*Caddo Nation*
Welcome to our Oklahoma casinos ....*Cherokee Nation*
The Texas Rangers shot all our horses .... *Quana Parker*

V 027
MULE & HORSE OWNERS
My kingdom for a horse .... *Richard Plantagenet*
My twenty-mule team Borax Wagon on
Death Valley Days had the best mules ever ....*Ronald Reagan*
Mule Train ....*Frankie Lane*

V 028

Seabiscuit was the world's best horse ever .... *Charles S. Howard*
No, Seattle Slew was .... *Karen Taylor*
No, Secretariat was.................................*Chris & Penny Chenery*
No, American Pharoah was.....................................*Elliott Waldon*
No, Justify was................................*Bob Baffert & George Soros*

V 029

Man O' War was the best horse of all............... *Samuel D. Riddle*
No, Whirlaway was the best .... *Calumet Farms*
Is a horse a horse? .... *Mr. Ed*
Yes, a horse is a horse of course .... *Alan Young*
My horse, my horse....Ahh! A...Ahh! AAhh! .... *Jack Woltz*

V 030

Some horses are good for racing and dressage, while
others are good only for mucilage .... *Lili von Shtup*
I made my horse a senator...*Caligula*
Marezy doats and doeszy doats...............................*Milton Drake*
May the horse be with you ....*Harrison Ford*
Best public school in town....................................... *Horse Mann*
Horseface... *Trumpski*

V 031

I now build houses for humanity ....*Jimmy Carter*
We are not butchers!.....................................*George H.W. Bush*
If you've seen one redwood,
you've seen them all .... *Ronald Reagan*
Ain't never gonna be any more Democrat
Supreme Court Justices.................................. *Mitch McConnell*
Our Constitution protects Aliens, Drunks, and
U.S. Senators..*Will Rogers*

V 032

Come see two lion tamers get eaten by lions ...... *Siegfried & Roy*
Send in the clowns...*Emmett Kelly*
OK, here I am, all the others can leave now ....*Bozo the Clown*

V 033

Send out the clowns. We are now shutting down
our Ringling Bros. Circus for the last time......................*Irvin Feld*
We will send all our animals to retirement homes .... *Roy &*
Siegfried
We will send all our lions to petting zoos............... *Gunther Gebel*

V 034

This land is my land, and this land is your land........ *Pete Seeger*
See the USA in your open sleigh .... *Dinah Shore*
Oh, what a beautiful morning................................ *Gordon McRae*
What a wonderful day.. *Satchmo*
It's a beautiful day in the neighborhood.......................*Mr. Rogers*

V 035

DOING & DOOIN

How am I dooin?..*Mayor Ed Koch*
Do do that voodoo that you do................................... *Cole Porter*
Doo wop ....*The Cadillacs*
Do wacka do wacka do... *Roger Miller*
Asparagus? Ugh! Gumby doo doo............................ *Joan Rivers*
You want me to do what? .... *Stormy Daniels*

V 036

Come up and see my weiner ....*Anthony Weiner*
I can't get it up anymore.. *Willy Nilly*
Too bad, much ado about nothing ....*The Bard*
It's a small world after all.....................................*Sherman Bros.*
I don't get no respect either ....*Rodney Dangerfield*
All hat and no cattle ....*Clint Murchison*

V 037

Beat it kid, you bother me ....*William C. Fields*
Come up and see me sometime Big Boy...................... *Mae West*
Ah, yes, my little chickadee, have you ever had this tooth pulled
before? .... *W.C. Fields (as the Dentist)*

V 038
Here's Johnny! ....*Ed McMahon*
Here's Johnny! ....*Jack Nicholson*
And Johnny, we hardly knew ye ....*Kenneth O'Donnell & David*
Powers

V 039
TRAINS & WINDS
Listen to the jingle, the rumble, and the roar,
of the Wabash Cannon Ball........................*P. Carter & Wm. Kindt*
In a lonely shack by a railroad track, he was born to
wander, the next of kin to the wayward wind .... *Gogi Grant*
I hear the train a coming, it's coming 'round
the bend.. *Johnny Cash*
Cast your fate to the winds.................................. *Vince Guaraldi*
Inherit the wind...................................*Jerome Lawrence & R. Lee*
They call the wind Mariah.................................... *Harve Presnell*
And the summer wind... *Sinatra*

V 040
I was born under a wandering star ....*Lee Marvin*
I'm a wanderer .... *Dion de Mucci*
Tomorrow, tomorrow, the sun will come up tomorrow..........*Annie*
The hills are alive with the sound of music ....*Julie Andrews*

V 041
POLITICS & POLITICIANS
Politics ain't beanbag ....*David Axelrod*
All politics are local politics... *Tip O'Neill*
All politics are national politics........................... *Alan Abramowitz*

V 042
Main Street... *Sinclair Lewis*
All we need is a good five cent cigar .... *Thomas R. Marshall*

All we need is a good business administration..... *George Babbitt*
All we need is more sales .... *Sears and Roebuck*
All we need is lots of different colored ice-cream ....*Ben & Jerry*
We've got plenty of ice cream without all that .... *Dairy Queen*
Down and out in Paris and London .... *George Orwell*

V 043
Love and marriage, love and marriage.................... *Frank Sinatra*
Go together like a horse and carriage................... *Petzel & Knish*

V 044
I did not sleep with Mavis Pruitt .... *Rubin Flood (he didn't)*
Elmer Gantry ....*Sinclair Lewis (he did)*
I did not have sex with that
woman... *Bill Clinton*
Yes, you did... *Monica Lewinsky*
Just what do you mean by sex?................................. *Slick Willy*

V 045
I didn't pay off any of those women........................*Donald Trump*
Yes, you did.. *Stormy Daniels*
That child ain't mine.. *Warren G. Harding*
So I stuped that woman, so what? Fake News ......*Donald Trump*
Maybe we could pay Trump to leave office ....*Karen Attiah*

V 046
FOREIGN RELATIONS
Trump is no longer welcome in Canada.................*Justin Trudeau*
Trump should stay home .... *Emmanuel Macron*
Trump is no longer of use for us .... *Vladimir Putin*

V 047
If Trumpski wants a trade war, he'll get one...................*Xi Jinping*
If Trump talks about nationalism, he should
do it elsewhere ....*Angela Merkel*
Come see our big Trump balloon here in London ..... *Teresa May*
Trump was very nice to me....................................... *Kim Jun Un*

V 048
What, me worry? .... *Alfred E. Newman*
I'm over 50 years old, and talkies are coming soon,
so why should I be worried? .... *Douglas Fairbanks*
No, I love your parties .... *Charley Chaplin*
On the power of negative thinking .... *Norman Vincent Peale*

V 049
Was that Mr. Hoover at our restaurant table?..... *Charley Chaplin*
Mr. Chaplin is now banned from re-entering
the United States... *J. Edgar Hoover*
I saw Mr. Hoover picking his nose last night
at Toots Shore .... *Emily Post*

W 001
I just finished my book on Aaron Burr......................... *Gore Vidal*
Shut up, you queer....................................... *William F. Buckley*

W 002
The president is a card-carrying
communist... *Tail Gunner Joe McCarthy*
No collusion, no pawing, no lying, no treason. I did nothing
wrong. Why don't people believe me?................... *Donald Trump*
I don't know how much money I paid her to
keep quiet? .... *Trumpski*
Donald Trump has defiled the office of president.............. *George
H.W. Bush*

W 003
I brought home the news on television .... *Tom Brokaw*
I always made Richard Nixon very uncomfortable......*Dan Rather*
I really did fly in that airplane during
the Falklands War .... *Brian Williams*

W 004

FAMOUS & INFAMOUS INITIALS

Bully! And carry a big stick.. *TR*
The New Deal will prevail...*FDR*
A chicken in every pot.. *HH*
Ich bin ein donut ....*JFK*
The buck stops here ....*HST*
I will go to Korea .... *IKE*
I have a dream...*MLK*
Light is at the end of the tunnel...*LBJ*
Guy next door with a barking dog ....*SOB*
Fake news...*DJT*
Electricity for all eastern Tenn.. *TVA*
Standard Oil of Fire Island .... *STD*
Now they all vote Republican... *DNC*
United Airlines .... *UAL*
A room, a gym, and a swimming pool .... *YMCA*
Youth Conservation Corps..*YCC*

W 005

WOODEN PUPPETS

I'm not related to Joe McCarthy ....*Charlie McCarthy*
I am not related to Charlie McCarthy, and my heart
is not made of naughty pine................... *Calai-ja (Hank Williams)*

W 006

LOUISIANA

Down in Loosiana close to New Orleans, way back up in the
woods among the evergreens…Go Johnny go...Go Johnny go...
Johnny B. Goode...*Chuck Berry*

W 007

Best soul food in the Tremé ....*Aunt Jemima & Uncle Ben*
There is a house in New Orleans that's called

the Rising Sun... *The Animals*
Jambalaya, crawfish pie, and filé gumbo,
we'll have big fun on the bayou .... *Hank Williams*
Come to the Big Easy for Mardi Gras.................. *Mayor Landrieu*
Laissez les bon temps roller.. *King Creole*

W 008
Best Cajun chef in the Vieux Carré...................... *Paul Prudhomm*
I'm the new best Cajun chef on Bourbon Street........ *Isaac Toups*
I drove my Chevy to the levee, but the levee was dry, and them
good ole boys was drinkin' whiskey and rye.............*Don McLean*
Best chitlins and boiled catfish on the levee .... *Porgy & Bass*
Best Creole chef on Bourbon Street.................... *Emeril Lagasse*

W 009
Summertime, and the living is easy...................... *Ella Fitzgerald*
Sweet Georgia Brown .... *Ethel Waters*
Sweet Caroline.. *Neil Diamond*

W 010
Down in Arizona where the badmen are, nothing much to guide
them but the evening star...........................*Ragtime Cowboy Joe*
Buttons and Bows ....*Dinah Shore*

W 011
GEORGIA
Way down upon the Chattahoochee.................... *Stephen Foster*
Georgia on my mind.. *Ray Charles*
Izzat the Chattanooga Choo Choo? ....*Glenn Miller*
I don't know, let me think..*Fats Domino*
Roll me over in the clover...................................... *Sassy Lassies*
I'm looking over a four-leaf clover............................*Art Mooney*

W 012
I'm faster than a speeding bullet and am able to fly
over tall buildings .... *Superman*
I can jump over small buildings .... *Supergirl*

Don't park gasoline trucks where crop-dusters fly.......*Cary Grant*
Because we can .... *The Stepford husbands*

W 013
ACTRESSES & SINGERS
I was the best stage actress in the 1880s and 1890s..........*Sarah Bernhardt*
I was the "IT" girl in the 1920s.....................................*Clara Bow*
I was one red hot mamma .... *Sophie Tucker*
I made a successful transition from the stage
to movies...*Helen Hayes*
Come help me hold up this lamp post................ *Marlene Dietrich*
Do I have to take Stevie Wonder to lunch? ....*Wonder Woman*
Silence is golden when you can't think of a
good answer...*Muhammed Ali*

W 014
My big cheetah cat loves accompanying me on my walks along
the Champs-Élysées in Paris............................*Josephine Baker*

W 015
Henry VIII married half a dozen Queens, and I've married
twenty-one husbands..*Zsa Zsa Gabor*
Don't get angry, get it all .... *Ivana Trump*
Gypsies, tramps, and thieves.............................*Cher Sarkesian*
The way we weren't.......................................*Barbara Streisand*
You can learn a lot from Lydia
(the tattooed lady)............................... *George Burns & Groucho*

W 016
I sang a duet with my late father's recording.............*Natalie Cole*
I feel pretty, oh so pretty ....*Natalie Wood*
Let me entertain you... *Gypsy Rose Lee*

My centerfold in Playboy set a new sales record ....*Marilyn Monroe*

W 017

I was the Queen of Soul..Aretha Franklin
I was the Queen of Sod... Lee Liberace
The Queen of Sweden wants of come to SFO ....Cab Calloway
What we don't need here is another queen........... Joseph Alioto,
                                                            former mayor of SFO
I'm smarter than I look.................................... Marilyn Mansfield
Yes, that's all me.. Dolly Parton
I really just had to ask............................Barbara Wawa (Walters)

W 018

I wrote my advice column for many years in the
Chicago Tribune.. Abby van Buren
Do I ever read my sister Abbey's advice column? Oh, you know?
I never read the Tribune.. Ann Landers
                                                                of the Sun-Times

W 019

Come and see my twin 45s...Candy Barr
Come to the U. of Nevada at Reno and
study ecdysiasm.. Tempest Storm
Wilber Mills, a senator from Arkansas, once spent much of his
time in Washington watching the Argentine stripper, Fannie Fox,
who performed onstage for him in many of my exhibitions
of the ecdysiast persuasion.. Miss Fox
Come and see my new act in Las Vegas. It's the same,
but better...Stormy Daniels

W 020

Porn? I can't define it, but I knows it
when I sees it... Potter Stewart
They call me naughty ....Bettie Paige
Sex is good, but largely misunderstood....................Alfred Kinsey
Come and see my "act" in Salt Lake City..............Roseanne Barr
Vote for Earl .... Blaze Starr
Vote for Pedro...Napoleon Dynamite
Vote for Hillary ....Wm. J. Clinton

W 021
RODEOS & CIRCUSES
I can shoot a cigarette out of someone's mouth at 50 yards while
riding backwards on a horse ....*Annie Oakley*
Come and see my Wild West Show............................ *Buffalo Bill*
Come see the greatest show on earth ....*Barnum & Bailey*
There's no people like show people......................*Ethel Merman*
I once drove a stage coach and forgot
to pick up the passengers.......................................*Calamity Jane*
Aces and eights ....*Wild Bill*

W 022
The Fire Marshal says too many people are inside this tent, and
we gotta get a lot of people out of here, fast .... *J.A. Bailey*
OK, everyone come over here and
see the "Egress" .... *P.T. Barnum*

W 023
"Stuffed wild men from Borneo" and Egyptian mummies make
good side show and circus exhibits in America, along with
Schlitzie the micro-cephalic, who lived for most of his adult life
under the Big Top with his circus family ....*Tom Mix Circus*

W 024
We had lots of these things in my museum of oddities. I also built
the magnificent salt water baths and the second Cliff House
overlooking the Golden Gate ....*Adolph Sutro*

W 025
THE TWILIGHT ZONE
I've met two people I didn't really like........................ *Will Rogers*
Will Rogers never met number three:
Sen. Ted Cruz of Texas...*Mark Shields*
You're now in The Twilight Zone...............................*Rod Serling*
Go where no man has gone before.....................*William Shatner*
Live long and prosper .... *Leonard Nimoy*
I seldom attend my own garden parties .... *Jay Gatsby*
Stop the bubble machine ....*Lawrence Welk*

W 026
MODERN FOOD AVOIDANCES
Modern Chinese do not eat butter, cheese,
or milk .... *Frederick Simoons*
Christian Scientists don't consume alcohol,
coffee, or tea ....*Mary Baker Eddy*
We don't drink and we don't chew and we don't go
with the boys who do.................................. *Girl Scouts*
Mormons avoid drinking alcohol. They also used to
avoid hot drinks (tea or coffee), and caffeinated soft
drinks. A lot of this is now relaxed ....*Peggy Fletcher*

W 027
We consume over a thousand horses
every year .... *Chinese horsemeat purveyors*
Long ago in China, a particularly well-flavored
breed of dog was given the
name "Chow" .... *Ancient Chinese dog breeders*
Vietnamese and Koreans also like dog meat
BBQ served in restaurants that specialize in
different kinds of dog............. *Vietnamese and Korean dog chefs*

W 028
Modern Europeans generally do not eat horsemeat or certain
other animals that are considered to be pets.................*Frederick
Simoons*
Southern Baptists, Mormons, Muslims, Sikhs, and Brahmins are
taught to avoid consuming alcohol ....*World food avoidances*
Who took the cork out of my lunch? .... *W.C. Fields*

W 029
High caste Brahmins in India must not
drink wine or eat meat.......................................*The Manu Smriti*
Orthodox Jews must not eat pork, oysters, clams, shrimp,
lobsters, and any other bottom-feeding aquatic animals,
or the rear half of cows, and anything else that's
non-kosher ....*Book of Leviticus*

Most Muslims may not eat pigs, dogs, carrion,
donkeys, snakes, hyenas, insects, or
anything else not Halal .... *The Hadiths*

W 030
Most or many Brits, Irish, Americans, Canadians, Australians,
and Kiwis tend not to eat snails or frogs and are amused that the
French do. Most Europeans do not eat horsemeat, but the
French do ....*Frederick Simoons*

W 031
Have another cherry? ....*Daryl van Horne*
What's for dinner?... *Alfie Packer*
We're having Spotted Owl ....*Paul Bunyan*
Bon appetite ....*Julia Child*
Just one more bite, Mr. Creasote?......................... *Monte Python*
Please help us to get rid of all these murderous gulls and
crows on Bodega Bay. We don't want them around
anymore ....*Jessica Tandy, Tippi Hedron, & Mitch*

W 032
OVER & UNDER THE WATER
The rising tide will lift all boats ....*Jack Kennedy*
But if you don't have a boat,
you're gonna f___ing drown.......................... *Frank Fitzsimmons*
We finally found the Titanic....................................*Robert Ballard*
And there's Davy, whose still in the Navy,
and probably will be for life .... *Billy Joel*
I'm blue, navy blue, I'm as sad as I can be,
my steady boy said ship ahoy
and joined the Nay-aay-vee ....*Diane Renay*

W 033
It was sad when the great
ship went down............................... *Camp song about the Titanic*
Remember the Edmund Fitzgerald ....*Gordon Lightfoot*
We all live in a Yellow Submarine............................. *The Beatles*
They call me Mellow Yellow...*Donovan*

The Great Yellow Bird ....*Sean Garrison*
Everything is in the Yellow pages................*City telephone books*
Yellow pages? What are those?..........................*Jobs & The Woz*
Yellowstone is about ready to blow up again..........*Park Rangers*

W 034
SAN FRANCISCO
Open your Golden Gate,
San Francisco here I come ....*Jeanette McDonald*
Here I be from over the sea, I'm...............*Barnacle Bill the Sailor*
Come visit my City Lights Bookstore in North Beach........... *Larry
Ferlengetti*
I am the King of Torts...*Melvin Belli*
I stole them torts & took them clean away .... *The Knave of Harps*
I left my heart in San Francisco...............................*Tony Bennett*
Don't call it "Frisco".. *Herb Caen*
And don't call it "Cali" either......................... *Gov. Gavin Newsom*

W 035
The new Millennium Tower in San Francisco's financial
district is now called San Francisco's
Leaning Tower of Error......................... *Millennium Tower tenants*
Don't worry too much about
a building that leans ....*Michele Conti, Mayor of Pisa*
Not too hot, not too cold .... *Goldilocks*
The coldest winter I ever spent was a
summer in San Francisco...................................... *Mark Twain*
All the upper middle-class Hippies who came to San Francisco
for the 1960's Summer of Love froze their tushies
off in Golden Gate Park...*Mayor Alioto*

W 036
Along with Seattle, Portland, Los Angeles, and San Jose, we
have the greatest concentration of homeless people in the
United States, mostly on Market and
Mission Streets...*Mayor London Breed,
mayor of San Francisco*

W 037
I paid for printing all my books by myself. Also, come to
Oakland and see my bar in Jack London Square..... *Jack London*
Oakland? There's no there there .... *Gertrude Stein*
Think your theater show is good? Play Oakland ....*Jack Benny*
They're taking our God damned Oakland
Raiders away again ....*Raider Nation*
We are now suing the Raiders for all the money we spent
making improvements
to the stadium............................*Libby Schaaf, Mayor of Oakland*
Hey, leave them alone .... *Carolyn Goodman,*
Mayor of Las Vegas

W 038
Life's a whale of a tale .... *Kirk Douglas*
Some say I could not have written that
all by myself...*Christopher Marlowe*
All I really need to know I learned
in Kindergarten ....*Robert Fulghum*
In Chicago, not too many dead people vote in the
elections anymore .... *Mayor Richard Daley*

W 039
I cannot tell a lie...*George Washington*
I am not a crook...*Richard Nixon*
Here's my list of enemies.................................. *Richard M. Nixon*
Here's my list...*Trumpski*

W 040
That's Life... *Sinatra*
Life is nasty, brutish, and short .... *Thomas Hobbes*
Life's just a bowl of cherries....................................*Zachary Taylor*
Life is like a box of chocolates .... *Forrest Gump*
Life is like a river..*Atticus Finch*

Life is but a dream..*Rip van Winkle*
Can't buy me love............................*John, Paul, Ringo, & George*
I am proof that you can't buy friendship ....*Doris Duke*
This poor little rich girl has nothing left ....*Barbara Hutton*

W 041

THE ECONOMY

The economy is sound .... *Herbert Hoover*
Very soon, the stock market will crash. And I'm not called the
Great Bear of Wall Street for nothing.................*Roger W. Babson*
Most didn't survive The Crash and
lost everything..*John Pierpont Morgan*
The economy is sound. It would take a genius to
bring it down... *Richard Nixon*
Are you sure we've never met before? ....*Donald Trump*

W 042

Nobody is richer than I am ....*King Croesus of Lydia*
Living well is the best revenge.............................*George Herbert*
Better to live rich than to die rich ....*Samuel Johnson*
The man who dies rich dies disgraced ....*Andrew Carnegie*
I bought a lot of stuff I didn't need, nothing is left........*Mike Tyson*
I spent all my prize money and
I've got 11 kids to support ....*Evander Holyfield*
I spent all my money and
didn't pay any taxes ....*Floyd Mayweather*
The IRS took all the money I had and nothing was left...........*Joe
Louis*

W 043

On Broadway ....*George Benson*
It's Showtime folks...*Joe Gideon*
It's Showtime...*Betelgeuse*

W 044

Up, up, and away in my beautiful balloon ....*Montgolfier*
Come fly with me... *Sinatra*
I'm leaving on a jet plane.....................................*Mary Travers*

W 045

OF LABOR AND UNIONS

Coal miners put down your shovels ....*John L. Lewis*
Truck drivers park your trucks................................ *Jimmy Hoffa*
Auto workers unite.. *Walter Reuther*
My Pinkerton goons will break this strike .... *Henry Ford*
Read my new book "*Grapes of Wrath*"................*John Steinbeck*
Huelga, farm workers unite...................................*Caesar Chaves*

W 046

SOME FAMOUS & INFAMOUS PRESIDENTS

I studied dramatics under MacArthur .... *Dwight D. Eisenhower*
Burn the tapes. Your President
is not a crook.. *Richard M. Nixon*
There is no country today in Eastern Europe
under Communist rule .... *Gerald Ford*
Jerry Ford can't chew gum
and fart at the same time............................*Lyndon B. Johnson*
Human rights! .... *Jimmy Carter*
I'm the best President there ever was. And they won't let me
alone. Fake news, fake news, witch hunt. Let me alone.
I never met Stormy Daniels.. *D. Trump*

W 047

WALKING IN A WINTER WONDERLAND

Jack Frost's a-roasting on an open fire.
Frosty's melting near the pyre............................... *Nat King Cole*
Sleigh bells are a-ringing, and are you a-listening? In the lane
the snowploughs are glistening, while we're freezing in the winter
wonderland..*Richard Smith &*
Felix Bernard Jr.

X 001

BASEBALL NOTABLES & RECORDS

Did Americans actually pay adults to play a game
of rounders and name a team after me?.......... *The Artful Dodger*
Did I really invent baseball? ....*Abner Doubleday*
Baseball is sublime.. *Walt Whitman*

I filmed the best baseball TV series in history.............*Ken Burns*

X 002
Play them minor leaguers? Never! ....*John McGraw*
Nice guys finish last ....*Leo the Lip*
The Prez didn't have as good a year as I did................ *The Babe*
I am the father of Sabermetrics and Money Ball.......... *Bill James*
Take me out to the ball game.................................... *Harry Caray*

X 003
THE FIRST WORLD SERIES
Me and my Providence Grays won the 1884 World Series
against the New York Mets in a brand-new ballpark that
stunk (it was built on top of a large Manhattan
garbage dump)...*Ole Hoss Radbourne*

X 004
I made the lords of baseball change the rules in 1877 for my fair-
foul bunt play, which wore down the pitchers, and then I would
hit away.. *Ross Barnes*

X 005
Anyone in here want to play some cards?.....*Christie Mathewson*
Not in my club house you don't .... *Connie Mack*
First in war, first in peace, and last in
the American League .... *Charles Drydan*
Wrong, we won the American League
pennant twice...................................... *Walter "Big Train" Johnson*

X 006
Watch out Dutchman, I'm coming down .... *Ty Cobb*
Watch your nose, Cracker.....................................*Honus Wagner*
Hit 'em where they ain't.................................*Wee Willie Keeler*
What has _____ _____ and chases flies?.....................*Max Patkin*
Who's on first? ....*Abbot and Costello*
Best double play combo in baseball .... *Tinker, to Never,*
to Last Chance

X 007

EARLY & LATER BATTING AVERAGES
I hit four twenty-six in 1901 .... *Napoleon Lajoie (Lazh-a-way)*
Four twenty-four in 1924 .... *Rogers Hornsby for the Cardinals*
Four twenty in 1922 .... *George Sisler for the Browns*
Four twenty in 1911 .... *Ty Cobb of the Tigers*
Four oh eight in 1911 .... *Joe Jackson*

X 008

CHICAGO BLACK SOX
They say I set up the bribes for the
Black Sox .... *Chick Gandil (1b)*
They say I took a bribe in the
1919 World Series .... *Eddie Cicotte (p)*
I didn't take any bribe money,
but I didn't report it .... *Buck Weaver (3b)*
Did the Reds actually win
the World Series? .... *Only the Shadow knows*
Yes, they did, and we got paid for it .... *Eight Men Out*

X 009

It ain't so, kid .... *Shoeless Joe*
Best damn team I ever had .... *Kid Gleason*
Yer all out, all eight of you .... *Kenesaw Mountain Landis*
So long, suckers .... *Arnold Rothstein*
What happened to my White Sox? .... *Charlie Comiskey*

X 010

BATTING AVERAGE IN ONE RECENT SEASON
Four oh seven in 1941 .... *Ted "The Splinter" Williams*
Three ninety in 1980 .... *George Brett*
Three ninety-four in 1994 .... *Tony Gwynn*

X 011

HOMERS IN ONE SEASON

Sixty-one in 1961*, and I hate that damn asterisk..... *Roger Maris*

Sixty in 1927 ....*Babe Ruth*

I hit eleven in 1911 .... *Home Run Baker*

I hit four in 1917 ....*Jim Thorpe*

Fifty-eight in 1938.. *Hank Greenberg*

Seventy in 1998**...*Mark McGwire*

Fifty-eight in 1932..*Jimmie Foxx*

Seventy-three in 2001** .... *Barry Bonds*

Fifty-six in 1930..*Hack Wilson*

Fifty-four in 1961 .... *Mickey Mantle*

Fifty-one in 1956 ....*Willy Mays*

***Steroid era*

X 012

CAREER HOME RUNS

Five hundred and eleven...*Mel Ott*

Seven hundred and 55...*Hank Aaron*

Seven hundred and 62** .... *Barry Bonds*

Over eight hundred ....*Josh Gibson*

I hit eight hundred and 68......................................*Sadaharu Oh*

Seven hundred and 14 ....*Babe Ruth*

Six hundred and 96 .... *A-Rod Rodriguez*

Six hundred and 9** ....*Sammy Sosa*

Six hundred and 30 ....*Ken Griffey Jr.*

*** Steroid era*

X 013

EARLIER SEASONS PITCHING WINS

Thirty-five in 1895..*Cy Young*

Thirty-three in 1917 ....*Eddie Cicotte*

Thirty wins in 1934 .... *Dizzy Dean*

Thirty-one in 1931 .... *Lefty Grove*

Fifty-nine in 1884... *Ole Hoss Radburn*

Thirty-six in 1913...*Walter Johnson*

Thirty-seven in 1908......................................*Christie Mathewson*

Thirty-one in 1933.. *Satchel Paige*
Thirty-five in 1904 ....*Joe McGinnity*
Thirty-three in 1916.........................*Grover Cleveland Alexander*

X 014

MORE PITCHING WINS PER SEASON

Thirty-four in 1912 .... *Smoky Joe Wood*
Twenty-eight 1948-65... *Satchel Paige*
Thirty in 1891..*Kid Gleason*
Twenty-four in 1898.. *Clark Griffith*
Twenty-nine in 1908 ....*Mordecai Brown*
Twenty-eight in 1952 ....*Robin Roberts*
Twenty-seven in 1940... *Bob Feller*
Twenty-seven in 1966.. *Sandy Koufax*
Twenty-seven in 1956...*Don Newcombe*
Twenty-six in 1968...*Juan Marachal*
Twenty-five in in 1969.. *Tom Seaver*
Twenty-four in 1971 .... *Vida Blue*

X 015

Twenty-four in 1972... *Gaylord Perry*
Twenty-three in 1975...*Catfish Hunter*
Twenty-four in 1986...*Roger Clemens*
Twenty-three in 1988 .... *Oral Hershiser*
Twenty-four in 1917 .... *Babe Ruth*
Twenty-three in 1933...*Carl Hubbell*
Twenty-four in 1963 .... *Whitey Ford*
Twenty-three in 1950 .... *Bob Lemon*
Twenty-two in 2002..*Randy Johnson*
Twenty-three in 1953 .... *Warren Spahn*
Twenty-four in 1996 ....*John Smolz*
Twenty-one in 1988 ....*Dave Stewart*
Twenty-three in 1970 ....*Bob Gibson*
Twenty in 1978 ....*Dennis Eckersley*

X 016

PERFECT GAMES

In 1904, I pitched one for the Red Sox
against the Athletics .... Cy Young
In 1956, I pitched one for the Yankees
against the Dodgers .... Don Larson
In 1964, I pitched one for the Phillies
against the Mets... Jim Bunning
In 1965, I pitched one for the Dodgers
against the White Sox ....Sandy Koufax
In 1968, I pitched one for the A's
against the Twins .... Catfish Hunter
In 2004, I pitched one for Phoenix
against the Braves .... Randy Johnson
In 2012, I pitched one for the Mariners
against the Rays ....Felix Hernandez

X 017

Am I really the luckiest man in the world?................... Lou Gehrig
I like the night life in New York, more beer ....Babe Ruth
So do I, another beer .... Mickey Mantle
So did I, and much more beer .... Grover C. Alexander

X 018

Before the AL voted in the designated hitter rule in 1973, I was
once a designated player for the
St. Louis Browns in 1951...................................... Eddie Gaedel
We won the 1954 American League pennant with 111 wins, the
highest ever. Then we got shut out in the series in
four games by the Giants ....Al Lopez
Poor Al .... Peter Lorre

X 019

Fifty-six straight hits in 1941, and how do I look? ....Joltin Joe
Where have you gone, Joe Dimaggio?........... Simon & Garfunkel
I gave a lot of batters some friendly
crew-cuts.. Sal "the Barber" Maglie
Don't look back, someone might be gaining

on you .... *Satchel Paige*
I was Gato Grande at Mile High......................*Andreas Gallaraga*

X 020
We finally beat the Yankees in the World Series
at Ebbets Field...*Roy Campanella*
Life isn't a spectator sport................................... *Jackie Robinson*
I don't make history, I catch fly balls........................... *Willie Mays*

X 021
CAREER HOME RUNS PER TEAM
I hit 376 homers for the Cardinals...............*Stan "the Man" Musial*
I hit a total of 369 homers for the Pirates ....*Ralph Kiner*
I hit 331 homers for the Tigers .... *Hank Greenburg*
I hit 289 for the Dodgers ....*Duke Snider*

X 022
I hit 493 homers for the Braves...........................*Eddie Mathews*
I hit 733 homers for the Braves................................. *Hank Aaron*
I hit 252 homers for the Mets ....*Darryl Strawberry*
I hit 317 homers for Kansas City.............................. *George Brett*

X 023
I hit a career total of 251 for the Reds..................*Ted Kluszewski*
Eighty-seven homers for the Red Sox ....*Dom Dimaggio*
I hit a few for the Kansas City Monarchs.....................*Buck O'Niel*
I was faster than a speeding bullet........................*Cool Papa Bell*

X 024
I hit 230 homers for the Brewers........................... *Prince Fielder*
I hit 475 for the Pirates...*Willy Stargell*
I hit 369 homers for the Rockies .... *Todd Helton*
I hit 361 for the Dodgers .... *Gill Hodges*

X 025
I hit 563 home runs for the Athletics
and the Yankees...*Reggie Jackson*
I hit 548 homers for the Phillies.............................. *Mike Schmidt*

I hit 469 for the Giants.. *Willie McCovey*
I hit 431 for the Orioles.. *Cal Ripken Jr.*

X 026

MORE CAREER HOMERS PER HOME TEAM

I hit 659 homers for the Yankees................ *George Herman Ruth*
I hit 536 homers for the Yankees........................... *Mickey Mantle*
I hit 493 homers for the Yanks...................................... *Lou Gehrig*
I hit 452 homers for the Red Sox................... *Carl Yastrzemenski*
I hit 361 homers for the Yankees............................ *Joe Dimaggio*

X 027

I hit 583 homers for Oakland and St. Louis. I also took lots of
"vitamin supplements" while there .... *Mark McGwire*
I hit 559 for Minneapolis / Saint Paul .... *Harmon Killebrew*
I hit 399 homers for the Tigers... *Al Kaline*
I hit 358 homers for the Yanks.................................... *Yogi Berra*

X 028

STEROID ERA*

We all used steroids that enhanced our
playing statistics..........................*Jose Canseco*, Sammy Sosa*,*
Mark McGwire, Barry Bonds*, Roger Clemens*, and more....*

X 029

I'm not building you guys a new stadium in NY.......*Robert Moses*
Then I will take the Giants to San Francisco.... *Horace Stoneham*
And I'll take the Dodgers to Los Angeles............. *Walter O'Malley*
And we did much better in California
and got our stadiums.............................. *Stoneham & O'Malley*
Before Candlestick Park, there was
Seals Stadium...................................... *San Francisco Examiner*
Before Dodger Stadium and the baseball configuration of the
Coliseum, there was Gilmore Stadium
in Hollywood..*LA Daily News*
Before Anaheim Stadium, there was Wrigley Field south of
downtown LA .... *Los Angeles Times*
Before Mile High and Coors Stadium, there was

Bears' Stadium .... *The Rocky Mountain News*

X 030
I moved the Browns to Baltimore ....*Clarence Miles*
I took the Senators to Minneapolis-St. Paul .... *Clark Griffith*
I took the Braves to Milwaukee .... *Lou Perini*
I took the Braves to Atlanta...........................*William Bartholomay*
Before the Braves, was
Ponce de Leon Park ....*Atlanta Journal-Constitution*
I moved the A's to Kansas City ....*Arnold Johnson*
I took the Athletics to Oakland ....*Charles Finley*
I moved the new Senators to Dallas .... *Bob Short*
We moved the Expos to Washington DC .... *Bud Selig & MLB*
Before the Mariners was Sicks Stadium..................*Seattle Times*

X 031
The Browns finally won the AL Pennant in 1944 .... *St. Louis Post Dispatch*

The Indians finally won the
World Series... *Cleveland Plain Dealer*
The LA Dodgers won their first
World Series... *Los Angeles Times*
The A's won three straight World Series titles.... *Oakland Tribune*
The Mets finally won the World Series...........................*NY Times*

X 032
The Marlins won the World Series twice .... *Miami Herald*
The Cubs finally won the World Series .... *Chicago Tribune*
The A's won the Earthquake Series.................... *Oakland Tribune*

X 033
The earthquake series matched up the Oakland A's against the
Giants at Candlestick. The series was postponed on account of
an earthquake. Everyone in the stands cheered, and then we
went on to win that World Series...........*Dave & Ricky Henderson*
There was a whole lotta shakin' goin' on.................. *Elvis Presley*

X 034

The Rockies finally won the NL Pennant .... *Denver Post*
The Astros finally won the World Series .... *Houston Chronicle*
The SFO Giants finally won the World Series........ *San Francisco Chronicle*
The Diamondbacks win the World Series .... *Arizona Republic*

X 035

BASEBALL INJURIES
Beware the spit ball and the bean ball .... *Ted Williams, Ralph Kiner, Mickey Mantle*
I won thirty-four games in 1912, but then I fell and broke my thumb while chasing a bunted ball, and I never pitched again .... *Smoky Joe Wood*
I got hit in the face by a line drive, and I never pitched again as well .... *Herb Score*
I once hit a 500-foot home run. It was the longest home run ever over the right field fence at Seals Stadium in SFO .... *George "Ox" Eckhardt*
I also once missed a fly ball in the outfield, and it hit me on the top of my head and nearly knocked me out .... *Ox Eckhardt*

X 036

The doctor will see you now, Mr. Ox .... *Dr. Ruth*
The top of my head hurts when I blow my nose........ *Ox Eckhardt*
Take two aspirins and call me in the morning .... *Dr. Welby*
Plop plop fizz fizz, oh what a relief it is .... *The Ox*
No, it looks to me kind of like a gunshot wound .... *Doc Adams*

X 037

Wait a minute, it looks like his skull is fractured .... *Dr. Kildare*
OK, let's crack this guy's head open and see what's in there .... *Trapper John, M.D.*
If you need representation, here's my card .... *Melvin Belli, LL.B*
Here's something to really make his pain go away .... *Dr. Kevorkian*
That won't be necessary .... *Sanjay Gupta, M.D.*

X 038
Any questions after surgery? I'm your health and wellness
consultant. Does your scalp still hurt
when you blow your nose? ....*Dr. Oz*
Here's a list of foods and recovery pills you
can buy from me..*Dr. Mercola*
Tell me, Mr. Ox, what do you feel about that ball hitting you
on your head?..*Dr. Phil*
Nah, you're all wrong. Ox has a tapeworm near his
medusa oblongata and it's probably been there for
years. Now get me some coffee..........................*Dr. House, M.D.*
Get it yourself. I'm a doctor, not a busboy................... *Dr. McCoy*

X 039
The truth is that the mighty Casey actually didn't strike out.
He hit a double, and the Stockton Nine won the game.....*Earnest
Thayer*
Come to my baseball saloon on Geary Street in
San Francisco..*Lefty O'Doul*
A Giants gift shop has been added to Lefty's
restaurant ....*Lefty's sous chef*
Come to our Edinburgh Castle Scottish pub
on Geary Street ....*Clan Francisco*

X 040
Come see my seafood grotto at Fisherman's
Wharf in SFO..*Joe DiMaggio*
Come and see my baseball saloon overlooking
the Chicago River..*Harry Cary*
Come see my Darryl Strawberry's Sport's Bar
and Grill in Queens..*Darryl Strawberry*
Come to my Orioles BBQ restaurant in
Ocean City.. *Boog Powell*
Come to one of my Bronco steak houses
in Denver.. *John Elway*

X 041
I quit because I was too fat and couldn't run the

bases anymore..*Babe Ruth*
I had to quit because I couldn't be Joe Dimaggio
anymore ....*Joe Dimaggio*
And I quit because I couldn't play first base anymore and
because I couldn't hit anymore.................................*Lou Gehrig*
I had to quit because of a poison gas episode
in France during the Great War ....*Christie Mathewson*

X 042
The Dodgers could come back and live on as the Brooklyn
Cyclones at Coney Island, where everyone eats lots of my
famous hot dogs... *Nathan Handwerker*
In 2018, I won the third straight Nathan's hot dog
eating contest by eating 74 of them in ten minutes
(a world record)..*Joey Chestnut*

X 043
GOLF NOTABLES
The golf swing is the most complex muscle
action on earth .... *Bobby Jones*
Golf is the most relaxing thing I know........*Dwight D. Eisenhower*
The more I practice, the luckier I get .... *Gary Player*
When I couldn't run track any more,
I took up golf ....*Babe Didrikson*
Come to my golf restaurant in La Quinta, California .... *Arnold
Palmer*
I played best when I had no money in my pockets ....*Lee Trevino*

X 044
The income tax has made more
Americans liars than golf...*Will Rogers*
Jeramiah was a bullfrog, he was a friend of mine ....*Three Dog
Night*
I was a pretty fair golfer in my day.....................*Kathryn Hepburn*
Golf is a contact sport...*Tiger Woods*
My lawsuit against the PGA is finally over ....*Vijay Singh*

X 045

TENNIS NOTABLES

I won the amateur Tennis Championship
at Wimbledon... *Helen Wills*
I love Wimbledon ....*Helen Jacobs*
Clean underwear is the most important thing......... *Gussie Moran*
I beat Bobby Riggs ....*Billie Jean King*
I was once a pretty good tennis player...................... *Arthur Ashe*
Game, Set, Match................................ *Serena & Venus Williams*

X 046

SOCCER NOTABLES

Two or three goals at every match in Brazil
and New York...*Pelé Santos*
I love Manchester, Madrid, Paris, Los Angeles,
and Posh Spice .... *David Beckham*

X 047

BASKETBALL STARS

Love them Phillips 66ers......................................*Vernon Vaughn*
Love them New York Rens ....*Robert Douglas*
I loved being one of the Harlem Globetrotters.........*Goose Tatum*
Me too, and I made money doing it............... *Meadowlark Lemon*
Love them Lakers .... *George Mikan*

X 048

I played with the Celtics for thirteen years.................. *Bill Russell*
Basketball is a contact sport .... *Wilt Chamberlain*
Air Jordan .... *Michael Jordan*
Slam Dunk.. *Magic Johnson*
I played with Indiana State and the Celtics ....*Larry Bird*
Best point guard for WSU and the Portland
Trailblazers..*Damian Lillard*

Y 001

BEST COLLEGE FOOTBALL COACHES

I coached football at Notre Dame for many years. Then
Hollywood hired me to supervise some of their

football movies .... *Knute Rockne*
I coached the Oklahoma Sooners to three national
championships .... *Bud Wilkinson*
I also coached the Sooners to three national
championships .... *Barry Switzer*

Y 002
I coached nationally top-ranked Penn State to two national
champs .... *Joe Paterno*
My Ohio State Buckeyes won five national
championships .... *Woody Hayes*
My Gators and my Buckeyes both won national
championships .... *Urban Meyer*
I led the Alabama Crimson Tide to five national
 championships .... *Nick Saban*
I led the USAFA Falcons in their first three years
(18 wins) .... *Buck Shaw*
I led the University of Southern California to three national
champs .... *John McKay*

Y 003
WORLD HEAVYWEIGHT BOXING CHAMPIONS
I can lick any man in the bar .... *John L. Sullivan*
He knocked me out of the ring for a few seconds .... *Jack Dempsey*
I took the title away from Jack Dempsey in 1926 .... *Gene Tunney*
I'm told I was the best defensive boxer in history .... *Jack Johnson*
I went fifteen rounds with the Dancing Baer ...... *Jimmy Braddock*

Y 004
My opponents can run but they can't hide .... *Joe Louis*
I like to look at comic books because I can't read ..... *Joe Palooka*
Income tax? What the hell is that? .... *Joe Louis*
Float like a butterfly, sting like a bee .... *Mohammed Ali*
I was the first one in recent years to get the second
heavyweight title back .... *Floyd Patterson*

Y 005

He bit my ear off .... *Evander Holyfield*
Undefeated! .... *Rocky Marciano*
I KO'd Michael Spinks with one punch .... *Mike Tyson*
Somebody down there don't like me .... *Rocky Grazziano*
In our first title bout, I hit Sonny Liston so hard, he
wouldn't get off his stool for the next round. Then he
took a dive in the rematch .... *Cassius Clay*
I'm not going to any ^#@x* Vietnam. No Viet Cong ever
called me a nigger .... *Mohammed Ali*
I was Mohammed Ali's favorite news reporter .... *Howard Cosell*
I coulda been a contender .... *Brando (In: "On the Waterfront")*

Y 006

HEAVYWEIGHT BOXING CHAMPS FROM EUROPE
I was the European heavyweight champ from
1922 to 1924 .... *Georges Carpentier*
I won the heavyweight championship in 1930 ...... *Max Schmeling*
I caught Patterson with my Toonderbolt .... *Ingmar Johansson*
We won two world heavyweight titles for
Russia in 2004 and 2009 .... *The Klitschkos*

Y 007

NEW YORK SONGS & SAYINGS
East side, west side, all around the town, boys and girls together
on the sidewalks of New York .... *Charles B. Lawler*
New York is my kind of town .... *Fanny Brice*
New York, New York. If I make it here I
can make it anywhere .... *Kander & Ebb*
On Broadway .... *George Benson*

Y 008

Everyone in New York is Jewish,
whether they're Jewish or not .... *Marx Bros.*
Everyone in America is English,
whether they're English or not .... *HME*
Everyone in Utah is Mormon,
whether they're Mormons or not .... *Gov. Gary Herbert*

Y 009

SONGS ABOUT CITIES

Chicago, Chicago, that toddlin' town .... *Frank Sinatra*
Do you know the way to San Jose?.................... *Dionne Warwick*
By the time I get to Phoenix, I'll be sleeping .... *Glenn Campbell*
Man on the Run...*Little River Band*
And then they caught me down in
Juarez, Mexico.. *Johnny Cash*
Gary Indiana, Gary Indiana .... *Ron Howard*

Y 010

Meet me in St. Louie, Louie, meet me at the fair .....*Judy Garland*
Hello Buenos Aires...
What's new in Buenos Aires?........................... *Madonna as Evita*
We got trouble right here in River City,
and it's called pool..*Professor Hill*
I'm mad as hell and I'm not going to take it anymore .... *Albert
Finney*
Neither am I ... #@!%*|\\!#................................. *Iliza Schlesinger*

Y 011

BOREDOM

The Book of Mormon is chloroform in print and
the world's best antidote for insomnia....................... *Mark Twain*
Boredom is the awareness of time passing .... *Heidegger*
I am leaving this world because I am bored........*George Sanders*
Never be bored .... *The Boz*
The two antagonists of happiness are
pain and boredom .... *Shopenhauer*

Y 012

OBSCURE EXPLETIVES

Fee fi fo fum...*Hungry Giant*
Nemesis of all evil .... *Biff Baxter*
Ho, ho, ho .... *Green Giant*
Dum de Dum Dum ....*Dragnet*
Shazam...*Capt. Marvel*

Dit dit dit dah..*Beethoven's 5th*
Up, up, and away..*Superman*
Up Thine..*William Penn*

Y 013
ROADS & HIGHWAYS
Hit the road Jack, and don't you come back no more,
no more, no more, no more .... *The Raylettes*
What'd you say? ....*Ray Charles*
Road trip!.. *Otter & Boone*
Let's roll .... *Thelma and Louise*
And away we go .... *Jackie Gleason*

Y 014
OK, we're off to see the Lizard...*Dorothy*
Follow the yellow brick road............ *Head Munchkin (Jerry Mare)*
Tiptoe through the tulips .... *Tiny Tim & Peewee Herman*
Take the fork in the road.......................*Lawrence P. "Yogi" Berra*
Travels with Charley .... *John Steinbeck*

Y 015
Happy trails to you... *Roy Rogers*
Back in the saddle again... *Gene Autry*
On the road ....*Jack Kerouac*
On the commode again ....*Willy Nelson*

Y 016
This ain't the place..*Brigham Young*
Oh, when the Saints go marching out .... *Louis Armstrong*
Did Brigham Young really say that?..........................*Mark Russell*
All comedians are un-equal .... *Bertrand Russell*

Y 017
COUNTER CULTURAL NOTABLES FROM THE 1950s
I saw the best minds of my generation destroyed by
madness and starvation.......................................*Allan Ginsberg*
I saw the best root vegetables of my generation
plucked from the soil by evil machinery..................*The Beet Poet*

All of you mugs got plenty of bugs,
ain't got no bugs on me .... *Jerry Garcia*
Come to SFO and catch my act at the Bagel Shop
in North Beach .... *Lenny Bruce*
Come and read some books in my
basement bookstore .... *Ferlengetti*

Y 018
EARLY NINETEEN SIXTIES
We started out as the Quarrymen in Liverpool .... *The Beatles*
This is the Dawning of the
Age of Aquarius.. *The Fifth Dimension*
Break on through to the other side .... *Jim Morrison*
Tune in, turn on, drop dead .... *Timothy Leary*
I'm not trying to seduce you, Benjamin .... *Mrs. Robinson*
God bless you please, Mrs. Robinson .... *Simon & Garfunkel*

Y 019
How many times a must a man walk down before they can call
him a man? The answer my friend is blowing in the wind, the
answer is blowing in the wind......................... *Peter, Paul, & Mary*

Y 020
LATER IN THE 1960s
Where have all the flowers gone? .... *Peter Yarrow,*
Paul Stookey, & Mary Travers
Under the Boardwalk.................................... *The Motown Drifters*
The Queen of England is visiting San Francisco. Just what we
don't need: another queen .... *Mayor Joseph Alioto*
Come see my gay bar in San Fransisco................ *Quenton Crisp*
Is my proclamation good for another pint or two? .... *Emperor*
Norton

Y 021
ANIMAL HOUSE
What's the worst fraternity on campus? The one that
delivered a cadaver to the faculty luncheon?.......... *Dean Wormer*
Do you still want to show me your cucumber?......... *Mrs. Wormer*

Mrs. Wormer will be vacationing in Sarasota .... *Daily Faberian*
Louie, Louie.. *The Kingsmen*
Guess what I am now? .... *Bluto of the Omegas*
Food Fight! .... *In the Faber College Cafeteria*

Y 022
Toga, Toga, Toga ....*Bluto Blutarski*
You make me wanna dance,
you make me wanna shout..*Otis Day*
A little bit softer now....
A little bit louder now............................. *Otis Day and the Knights*
We're gonna to rock around the clock tonight .... *Bill Haley*
Lamma Lamma Ding Dong .... *Otis and the others*

Y 023
GRASS
Grass is good .... *Nebuchadnezzar*
Grass is very good.. *Cheech & Chong*
Guinness is good for you .... *Sir Edward Guinness*
Ganja is good for you.............................*Haile Selassie Rastafari*
Jah lives cause ganja .... *Bob Marley*

Y 024
Rocky Mountain high .... *Bob Denver*
Puff the Magic Dragon ....*Peter, Paul, & Mary*
Our new football field is covered
with Idaho Bluegrass ....*Boise State groundskeeper*

Y 025
And then she said, "On 34th and Vine,
all you need is Love Potion Number Nine." .... *The Clovers*
The High and the Mighty....................................*Dimitry Tiomkin*
Born to be wild...*Steppenwolf*
All you need is love.. *The Beetles*
Come on Baby, light my fire................ *Jim Morrison & The Doors*

Y 026
CAMPUS UNREST IN THE MID 1960's
Hey Hey, Ho, Ho,
Vietnam has got to go ....*1960s Campus Revolutionaries*
Come on down to my Straight Theatre
on Haight Street .... *Gene Williams (BHS)*
There will be no more loud speakers, bullhorns,
rioting, arson, hoe downs, sit-ins, or
shivarees on my campus......................................*S.I. Hayakawa*

Y 027
Higher education is ever-changing. Sometimes you
need to be Mother Theresa and sometimes you
need to be Dirty Harry ....*Dr. Clark Kerr*
Oh, you're from the 60s.
Peace, Love, Dope. Get outta here! ....*James Earl Jones*

Y 028
What did you mean when you e-mailed me a message saying,
"Is Jumping Jack Flash a gas gas gas?"......... *Whoopie Goldberg*
I don't get no satisfaction...*Mick Jagger*
You're so vain .... *Carly Simon*

Y 029
GUNS IN TOWNS
Don't bring your guns to town..................................... *Virgil Earp*
But all god's chilluns gots to have some guns ... *Smith & Wesson*
From my cold dead hand!..............*Charlton "Shootemup" Heston*
But guns are good for everyone ..... *Remington, Browning, & Colt*
Charlton Heston's movies are no longer in demand. They
couldn't get the gun from his cold dead hand .... *Jim Carrey*

Y 030
A JELLY DONUT?
IN YOUR F...ING FOOT LOCKER? ....*Sgt. R. Lee Ermy*
Show me your war face!!............... *USMC Drill Instructor Hartman*
Get your sorry fat ass
off my obstacle!................................. *Gunnery Sgt. Lee Hartman*

You slapped a fly on your face?
Let's go find it .... *DI Gunnery Sgt. Jack Webb*
I am not a conniving worthless
USAF master sergeant .... *Sergeant Bilko*

Y 031
In like Flynn .... *Russell Mulcahy*
In like Beckham .... *Los Angeles Times*
In like Flynt .... *James Coburn*
In & Out Burgers .... *Harry & Esther Snyder*

Y 032
Beware the Gremlins from the Kremlin .... *Thomas Dewey*
Extremism is no vice, and I am not insane .... *Barry Goldwater*
The California state budget has been looted
by the Democrats .... *Ronald Reagan*
Hey, c'mon Ron, the election's over .... *Jeth Unruh*
Beware the House Un-American Intelligence Committee .... *Joe*
McCarthy

Y 033
ASTRONAUTS
Who's the greatest pilot you ever saw? .... *Gordo Cooper*
Anyone going up in that thing is just
spam in a can .... *Chuck Yeager*
I've got a full bladder and I'm not afraid to use it .... *Hugh Laurie*
First American into outer space .... *John Glenn*
Who says we never landed on the Moon? .... *Neil Armstrong*
Sorry I couldn't make it, guys .... *Gus Grissom*

Y 034
Beware the Frozen Chosen .... *GI combat troops in Korea*
Beware the military industrial complex .... *Eisenhower*
Beware the Ghost Riders in the Sky .... *Riders of the Purple Sage*

Y 035
Beware the Satanic Verses .... *Salman Rushdie*
Beware my fatwas .... *Ayatolla Khomeini*

Beware our demolition squad
zeroing in on evil-doers ....*Navy Seals (PB&J)*

Y 036
ENTERTAINERS ON THE EDGE
Like a virgin...*Madonna*
Like a sturgeon........................... *Weird Al Yankovic*
Wake me up when it's time to hatch this egg.............. *Lady Gaga*
Welcome to Lower Slobovia...*Al Capp*
To most of you, I'm an atheist.
But to God, I'm the loyal opposition..........................*Woody Allen*

Y 037
EXCELLENT ENTERTAINERS
What a country. In America, you can always find a party.
In Russia, Party always finds you........................*Yakov Smirnoff*
I love New York: it's theatres, it's speakeasies,
it's hookers..*Mayor Jimmy Walker*
The sounds of silence are written on the
subway walls.. *Simon & Garfunkel*
Joy to the fishes in the deep blue sea,
joy to you and me..*Three Dog Night*
Will you still need me, will you still feed me
when I'm 65?..*The Beatles*
If not, then the Candyman can ....*Sammy Davis Jr.*

Y 038
ICONIC TUNES
When you wish upon a star, it doesn't
matter who you are ....*Walt Disney*
I'd like to teach the world to sing
in perfect harmony .... *Billy Davis*
Like a limestone cowboy .... *Glenn Campbell*
Like that'll be the day...*Buddy Holly*
Danke Schoen ....*Wayne Newton*
Hey, Macarena... *The Los del Rio*
Ommmmmmm ....*Don Draper (in the last episode)*

Y 039
MANY, MANY, MANY

Hundred and hundreds .... *Henry Ford*
Thousands and thousands...*Ray Kroc*
Millions and millions................................... *John D. Rockefeller*
Billions and billions .... *Carl Sagan*
Trillions and trillions .... *Warren Buffet*
Oodles of Googles.. *Ronald Graham*
Gazillions & gazillions ....*Aristotle Onassis*
Parsecs and Parsecs....................................... *James T. Kirk*

Z 001

Baby, the rain must fall ....*Glen Yarborough & Steve McQueen*
I like piña coladas and walkin' in the rain ....*Jimmy Buffett*
Drinking Rum and Coca Cola,
workin for da Yanqui dollah.................................*Andrews Sisters*
That new guy isn't interesting. I'm still the world's
most interesting man of all.
Stay thirsty, my friends. ....*Johnathon Goldsmith*
Tequila... *The Flores Trio*

Z 002
INFAMOUS SOUNDS

Roar grrr..rr snort..................................... *Leo the MGM Lion*
Aaa-ah-ah-aaa!... *Tarzan*
Great balls of fire .... *Jerry Lee Lewis*
Para bailar a la la Bamba ....*Ritchie Valens*
Hoo Ahh ....*Al Pacino (In: "Scent of a Woman")*
Arff...*Annie's dog, Sandy*

Z 003
ICONIC INITIALS

National League .... *NL*
British Broadcasting Corp. .... *BBC*
American Legion .... *AL*
United Press International .... *UPI*
Associated Press .... *AP*
Worst city on Earth for s__t on the sidewalks .... *SFO*
Lights out .... *KO*
Brexit .... *OUT*
French Foreign Legion .... *LE*
Bad people .... *KKK*

Z 004
MORE INITIALS

China, Burma, India .... *CBI*
Flying Tigers (Fei Ho) .... *FLT*
Grand Army of the Republic .... *GAR*
British European Airlines .... *BEA*
Union of Confederate Veterans .... *UCV*
The Flying Dutchman .... *KLM*
Veterans of Foreign Wars .... *VFW*
The Royal Air Force .... *RAF*
Disabled Americans Veterans .... *DAV*
The Flying Chicken .... *KFC*
Expensive German car .... *BMW*
Cheaper German Car .... *VW*
Captured & survived .... *POW*
Much too much to process .... *ADD*
Skilled labor unions .... *AFL*
We have ignition .... *NASA*
Unskilled labor unions .... *CIO*
Industrial Workers of the World .... *IWW*
American Fed. of Teachers .... *AFT*
OD'd .... *RIP*

Z 005

MEDIA NOTABLES

Oh, there's rioting in Africa and there's strife in Iran. The French
hate the British, and the Brits hate Sudan.
And we don't like anybody very much............. *The Kingston Trio*
This is the city. Everyone who lives here must play by
the rules. When they don't, then that's when I
go to work. I'm a cop.. *Sgt. Joe Friday*
Tune in sometime to our famous copper
clapper routine...............................*Johnny Carson & Jack Webb*
Dos Equis my ass, I'm still the world's most
interesting man..*Jonathon Goldsmith*
We try to avoid seeing our homeless
encampments................................. *Mayor Jen Durkan of Seattle*

Z 006

We didn't need no welfare state, everybody pulled his weight,
those were the days...................................*Edith & Archie Bunker*
I can fly on forever................................... *The Music Box dancer*
The Lord of the Flies...*William Golding*
All God's chillins gots to have a gun................... *Smith & Wesson*
Nah, you'll shoot your eye out.................................... *Santa Claus*

Z 007

RICHARD NIXON

Dick Nixon has left a trail of s__t behind him so deep it can
fertilize the entire Sinai .... *General Taylor in*
"Good Morning Vietnam"
We're going to put Watergate behind us and get along with the
important business of America, like getting chiselers off the
welfare roles .... *Richard M. Nixon*

Z 008

Follow the money .... *Deep Throat*
This is my last news conference, and you won't have
Nixon to kick around anymore .... *Dick Nixon*
I was Deep Throat .... *W. Mark Felt*

Z 009

I don't know but I've been told
*>#*_* "*x*^*+@+^* %xz .... *Drill Sgt. Hartman's Boys*
Ho Chi Minh is a sonnuva bitch, he's got the clap
and the seven-year itch ....*Sgt. Hartman*
Pin silver wings upon his chest, make him
one of America's best...*Barry Sadler*
Too many years, too many tears .... *Vietnam War Vets*

Z 010

Stop calling me a Vietnam War draft dodger. A crooked
physician, fake bone spurs, and several thousand dollars will
work every time.. *Donald Trumpski*
The three of us joined the National Guard or ROTC to avoid
compulsory service in Vietnam...................... *J. Danforth Quayle,*
Bill Clinton, & George W. Bush

Z 011

TAX EVADERS

Only little people pay taxes .... *Leona Helmsley*
You, madam, are a feculent wretch.....................*James Michener*
I don't pay taxes either .... *Donald Trump*
You, sir, are a national disgrace ....*Truman Capote &*
Wm. C. Fields

Z 012

HIKERS & CONSERVATION WORKERS

I ran and jogged all the way from Alabama to the
Santa Monica Pier...*Forest Gump*
I never did get to hike that Appalachian Trail.............*Eliot Spitzer*
The John Muir hiking trail along the Sierras
is the best..*Yosemite Sam*
During the 1930s, we did a lot of conservation work
and built many of these wilderness trails
during the Depression .... *Youth Conservation Corps*

Z 013

OCEANIC FLOATING WEEDS

In the 1920s and 1930s, I was the first to study the
floating prairies made of different kinds of seaweed, ghost ships,
and downed airplanes, called the Sargasso Sea and
the Bermuda Triangle ....*William Beebe*

Z 014

OCEANIC FLOTSAM & JETSOM

Today, and for a decade or two in the middle of the Pacific
Ocean Gyre, there is another swirling vortex of over six
hundred thousand square miles made up of 1.8 trillion tiny
pieces and large chunks of non-biodegradable plastic objects,
packages, wrappers, containers, used condoms, and garbage
between Hawaii and California that is larger than Germany,
France, and Spain combined. And there are
also five more such patches, including oil spills around
the world... *P. Galey, M. Hood,*
L. Lebreton, et al.

Z 015

TRAITOROUS DOGS

I switched sides during the Revolution................. *Benedict Arnold*
In 1812, I became a man without a country .... *Philip Nolan*
I stayed in North Korea after the war .... *John Roedel Dunn*
We gave secret nuclear information to
the Soviets.. *Julius and*
Ethel Rosenberg
I joined the ISIS terrorists to fight against
America in Iraq ....*John Walker Lindh*

Z 016

INFAMOUS ABBREVIATIONS

All is deception *M16*

All are the walking dead ....*HIV*

All are gangs *M13*

All is news .... *BBC*

All is hidden... *NSA*

All is security .... *NSA*

All are spooks .... *KGB*

All is spying .... *CIA*

All is everywhere .... *FBI*

All is radio .... *RCA*

All are missing... *MIA*

All is driving..*DMV*

All is dilation & curettage .... *D&C*

All aren't coming back ....*KIA*

All is over ....*DOA*

All is disinformation .... *FOX*

All we saw, we saw the sea... *USN*

All is sign language ....*ASL*

All lights out... *KO*

All is sleep..ZZZ

All is unidentified .... *UFO*

All is underwear.. *BVD*

All is Bert & Ernie .... *B&E*

All is no more plumber's butt .... *DUL*

All is football..*NFL*

All is baseball ....*MLB*

All is basketball .... *NBA*

All is hockey.. *NHL*

Z 017

AMERICAN CITIES

Cheers...*BOS*
Beantown ....*BOS*
Da Big Move.. *LAX*
The Windy City .... *CHI*
Da Big Apple..*NYC*
Porkopolis.. *CIN*
The Forest City ....*CLE*
Tinseltown ....*HOL*

Z 018

The Silicon City... *SJC*
The Saintly City .... *SLC*
The Biggest Little City .... *RNO*
The Strip.. *LAS*
City of Brotherly Indifference............................ *PHL*
The Big Easy ....*NOL*
The Aloha City ....*HNL*
The Emerald City ....*SEA*
The Other Emerald City ....*PDX*
The Beer City...*STL*
The Oil City.. *OKC*
The Other Beer City .... *MKE*
The Other Oil City .... *TUL*
The Dry Heat City..*PHX*
The Biggest Oil City ....*HOU*
Motown..*DET*
The Seismic City..*SFO*
The Music City...*NAS*
The Old Steel City ....*PIT*
Big D ....*DAL*
The Insurance City .... *OMA*
The Hurricane City...*MIA*
The High & Dry City..*DEN*
The Glass City .... *TOL*
The Grass & Snow City .... *BOU*

Z 019

Petrified Forest.. Forest Lawn
Cave of the Winds... The Green Latrine
Quantico... USMC
Ft. Benning.. Infantry
Ft. Sill.. Artillery
Ft. Leavenworth .... Bad Apples
San Diego .... All the Ships
Ft. Knox .... All the Gold
The Pentagon .... All the Brass
Old Navy Yard... Brooklyn
Old Ebbets Field.. Brooklyn
The Tornado City .... Moore, OK

Z 020

MISCELLANEOUS INITIAL COMBOS

BnB .... Bed & Breakfast
B&F .... Back & Forth
I&O.. In & Out
B&W.. Bob & Weave
R&R .... Rest & Relaxing
B&T .... Block & Tackle
D&C .... Dusting & Cleaning
B&G .... Bump & Grind
BLT .... Bacon & Tomato
S&J .... Shuck & Jive
P&Q .... Peas & Queues
C&P .... Cut & Paste
W&D .... Wattle & Daub
S&A.. Shock & Awe
S&M .... Sad & Morose
C&B .... Crash & Burn

Z 021

AOK .... Time to Go
GI.. Gilligan's Isle
UFO .... Air Force One
TYT .... Young Turks

BOM ....Book of Monsters
T4T .... Tee Time
D&D...Down & Dirty
COLT 45.. Peacemaker
CIB .... Combat Infantry
P 51 ....The Mustang
SOB..Opponent's Lawyer
P 47 .... The Jug
P 38 .... Fork-Tailed Devil
B 29 .... Stratofortress
B 52 .... Old Buff
TDY .... Tedious Duty
BS .... Not True
PCS..Forever

Z 022
SOL .... Out of Luck
PDQ ....Bach
AA .... Drunkards club
OD'd .... Too much
B&S .... Bait & Switch
AFA .... Air Force Academy
ND .... Notre Dame
OU .... Oklahoma
USC...Southern Cal
KU .... Kansas

Z 023
OSU .... Ohio State
KSU..Flaw on the Kaw
WTF .... Wichita Falls
OSU .... Oklahoma State
PB&J ....Peanuts & jelly
DU .... University of Denver
PBR..Inexpensive beer
CU .... University of Colorado
R&B.. Rhythm & blues

UC.. *University of California*
IBM ....*I've been moved*

Z 024
KO... *Kick Off*
RK... *Road Kill*
VMI ....*Military School*
K9 ....*Smart Dogs*
STD..*Unclean*
FOB ....*Fresh off the boat*

Z 025
N&W ....*Norfolk & Western*
C&O..*Chesapeake & Ohio*
AT&SF ....*Santa Fe RR*
SP...*Southern Pacific*
UP..*Union Pacific*
D&RG ....*Denver & Rio Grande*
MOP..*Missouri Pacific*
NYC ....*New York Central*
PRR ....*Pennsylvania Railroad*
L&N..*Louisville & Nashville*
OBS ....*Orange Blossom Special*
SR...*Southern Railway*
NP..*Northern Pacific*
GN ....*Great Northern*
MKE...*Milwaukee Road*
BNSF ....*Burlington Northern & SF*
IC ....*Illinois Central*
B&O ....*Baltimore & Ohio*
AMT ....*Amtrack*
BO...*Body Oder*

Z 026
Good morning, America, how are you? I'm the train they call the
City of New Orleans, and I'll be gone 500 miles
when the day is done ....*Arlo Guthrie*

Z 027

LIKE IT OR NOT

I love a parade.. *Professor Hill*

Everybody loves somebody sometimes..................... *Dino Martin*

Everybody likes me... *Trumpski*

I don't like you.. *Taylor Swift*

Z 028

HUSTLING & HUSTLERS

How about a nice friendly game of pool? .... *Minnesota Fats*

Yeah, let's do it... *Fast Eddie*

A fool and his money are soon parted ....*Thomas Tusser*

What's strip pool? Is it like strip poker?..................... *Prince Harry*

Ahh, well, we live and learn, or anyway, we live.......... *Will Cuppy*

All you really need to know, you
learned in Kindergarten ....*Robert Fulghum*

Please Brer Bear, don't throw me
into that briar patch.. *Brer Rabbit*

Z 029

BAD BOYS

Bad, bad, Leroy Brown, the baddest clown in the whole
damn town, meaner than a junk yard dog..................... *Jim Croce*

Big Bad John .... *Jimmy Dean*

Z 030

Whom the gods would destroy, they first remove reason,
sanity, and a functioning putzsickle......................... *Sopheronias*

Stop calling me a fake president
and a collusionist...*Donald the Bad*

Bulls__t, Trump is the enema of the people................. *Bill Maher*

Trumpski has to go .... *David Pakman*

Z 031

The President yells at me all the time .... *Gov. Chris Christie*

Aw come on Chris... cry, whine, piss,
moan, act like a man... *Cenk Uyger*

Shouldn't certain presidents go to president school first? ...... *Ana Kasperion*

Z 032

Trump is a big con-artist, and I just quit
being a Republican .... *George F. Will*
Too bad Trump isn't Catholic, he could be
excommunicated .... *Megyn Kelly*
Trump should step down .... *Pope Francisco*
Perhaps we can pay Trump to leave office .... *Karen Attiah*
Trump is a cretin .... *Rosie O'Donnell*
You betchum, Red Rosie .... *Little Beaver*

Z 033

Trump is a dangerous demagogue .... *Michael Bloomberg*
Trump is a f___ing moron and a liability .... *Secretary Rex Tillerson*
Trump is an idiot and a lout .... *General John F. Kelly*
Is Trump as bad as King John? .... *Only the Shadow knows*
Trump is unfit to dictate
anything on defense matters .... *General James Mattis*
Let's all call the President and tell him how
well he's doing .... *Kellyanne Conway*
Trump promised everything, and you all bought it .... *Carl Ichan*

Z 034

Trump is a fake, a fraud, and a liar .... *Keith Olbermann*
Yeah, even Ray Charles can see that .... *Cenk Uygur*
So can Mr. Magoo .... *Mel Blanc*

Z 035

Could I have won that election? .... *Joe Biden*
Don't ask .... *Hillary*

Even the Shadow doesn't know........................*Lamont Cranston*
How should I know?................................. *Mandrake the Magician*
I know .... *Vladimir Putin*
So do I... *The Amazing Randi*

Z 036
The GOP is now just a one-ring circus with a delusional
Ring Master..*J.R. Forrest*
Trump's Rah-Rah squad on Fox Fake News is just
a cover up.. *Eugene Robinson*
Without the Russians, Trumpski would not have
won the election... *Max Boot*
It's time for a closer look .... *Seth Myers*
Born in the USA.. *Bruce Springsteen*
I was born in the USA,
but Donald Trumpski wasn't..................................*Barack Obama*
I didn't say that Trump was born here.............. *Bruce Springsteen*
Trump wasn't born, he was decanted ....*Aldous Huxley*

Z 037
CASABLANCA
Most of the people in Casablanca are trying
to get out ....*Sydney Greenstreet*
As time goes by................................. *Sam on the piano at Rick's*
We Germans must learn to operate
in all kinds of conditions...................................... *Major Stroesser*
There are some neighborhoods in New York I
wouldn't advise you to invade .... *Rick Blaine*
Maj. Stroesser has been shot. Round up the
usual suspects...*Capt. Renault*
Louie, I think this is the beginning of a beautiful
friendship...*Bogart*

Z 038
QUOTATIONS FOR OLD PEOPLE
When did you notice that the Roman numerals
for "40" are XL? .... *George Carlin*
When all things either dry up or leak................*Iliza Schlessinger*

246

When you can't tie your shoes or cut your
toenails anymore...*Many of Us*

Z 039
FAMOUS & OBSCURE ENDINGS
Thanks for the memories...*Bob Hope*
Hi-yo Silver, away ....*Lone Ranger*
Gitemup Scout ....*Tonto*

Z 040
Frankly my dear, I don't give a damn........................*Rhett Butler*
In the end, we are all dead .... *John Maynard Keynes*
Dead men tell no tales... *Capt. Morgan*
The past is never dead...*Wm. Faulkner*

Z 041
Rosebud..*John Foster Kane*
There are no second acts.............................*F. Scott Fitzgerald*
Oh? Izzat so? Did I get one or not? ....*Lazarus*
What kind of second acts? I was reincarnated ......*Bridey Murphy*

Z 042
COMING TO AN END
All good things must come to an end............................. *Chaucer*
That's life, and it was a very good year,
and I did it my way .... *Frank Sinatra*
What's it all about, Alfie?.................................. *Dionne Warwick*
At the end of time, we will play the Funeral March of the
Marionettes ....*Alfred Hitchcock*
We are born alone, we live alone, we eat alone, we die alone.
Everything in between is a gift from somewhere........ *Yul Brynner*
Life is a dead-end street.....................................*H.L. Mencken*

Z 043
I retired to my Florida estate on Key Mosabe ....*Jay Silverheels*
Said the Alligator King to his seven sons, "I'm feeling mighty
down, if any of you can pick me up, you can wear my golden
crown." ....*Berl Ives*

Z 044

GOOD NIGHT

Good night Mr. and Mrs. America and all
the ships at sea ....*Walter Winchell*
Say good night, Chet ....*David Brinkley*
Good night, Chet ....*Chet Huntley*
And that's probably the way it wasn't ....*Walter Cronkite*
This is London, and we are still here,
good night..*Edward R. Murrow*
Goodnight Irene, goodnight Irene,
I'll see you in my dreams .... *The Weavers*
All you have to do is dream, dream, dream........ *The Everly Bros.*

Z 045

IT'S ALL OVER FOLKS

And all the crooks on Wall Street will be
disemboweled..................................... *The Bankrupt Angel Lucifer*
And all crooked television evangelists will
be hanged .... *Marjoe Gortner*
And all big pharmaceutical pill gougers and
lobbyists will be expunged .... *George Carlin*
And the sea shall give up her dead....... *Book of Common Prayer*

Z 046

And everyone will live on forever
on Facebook.. *Mark Zuckerberg*
It ain't over till it's over .... *Yogi Berra*
It isn't over till we say it's over..............................*Bluto Blutarsky*
It's over...*The Book of Benediction*
T-That's all, folks .... *Pork Chop*
That is all...........................*M*A*S*H* public address announcer*

Z 047

AND NOW IS THE END OF EVERYTHING

At the end of time, I will blow my gigantic horn to
announce the coming of the
terrible Judgment Day...............................*The Archangel Gabriel*
And at the end, there will be a terrible battle

called Armageddon .... *Book of Reparation*
At time's end, the heavens and earth will come
to an end...*The Ring of the Nibelung*
At the end of days will come
Gotterdammerung....................... *Germanic Twilight of the gods*
And Lord Shiva will then come to destroy
everything .... *The Mahabharata*
Bye Bye, Blackbird... *Irving Kaufman*

Z 048
And after the end of time will come the Norse Ragnarok, where
the cosmos and all the gods will be destroyed and Yggdrasil (the
invisible great supernatural tree that holds everything in its trunk,
branches, and roots) will start to tremble and then fall and
collapse into the universal ocean .... *The Norse Autumn*
of the gods

Z 049
Then will come War, Pestilence, *E. coli*, Baldness, Crab Grass,
Herpes, Curmudgeons, Cataracts, Impotence, Famine, and
Death .... *The Ten Centaurs of the Apocrypha*
At the end of time, Satan will be
defeated and extricated........................... *The Archangel Michael*
And then the next Mayan Long Count calendar
will run out of time, and then worlds and continents
will collide and disappear. And then we will just start up another
Long Count calendar...................... *Olmec & Mayan time keepers*

Z 050
I went riding out one dark and windy night, when all at once, a
mighty herd of red-eyed cows I saw a-flying through the ragged
sky and up the mighty draw. Their brands were still on fire, and
their hooves were made of steel. Their horns were black and
shiny, and their hot breath I could feel. And then I saw the riders
and heard their mournful cries. Yippie eye-ohh, Yippie eye-yay,
ghost riders in the sky ....*An old cowboy*

Z 051

One day, I saw heaven open, and out came a flying white horse
whose eyes were flaming. Upon his head were many crowns,
and his linen clothes were dipped in blood. I then fell at his feet
to worship him. Then an angel from heaven appeared carrying a
chain and a key to the bottomless pit below.
He then cast the Devil into the pit and bound him up
for a thousand years.................................*Saint John the Divine*
The worst pit I've ever known is the one
with that pendulum ....*Edgar Allan Poe*

Z 052

Tell me why you're crying, my son. I know you're frightened like
everyone. Is it the thunder in the distance you fear? Will it help if
I stay with you very near? And if you take my hand, my son, all
will be well when the day is done. Do you ask why I'm crying, my
son? You will inherit what mankind has done. In a world filled
with sorrow and woe. If you ask me why this is so, I really don't
know, and if you take my hand, my son, all will be well when day
is done..*Peter Yarrow*

Z 053

NEW BEGINNINGS

At exactly 12:00 midnight at the end of New Year's Eve, time will
stop and I will be there to welcome in the New Year's baby, who
will come back into existence at exactly at 12:01 on New Year's
morning. I will appear at Times Square in Manhattan where
everyone standing in the freezing cold will start singing.
Then automobile horns will start making noise along with
firecrackers, train whistles, gun shots, etc., and time will start up
again .... *Grandfather Time*
Waaa.. *The New Year's Baby*
Then, after many eons, the inhabitable earth will rise up out of
the primeval ocean again and become more lush and fruitful than
before. And a new first human pair, to be named Lifa and
Lifthrastrudel, will be awakened into the new green world
and will replace the previous incarnate
human pair, Ash and Elm ....*The Norse Eddas*

Z 054
And then Lord Brahma will come and start
everything up again.. *The Beef Veda*
And I saw a new heaven and a new earth, and
there was no sea.. *St. John the Divine*
And there will be a new beginning and a new Adam
and a new Eve (but they won't have
the same names) ....*Nathaniel Hawthorne*
Would you like some new magic mushrooms
and some zucchinis?.. *The new Eve*
Yeah, why not? They're both
big and they taste good .... *The new Adam*

Z 055

AND THEN AFTER THE NEXT END OF TIME
It's reveille, by the boogie woogie bugle boy
in company B .... *Andrews Sisters*
Hello, what time is it? Is it time for me to wake up? ......*Morpheus*
Happy days are here again .... *Harry S. Truman*

Z 056

In his shoemaker's shop, his work would never stop, as he
tapped away, working all the day. Then a dancing girl came in
his little shop, and his heart went pop inside his shop. Then he
heard her say in a friendly way, "Shoes to set my feet a-dancing,
dancing, dancing, dancing all the day, shoes to set my feet a-
dancing, dancing, dancing all my
cares away"....................................*Petula Clark & The Gaylords*

Z 057

High ho, hi ho, it's back to work we go.............*The Seven Dwarfs*
And I'll start dancing again until
the next end of time.................................. *The Music Box Dancer*

Z 058
And good and evil will again contend........*The Magian Scriptures*
Hi dee hi dee hi dee ho........................... *Cab Calloway*
Tutti-fruitie, alla-rootie ....*Little Richard*

HISTORICAL, NATURAL, AND GEOGRAPHIC POST SCRIPTS

BEGINNING DATES OF WORLD CALENDARS, SELECTED HUMAN EVENTS, ANCIENT & MORE RECENT CITIES, MONUMENTS, BUILT-STRUCTURES, & ENVIRONMENTAL DISASTERS THROUGHOUT DIFFERENT TIME PERIODS OF OUR SPECIES

Ω 001

NOTABLE ASTRONOMICAL EVENTS & NATURAL DISASTERS AFFECTING ANCIENT & MORE RECENT HUMAN POPULATIONS

BC = Before Common Era; CE = Common Era

Toba Meer Mega-Volcano (eruption) .... ca. 67000 / 74000 BC
Beginning of the Sundaland flooding .... ca. 19000–13000 BC
Beringia land bridge flooding (started) .... ca. 19000 BC
End of the last Ice Age .... ca. 13000–10000 BC
Lake Bonneville flood .... ca. 12500 BC
Lake Missoula (last flood) .... ca. 11000 BC
The Y-Dryas (cold period) .... ca. 9600–9000 BC
Mt. Mazama (eruption) (Oregon) .... ca. 5677 BC
Lake Lahotan (dried up) .... ca. 5000 BC
Burckle Crater & Mega-tsunami
(S. Indian Ocean) .... ca. 2807 BC

Ω 002

Northward shift of the northern African Summer monsoon belt into the Sahara (bringing savannah &
wetter conditions) .... ca. 8000 BC
Cessation of flooding in Sundaland .... ca. 8000–4900 BC

Cheddar Man died in Somerset, England................. ca. 7150 BC
Start of great flooding of Doggerland (North Sea)..... ca. 6500 BC
End of Doggerland flooding...................................... ca 6200 BC
Catastrophic Black Sea flooding............................ ca. 5600 BC

Ω 003
Southward shift of the northern African summer
monsoon away from the Sahara (bringing another age of
desert conditions there)... ca. 5000 BC
As an island, a small part of Doggerland
survived until .... ca. 5000 BC
Dogger Bank under the North Sea is
now all that remains ....after 5000 BC
Oetzi the Iceman died in the Austrian/Italian Alps..... ca. 3200 BC
Great Huabei Flood in northern China................. before 2070 BC
Santorini / Thera (eruption) .... ca. 1610 BC

Ω 004
Halley's Comet (as seen in Greece & Rome) ....466 or 475 BC
Mt. Etna Italy (eruption)..475 BC
Halley's Comet (seen in China)..240 BC
Halley's Comet (seen in Babylonia)...................................164 BC

Ω 005
Halley's Comet (seen in Babylon) ....87 or 90 BC
Popocatepetl (Mexico) (eruption) ....060 BC
Halley's Comet (seen in Rome)...012 BC

Ω 006
Halley's Comet (seen in Rome) by Flavius Josephus.......066 CE
Halley's Comet (seen in Mesopotamia) in the
Bavli Talmud ....070 CE
Halley's Comet (seen in Rome) by Vespasion.................079 CE
Mt. Vesuvius (eruption) ....079 CE

Ω 007
Halley's Comet.. 141 CE, 218 CE
Halley's Comet............................... 240 CE, 295 CE, 374 CE

Halley's Comet (Chalons in Gaul)...................................... 451 CE
Halley's Comet .... 530 CE

Ω 008
Mt. Ilopango (El Salvador) (eruption) .... 536 CE
Halley's Comet ....607 CE, 684 CE, 760 CE
Halley's Comet ....837 CE, 912 CE, 989 CE
Halley's Comet (England).. 1066 CE
Halley's Comet .... 1145 CE
Mt. Etna (earthquake)... 1169 CE

Ω 009
Halley's Comet .... 1222 CE
Popopcatepetl (eruption) .... 1245 CE
Halley's Comet .... 1301 CE
Black Death in England .... 1348 CE
Halley's Comet .... 1378 CE
Halley's Comet (Constantinople).................................. 1456 CE
Bubonic Plague in England...1500s CE

Ω 010
Halley's Comet (Switzerland) by Huldrych Zwingli .... 1531 CE
Halley's Comet (England & Scotland) by John Knox...... 1572 CE
Huaynaputina (Peru) (eruption) .... 1600 CE
Halley's Comet (England) by
Edmund Halley & Johann. Kepler .... 1607 CE

Ω 011
Halley's Comet (Basel in Switzerland) .... 1618 CE
Santiago (Chile) earthquake .... 1647 CE
Great Plague in England... 1655 CE

Ω 012
Halley's Comet (Massachusetts) by Increase Mather .... 1682 CE
Mt. Fuji (eruption) .... 1700 CE
Halley's Comet (Saxony) by
Nicolas de Lacaille & J.G. Palitzsch.............................. 1759 CE
Halley's Comet (France) by Napoleon & Tolstoy............ 1811 CE

Mt. Tambora (eruption)...1815 CE
Halley's Comet (France) by
LaPlace, Clairaut, Mark Twain (born) ....1835 CE
Krakatoa (eruption) ....1883 CE
Halley's Comet (New York) Mark Twain (died) ....1910 CE
Halley's Comet seen by spacecraft ....1986 CE

Ω 013
WORLD CALENDARS*, STARTING DATES OF ERAS, DYNASTIES, AND OTHER WORLDLY TIME PERIODS

* indicates a calendar

Byzantine (Alexandria)*..5492 BC
Sumerian King List.. ca. 4500 BC
Egyptian (start of 1st Sothic
cycle)* *(see below in Ω 038 on page 263)*........4416 or 4242 BC
Archbishop of Usher* ....4004 BC
Anno Mundi (Bede)*...2952 BC
Egyptian (start of 2nd Sothic Cycle)* ....2891 or 2782 BC
Start of the Chinese 3 sovereigns &
5 emperor periods..2852 BC

Ω 014
Chinese (Fu-xi)* ....2852 BC
Egypt (Pre-dynastic)..2800 BC
Jewish (Biblical)* ....2761 BC
Anno Mundi (Septuagint)* ....2750 BC
Coptic* ....2670 BC
Mayan Long Count* ....2114 BC
Hindu (Kali Yuga)*...2102 BC
Egyptian (1st dynasty...2100 BC

Ω 015
Chinese (Huang di)*...2627 BC
Armenian* ....2492 BC
Akkadian (Sargon I) ....2224 BC
Xia Dynasty (China) ....2070 BC

Ω 016
Neo Sumerian (Umma)* .... 2000 BC
Babylonian (Hammurabi)*.. 1792 BC

Ω 017
Shang Dynasty (China)* .... 1600 BC
Delphic Oracle (origin)*..ca. 1400 BC
Egyptian (end of the 2nd Sothic Cycle)*............ 1374 or 1322 BC

Ω 018
Zhou Dynasty (China)* .... 1046 BC
Carthage (founded)* .... 846 BC
First Olympiad* .... 776 BC
Rome (founded) AUC* .... 752 BC
Babylonian (Nabonassar)* .... 747 BC
Japanese Amaterasu (Jimmu)* .... 660 BC

Ω 019
Byzantium (colonized) .... 653 BC
Zoroastrian (Achaemenid)* .... 650 BC
Buddhist (Siamese)* .... 542 BC
Han Dynasty (China)* .... 206 BC
Islamic (Hegira)* .... 622 CE

Ω 020
EARLIER FOUNDING DATES OF ANCIENT WORLD CITIES AND NOTABLE HUMAN STRUCTURES

BC = Before Common Era; CE = Common Era

Gobekli Tepe (built) ....ca. 9000 BC
Nevali Cori monuments (Turkey) ....ca. 8400 BC
Catal Huyuk (settled)...ca. 7500 BC
Ninevah (settled) ....ca. 6000 BC
Ashkelon (occupied) .... 5900 BC

Ω 021
Nekhen (Upper Egyptian tomb) ....ca. 5600 BC
Jaffe (inhabited)..ca. 5500 BC
City of Eridu (founded)..ca. 5400 BC

City of Nippur (founded) ....5262 BC
Nabta Playa stone circle (upper Egypt) .... ca. 5000 BC

Ω 022
Ubaid settlements .... ca 5000 BC
Great Sphinx of Giza .... ca. 4500 BC
City of Nekhen (built)................................. ca. 4400 BC
Elamite city of Sussa .... by 4200 BC
City of Uruk (founded) ....4100 BC
Hierakonpolis (settled)............................... by 4000 BC
City of Ur (founded).................................. by 3800 BC

Ω 023
Anatolian city of Hattusha (settled)........................... by 2750 BC
Chinese city of Hangzhou .... by 2700 BC
First Pyramid in Egypt (Djoser's) .... ca. 2700 BC
Indian city of Dholavira
(Rann of Kutch).. ca. 2650 BC–1450 BC
Byblos (founded)...................................... ca. 2600 BC
Tarxien Temples (Malta) .... ca. 2600 BC
Mohenjodaro (occupied)............................... ca. 2600 BC

Ω 024
City of Lagash (founded)...............................2500 BC
Stonehenge (built).................................... ca. 2400 BC
Babylon (founded)....................................2200 BC
City of Eridu .... ca. 2200 BC
Carnac stones (built) .... ca. 2200 BC
Harappa (occupied)................................... ca. 2200 BC

Ω 025
Agar Quim (Malta)..................................... ca. 2200 BC
Athens (settled)......................................2000 BC
Newgrange (built).................................... ca. 2000 BC
City of Kish (founded)................................ ca. 2000 BC
City of Troy (founded)................................ ca. 2000 BC
Laguna Pueblo (settled) .... ca. 2000 BC
Jerusalem (founded) ....2000 BC

Ω 026

LATER FOUNDING DATES OF WORLD CITIES AND ANCIENT STRUCTURES

BC = Before Common Era; CE = Common Era

Knossos (settled)..by 2001 BC
Mecca (settled)..ca. 2000 BC
Hattusa (settled) ....ca. 2000 BC
The Great Ziggurat of Ur (built)................................ca. 2000 BC
Ring of Kerry standing stone alignments...................ca. 1700 BC
Mycenae (occupied) ....ca. 1600 BC
San Lorenzo, Mexico (Olmec) ....ca. 1500 BC
Miletus (founded)..ca. 1450 BC
Sidon & Tyre (founded)..ca. 1250 BC
Town of Lygos (Byzantium) ....ca. 1200 BC

Ω 027

Town of Gaza (founded)..ca. 1200 BC
Olmec settlements...ca. 1200 BC
Lucknow (Lakhanpur) ....ca. 1000 BC
Varanasi (orig. Benares).......................................ca. 1000 BC
Sparta (founded)..ca. 900 BC
Old city of Jin & Dadu (Beijing) .... 771 BC

Ω 028

City of Maghada (founded) .... 684 BC
Byzantium (founded)... 667 BC
The Great Ziggurat of Babylon (built)........................ca. 610 BC
Babylonian Captivity .... 586 BC
Odessos founded by Greeks (now Varna in Bulgaria)...... 570 BC
Pompeii (founded) ....ca. 550 BC
Pasargadae (built) .... 520 BC
Persepolis (built).. 518 BC

Ω 029

The Great Ziggurat of Ur (rebuilt)............................ca. 500 BC
Monte Alban, Mexico (built) ....ca. 500 BC
Nanjing (founded)... 495 BC

Patna (orig. Patilaputra) .... ca. 490 BC
Parthenon (built)...447 BC

Ω 030
MORE RECENT FOUNDING DATES OF
WORLD CITIES AND ANCIENT STRUCTURES

CE = Common Era

Cologne, Germany ....038 CE
London (founded)...050 CE
Constantinople (founded) ....220 CE
Tikal (Yucatan) (built) .... ca. 300 CE

Ω 031
Kiev (founded)..482 CE
Mesa Verde (Colo) .... ca. 600 CE
Dublin, Ireland...837 CE
Chaco Canyon Pueblo (AZ)... ca. 850 CE
Moenkopi Pueblo (AZ)... ca. 900 CE
Walpi Pueblo (AZ .... ca. 900 CE
Aix la Chapelle (Aachen)..936 CE
Taos Pueblo (NM) .... ca. 1000 CE
Vinland (Leif Ericson) .... ca. 1000 CE

Ω 032
Cuzco (constructed) .... 1000 CE
Lucknow, India (originally)... ca. 1000 CE
Mixtec Codices.. ca. 1050 CE
Zimbabwe (built).. ca. 1050 CE
Halley's Comet (China, England, France)........................1066 CE
Timbuktu (built) .... ca. 1100 CE
Angkor Wat (built) ....1112 CE
Moscow (founded)..1147 CE
Old Oraibi (AZ).. ca. 1150 CE

Ω 033
Hiedelberg, Germany ....1196 CE
Hovenweep (Utah) (built) .... ca. 1200 CE
Cahokia Mounds (settled) .... ca. 1200 CE

Natchez Mounds (settled)...ca. 1200 CE
Tenochtitlan (built).. 1225 CE
Berlin (founded).. 1237 CE
Beijing (founded) .... 1268 CE

Ω 034
Shanghai (original settlement) .... 1291 CE
Machu Picchu (Peru)...ca. 1450 CE
Istanbul (formerly Constantinople) .... 1453 CE
Edo/Tokyo (founded) .... 1457 CE
Bahamas, Columbus .... 1492 CE

Ω 035
Santo Domingo (founded)... 1496 CE
Havana (founded)... 1515 CE
Mexico (Hernan Cortez).. 1518 CE
Vera Cruz (founded) .... 1519 CE
Acapulco (founded)... 1521 CE
Peru (Francisco Pizzaro) .... 1522 CE
Delhi (founded)... 1526 CE
Fort Caroline (founded)... 1564 CE

Ω 036
St. Augustine (founded) .... 1565 CE
Fatehpur Sikri (built) .... 1571 CE
Roanoke Colony... 1585 CE
Jamestown Colony .... 1607 CE
Quebec City.. 1608 CE
Newfoundland... 1610 CE
Santa Fe... 1610 CE

Ω 037
Ft. Nassau / Beverwijck .... 1614 CE
Plymouth Colony .... 1620 CE
New Amsterdam.. 1625 CE
Montreal .... 1642 CE
New York... 1664 CE
New Orleans.. 1718 CE

THE EGYPTIAN SOTHIC CYCLE

An ancient astronomical phenomenon where the dog star Sothis (aka, Sirius) rose above the horizon at the same time as the sun, originally marking the yearly rise of the River Nile (initially observed at Aswan and followed eight days later by observations at Memphis). Every year, this conjunction would appear later and later until it disappeared and then rose again in the expected place after 1460 (or 1461) years.

ABOUT THE AUTHOR

Hal Elliott is an emeritus professor of geography from Weber State University in Ogden, Utah. He graduated from San Francisco State University with a BA degree in History & Philosophy, and an MA degree in Geography. He later studied Chinese (Mandarin) from the University of California Extension, and graduated from the University of Oklahoma with a PhD in Geography & Asian Studies. He has taught courses in World Geography, Geography of Europe, the U.S. & Canada, India & the Middle East, and China & Japan. He also has taught courses on the History of Early Western Civilization, the History of Early Eastern Civilization, Urban Geography, Cultural Geography, Historical Geography, Economic Geography, Cartography, and Quantitative Methods. He has publications in *Geographical Analysis, The Journal of Geography, Economic Geography, Urban Geography, The Professional Geographer, The Yearbook of the Association of Pacific Coast Geographers, The California Geographer, The Annals of Regional Science, Ecumene, The Scottish American Patriot, The Florida Geographer, The Ohio Genealogy Quarterly, The Southeastern Geographer*, and the *Nova Scotia Genealogist*. Before coming to WSU, he taught classes at the College of San Mateo (CA), Cameron State College (OK), and Florida International University (FL)

Greatest thanks to my dear colleague, Dr. Sarah A. Elliott of the University of Utah and the University of Pennsylvania, for helping to bring this book into print.

HME, August 2019